Day Budget Vacations

IN NEW ENGLAND

Praise from the Press

"An excellent guide to New England's many attractions, and will save many an argument about which restaurant to try or what route to take." — **New England Living Magazine**

"Not just any guidebook . . . it exposes the little-known, little-travelled cubbyholes of tradition and caches of avant-garde." — **Cambridge (Massachusetts) Express**

"Offers six itineraries for seeing some of the best of this region." — **Berkshire Courier**

"Of special interest to Floridians, as they flock to New England . . ." — **WXFL, Channel 8 Winter Haven, Florida**

"Each section is a mixture, with small doses of history, literature and legend and large quantities of practical information." — **Glens Falls (New York) Post-Star**

"A dependable, well-arranged guide." — **Sunday Cape Cod Times**

Daytrips and Budget Vacations

IN NEW ENGLAND

by Patricia & Robert Foulke

The Globe Pequot Press

Chester, Connecticut 06412

Cover photograph taken by Oliver Denison at Mystic Seaport®
of Mystic, Connecticut
Cover designed by Barbara Marks

Text designed by Kathy Michalove

Copyright © 1983 by Patricia and Robert Foulke

All rights reserved. No part of this work may be reproduced or transmitted
in any form by any means, electronic or mechanical, including photocopying
and recording, or by any information storage or retrieval system, except as
may be expressly permitted by the 1976 Copyright Act or in writing from the
publisher.

Library of Congress Cataloging in Publication Data

Foulke, Patricia.
   Daytrips and budget vacations in New England.

   Bibliography: p.
   Includes index.
   1. New England—Description and travel—1981-
—Guide-books. 2. Automobiles—Road guides—New
England. 3. Family recreation—New England.
I. Foulke, Robert, 1930-   . II. Title.
III. Title: Day trips and budget vacations in New
England.
F2.3.F68   1983   917.4'0443   83-80633
ISBN O-87106-978-4 (pbk.)

Manufactured in the United States of America
Third Printing, July 1986

Contents

Acknowledgments vii
Author's Note. viii
Using the Book ix
Southern New England Map x
Northern New England Map xii
Information Sources xvi
Your Route. xvii
Your Expenses xviii
Eating. xviii
Activities xix
Letting Go xx
Readings. xx

ITINERARY A
The Southern Shore 1
ITINERARY B
The Cape and the Islands 35
ITINERARY C
Historic Boston and the Bay Colonies 73
ITINERARY D
Down East 127
ITINERARY E
The Green and White Mountains 159
ITINERARY F
The Western Circuit 189
APPENDIX I
New England Under Canvas. 221
APPENDIX II
Bed and Breakfast in New England 241

Index to Attractions 255

Photo Credits

Page	Credit
1	Mary Anne Stets Photo, Mystic Seaport, Mystic, CT
13	Connecticut Department of Commerce (*top*)
13	Frank W. Schlegel (*middle*)
13	Connecticut Antiquarian & Landmarks Society (*bottom*)
19	Claire White Peterson Photo, Mystic Seaport, Mystic, CT (*top and bottom*)
19	Mary Anne Stets Photo, Mystic Seaport, Mystic, CT (*bottom*)
29	U.S. Coast Guard (*top*)
29	The Preservation Society of Newport (*middle and bottom*)
35	Cape Cod National Seashore
49	Massachusetts Department of Commerce & Development (*top and bottom*)
49	Elwood Mills Jr. (*middle*)
65	Massachusetts Department of Commerce & Development (*top, middle and bottom*)
73	Massachusetts Department of Commerce & Development
81	Massachusetts Department of Commerce & Development (*top and middle*)
81	Plimoth Plantation (*bottom*)
95	Massachusetts Department of Commerce & Development (*top, middle and bottom*)
113	Lowell National Historical Park (*top*)
113	National Park Service (*middle*)
113	House of Seven Gables (*bottom*)
127	National Park Service
143	Maine Department of Commerce & Industry (*top and bottom*)
143	State of Maine Development Office (*middle*)
155	Maine Department of Commerce & Industry (*top and middle*)
155	National Park Service (*bottom*)
159	State of New Hampshire photo by Dick Smith
171	State of New Hampshire photo by Dick Smith (*top*)
171	State of New Hampshire photo by Dick Hamilton (*middle*)
171	State of Vermont Travel Division (*bottom*)
183	State of Vermont Travel Division (*top, middle and bottom*)
189	Old Sturbridge Village photo by Robert S. Arnold
197	Massachusetts Department of Commerce & Development (*top*)
197	Berkshire Music Center (*middle*)
197	Connecticut Department of Economic Development photo by Dominick J. Ruggiero (*bottom*)
213	Connecticut Department of Commerce (*top and bottom*)
213	Wadsworth Atheneum (*middle*)
217	Old Sturbridge Village photo by Donald F. Eaton (*top and bottom*)
217	Old Sturbridge Village photo by Robert S. Arnold (*middle*)
221	State of New Hampshire photo by Dick Smith

Acknowledgments

We are extremely appreciative of the information, suggestions, and maps sent by friends. Among the many who have helped enhance this book we especially thank the following:

Phyllis and Alexander Aldrich; Jo and Verner Alexanderson; Anne and William Barclay; Vondee and David Beeman; Elinor and Richard Berke; Ann and Werner Berthoff; Mona Bradley; Grethe and Maria Certain; Betty and Woodbridge Constant; Shirley, Barrie, and George Davidson; Shirley and Howard DeLong; Anne and Terrence Diggory; Judith and Bruce Eissner; Alberta and Jack Feynman; Patricia and Thomas Fox; Stuart Frank; Gay and Alvin Gamage; Sue and Robert Gorton; Anne Gwynn; Diane and William Hall; Thomas Holmes; Nancy and John Kendall; Linda and Benjamin Labaree; Ardyth Lewis; Polly and Charles Longsworth; Mary Maynard; Janet and Curt Mayott; Marjorie and Bard McNulty; Virginia and Stephen Minot; Juliet Mofford; Diane Nolan; Joan Orton; Barbara Pitnof; Mab and Charles Owen; Anne and Joseph Palamountain; Judith and James Potter; Charles Putney; Elizabeth and David Ratcliff; Jean and Donald Richards; Phyllis Roth; Kenneth Rothwell; Ardene Scroggy; John Sheldon; Sandy Shephard; Mary and Sanford Sistare; Eileen and Elwood Stitzel; Mary Lou and Robert Strode; Jean and Leonard Tomat; Charlotte Turgeon; and Philip West.

Author's Note

A New England vacation offers remarkable variety. Whether you live across the country or around the corner, you'll find something new on each trip. You may enjoy an Atlantic sunrise or a Green Mountain sunset, saltwater marshes or a busy village green, fresh lobster in Maine or cheese in Vermont. You can hike the Appalachian Trail, run white water in a canoe, climb the Presidential Range, and surf on white Cape Cod beaches. Or explore whaling museums and reconstructed colonial villages, walk historic trails in old cities, trace local legends and the lore of shipwrecks, and collect valuable memories everywhere.

For over thirty years we've enjoyed these many pleasures of New England. During this time we've traveled with babies and toddlers, children and teenagers. We've discovered both the pleasures and the problems of traveling light. At times we've tried to do too much, planning our trips in great detail. At other times we've simply taken off on an impromptu voyage of discovery. But no matter how we've traveled, and no matter how often we've been, we've never exhausted the possibilities of a region blessed by mountain, sea, city, and rich cultural heritage.

Using the Book

This book is meant to be useful to all kinds of travelers. For those who live in other parts of the country, our planned itineraries save time, and our camping and bed-and-breakfast information saves money. For New Englanders, our suggestions help locate places off the beaten track. There's even something here for the armchair traveler: legends, sea yarns, ghost stories, and historical tales of the people who walked these streets long ago.

The Itineraries

Each of the trips provides a variety of activities within a relatively small driving area. You can choose to explore and enjoy one small area, or extend your range by moving from one itinerary to the next.

Every itinerary includes a suggested route, total mileage, a map, sightseeing tips, information about sports and other activities, and sources of information. We've selected a wide range of activities and patterned them into a practicable sequence. But the outline is there for you to modify. You can work back and forth between itineraries, or within them. You can hit the highlights, or search out less well known pleasures.

There are six itineraries to work with:

A. The Southern Shore: The coastline along this two-state section is interesting and varied. There are fjordlike fingers of the sea, major rivers and seaports, miles of beautiful beach, small rural villages, and cities with a rich historic heritage.

B. The Cape and the Islands: This itinerary begins at the Rhode Island border, pauses in New Bedford,

Southern New England

WILLIAMSTOWN

MASSACHUSETTS

Itinerary F

CONNECTICUT

O ROCKY HILL

NEW HAVEN

Itinerary A

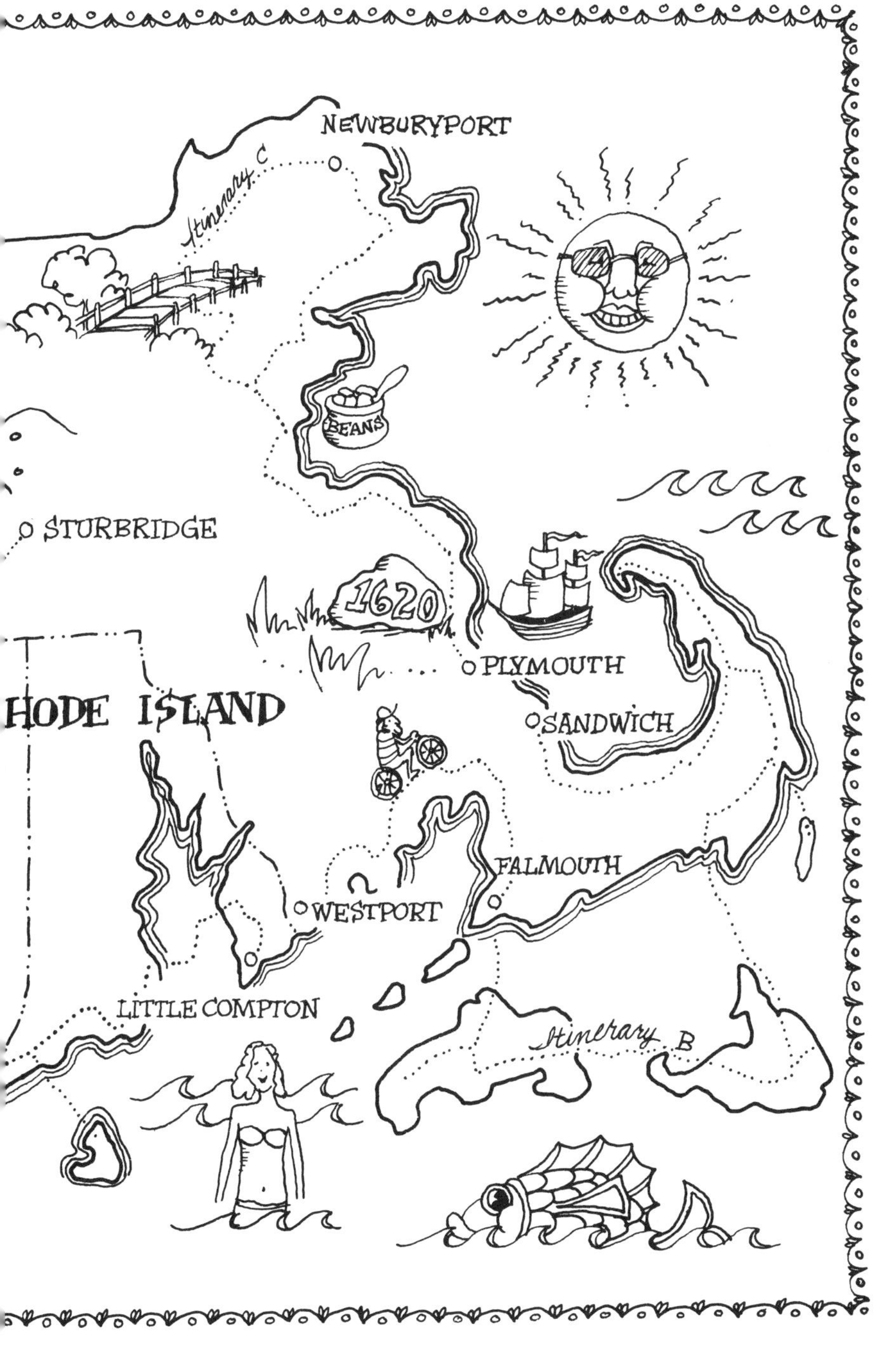

NEWBURYPORT
Itinerary C
BEANS
STURBRIDGE
1620
PLYMOUTH
HODE ISLAND
SANDWICH
FALMOUTH
WESTPORT
LITTLE COMPTON
Itinerary B

Northern New England

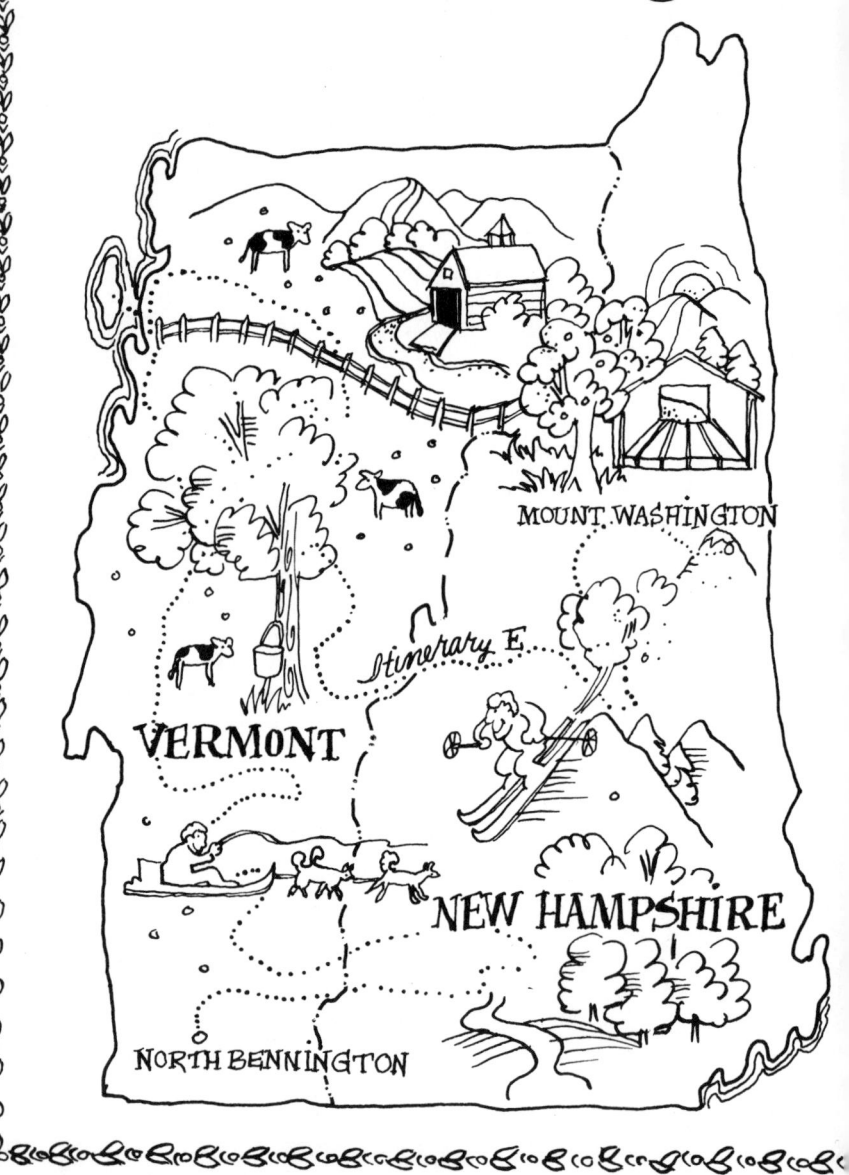

MOUNT WASHINGTON

Itinerary E

VERMONT

NEW HAMPSHIRE

NORTH BENNINGTON

xiii

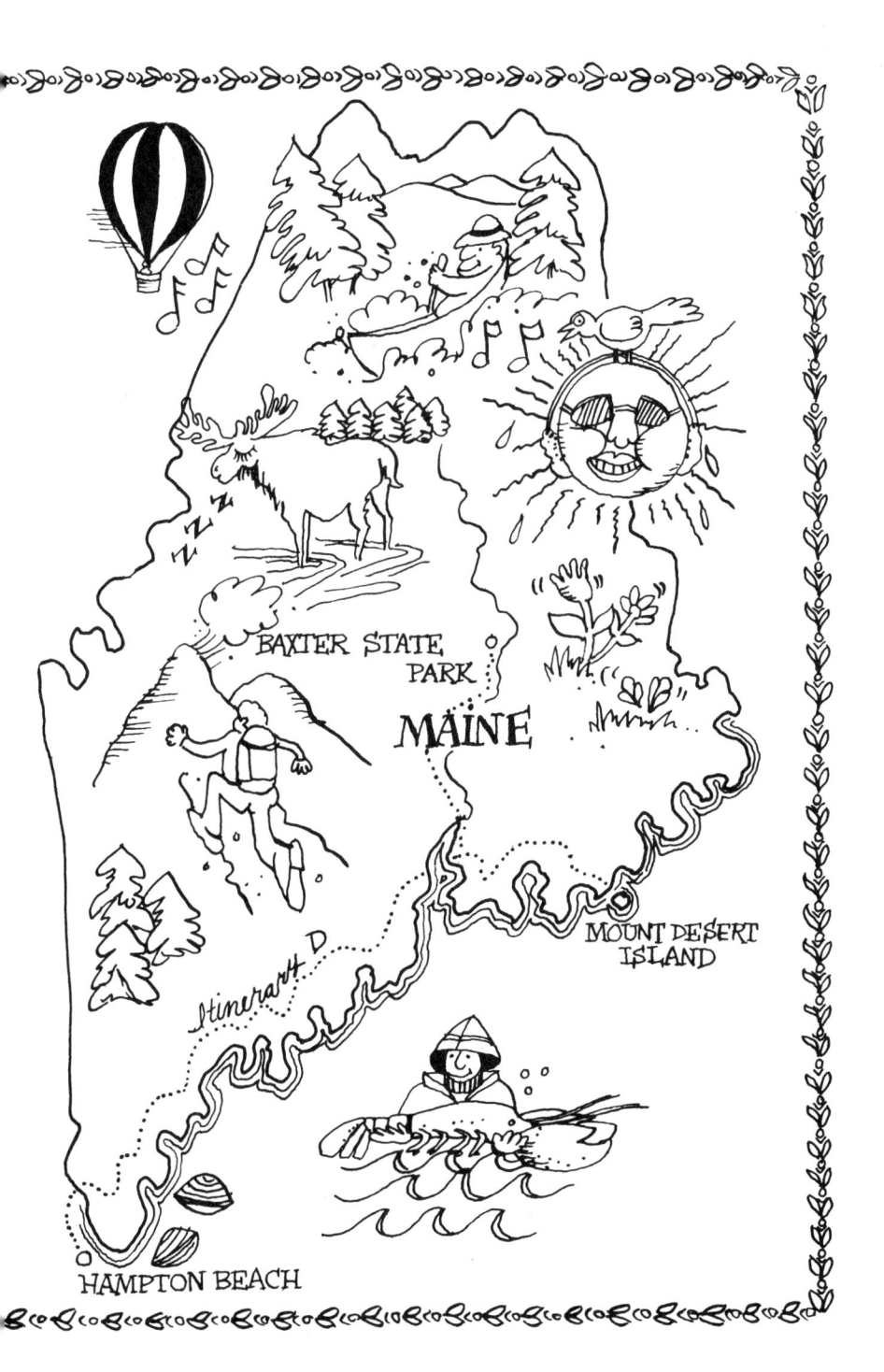

and continues on to Cape Cod. There we follow the southern coast from Falmouth and the islands to Hyannis, Chatham, and out to Provincetown, returning along the bay to Sandwich. The Cape means beaches and boating, historic sights, and a rich natural beauty that keeps drawing visitors to it year after year.

C. Historic Boston and the Colonies: In this area, from Plymouth to Newburyport, were the first settlements in our country. Here you can trace our history: the relationship between Indians and Pilgrims, the problems of the early colonists, the development of education and culture, the battles between theocracy and democracy, the growth of early industries, the events leading to the Revolutionary War, and the beginning of the Industrial Revolution in America.

D. Down East: A touch of New Hampshire, and then the Maine coast—waves dashing on rugged rocky shores, long fjords, cold water, and plentiful fresh lobsters. Yes, there are towns (even a city now and then) to visit, but most of all there's the sheer beauty of the place.

E. The White and Green Mountains: Come to the mountains of New Hampshire and Vermont for superb hiking, camping, and fishing. We begin at the Maine border, and travel west through the Presidential Range and lovely New Hampshire villages to Vermont. Here we follow Ethan Allen's beautiful mountains up to Lake Champlain and down again to Bennington.

F. The Western Circuit: Our last itinerary begins in the Berkshires, a lovely region of rolling hills and quiet New England towns, touched during the summer by marvelous music, theater, and art. Then we wind through the hills of western Connecticut, past tiny hamlets and striking colonial towns to Hartford, "Insurance City." The arts, history, and the great outdoors—all here for your pleasure.

The Legends and Tales

It's impossible to think about New England without thinking about the history of the area — a history embellished with centuries-old folktales and legends. Throughout the book we've scattered sea chanteys, ghost stories, legends, and more — all to whet your appetite for this marvelous region. Look for the symbol as you're reading; it marks a legend or story about the area we're describing.

The Overnight Suggestions

Camping is one way to stretch your vacation dollars. For novices and old hands alike, we've listed the wheres and how-tos for the area in New England Under Canvas, which begins on page 223. Noncampers may look for something a little different in the way of accommodations. We've provided a list of sources for finding bed and breakfast places, starting on page 243. Other thoughts: Try a budget motel. Stay in a college dorm — a plentiful resource in New England. The local Y can be a good buy too. Of course quality varies from city to city, so you may want to write to the national boards for more detailed information. Regardless of where you stay, remember you'll need reservations if you are going in season.

National Board of YMCAs
291 Broadway
New York, NY 10007
212-406-0090

National Board of YWCAs
135 W. 50th St.
New York, NY 10022
212-621-5115

The Readings

An area as rich as New England cannot begin to be explored in a single book. If you want to know more about the history and legends, the natural history, the sites, and the activities, look through the list of readings that begins on page xx.

New England delights most travelers because, like England itself, it encompasses a great variety of scenery and activity within a small area. You can drive from the suburbs of Connecticut to the wilderness of Maine in a day if you want to; you can easily combine time in the mountains, at the ocean, and in cities. Or you can concentrate on one area, delving into its people, terrain, and history.

Whatever the scope of your trip, planning is essential to its success. And good planning begins with anticipation. Yes, it's important to get organized, to make clear choices at some stage of the planning process, but it's wonderful to savor a whole range of possibilities before you do.

Collect brochures, articles, and ideas from friends. Entertain a wild dream or two (we once thought of traveling to England by way of Hawaii and Japan). Then let the mix mull for a while before finally pulling it all together into a workable plan.

Information Sources

We usually begin by attacking the travel section in our local library, with a sturdy canvas bag in hand to carry home our selections. Later we buy some of these books to take on the trip, along with other new books we've found in local bookstores. Then we may visit a travel agency for free brochures and information.

State Tourist Offices

State tourist offices offer maps, information about historic sites, and lists of campgrounds and other accommodations, restaurants, and sightseeing suggestions. It's a good idea to write before you go.

Connecticut: Connecticut Division of Tourist Information, 210 Washington Street, Hartford 06106, 203-566-3948.

Maine: State Development Office, State House, Augusta 04333, 207-289-2423.

Massachusetts: Massachusetts Department of Commerce and Development, 100 Cambridge Street, Boston 02202, 617-727-3201.

New Hampshire: New Hampshire Office of Vacation Travel, State House Annex, Box 856, Concord 03301, 603-271-2665.

Rhode Island: Rhode Island Department of Economic Development, 7 Jackson Walkway, Providence 02903, 401-277-2601.

Vermont: Vermont Travel Division, 61 Elm Street, Montpelier 05602, 802-828-3236.

You can also write to individual chambers of commerce in the towns you intend to visit (addresses are in the itineraries). They too offer maps and information about historic houses in the area (days and times sites are open), restaurants, accommodations, and special activities.

Chambers of Commerce

A number of organizations publish information about wildlife sanctuaries, wilderness expeditions, hiking trails, and outdoor recreation.

The **Appalachian Mountain Club** is the oldest conservation club in the United States. It publishes guidebooks on hiking trails and canoe routes, a monthly newsletter, and a semiannual journal. The **National Audubon Society** maintains wildlife sanctuaries all over the country. Its programs include conservation education, research on current wildlife issues, and natural history films. The society also operates libraries and stores where you can buy nature-related gifts. The **Green Mountain Club** maintains and protects the Long Trail system, and offers guidebooks and maps. **American Youth Hostels** offers hiking and bicycle tours, and a network of low-cost hostels.

Organizations

American Youth
  Hostels
132 Spring Street
New York, NY 10012
212-431-7100

Appalachian
  Mountain Club
5 Joy Street
Boston, MA 02108
617-523-0636

National Audubon
  Society
950 Third Avenue
New York, NY 10022
212-832-3200

Green Mountain Club
Box 889
Montpelier, VT 05602
802-223-3463

Your Route

If you choose to follow part or all of one of our itineraries, or to link two of them together, you have a route that works. We've traveled all of them many times. But remember that the itineraries can and should be modified—by your own interests and time limitations. And there are other factors to consider too: weather and road conditions, crowds in high season (travel off season if you can), ferry schedules, and the days and hours sites are open. And on longer trips, a day of relaxation is a must.

Once we've worked out all these factors, we make a list of the areas we want to cover, the activities we would like to do, and possible side trips. Then, after a lot of erasing and reconsidering, we write down our planned destination for each night on an index card, adding estimated mileage and driving time. Addresses and phone numbers we'll need en route are copied onto another card. Then we put cards, brochures, travel articles, books, and other information we've collected into a large envelope for easy reference along the way.

Your Expenses

Plan to carry enough money in traveler's checks, credit cards, and cash to get you through your trip. (Remember weekends and holidays if you need access to a bank to replenish your supply.) We estimate expenses — gas, tolls, ferries, entrance fees, camp food, meals out, snacks, gifts, accommodations (campsite fees or other overnight lodgings) — and add a slush fund for miscellaneous expenses and a reserve for emergencies. We list them all on yet another index card, which becomes our working budget. Of course it's easy to spend a little more, but we find this saves a frantic search for money once we're on our way.

Eating

If there's a special restaurant you've heard wonderful things about, it doesn't hurt to write or phone ahead for a reservation. (We list phone numbers for all our suggestions.) Or, once you get into town, ask a native for a good place to eat.

If you want to try regional foods and sample some terrific home cooking, look in the local papers or on bulletin boards around town for notices of church or grange suppers. Craft fairs and bazaars often sell homemade baked goods and preserves too.

Activities

Enjoy! Let the ages and interests of your family set the focus of your trip. But leave some time free for relaxation (defined as time to do nothing) and flexibility (the freedom to change your mind according to weather and mood).

When our children were little, we chose activities to appeal to their interests and levels of understanding. We visited zoos, county fairs, beaches, whaling museums, aquariums, restored villages, dinosaur traces, amusement parks, and planetariums; we took train rides and steamboat trips; we saw theater and puppet shows, baseball games, and historical reenactments; and we canoed and sailed and swam and rowed. Whenever we could we prepared them for an activity—showing them pictures and talking about the historic sites we intended to visit. They especially loved hearing stories about the children who once lived in these old houses.

We let them guide us through museums, picking out displays that intrigued them rather than stopping them (shifting from one foot to the other) in front of every exhibit. Then we would head for the museum shop and select postcards for our collections.

Children love nature trails with buttons to push and signs to read. They also love hikes, especially when they're well supplied with goodies for energy. Ours carried hard candies, raisins, fruit, and gorp, and a jacket, in a child-sized rucksack. And as we'd go along, we'd decorate the rucksack with souvenir patches from places we visited.

Whether you're traveling alone or with family, try something new on each trip. For starters think about gravestone rubbing, hang gliding, white-water canoeing, kayak surfing, saltwater fishing, needlepoint, polishing stones, or collecting shipwreck lore and local legends.

Most of us have a strong impulse to return with some booty from our adventures. You may want to collect postcards, decals, demitasse spoons, T-shirts, local books, cookbooks, state emblems, shells, rocks, or things for a special hobby.

While you're traveling, take the time to write about the day's discoveries, to reflect on your everyday life from the distance of travel. We keep journals ourselves, and have encouraged our older children to keep them too. We've found their postcard-illustrated narratives a big help in planning future trips, and a happy way of remembering past ones.

Letting Go

We've found that our most successful trips are those that strike a balance of sports, historic touring, and unplanned time. You may find, as we sometimes do, that unexpected local activities are more fun than preplanned ones. New friends may suggest a new treat, and circumstances may put local drama in your way. The key to full enjoyment is receptiveness—a childlike naiveté that looks out on a world where anything might happen.

Vacations are supposed to be relaxing. Of course it's easier to say so than to make them so—to fight compulsiveness when you want to see and experience more than you possibly can in one trip. Tentatively select what you want to do *before* you go, but allow yourself the flexibility to change your mind *as* you go. And most of all, enjoy!

Readings

Literature, Legends, and History

Bolte, Mary. *Haunted New England*. Chatham, MA: Chatham Press, 1972.

Botkin, B. A. *A Treasury of New England Folklore*. New York: Bonanza, 1965.

Deedy, John. *Literary Places: A Guided Pilgrimage, to New York and New England*. Kansas City: Universal Press, 1978.

Harting, Emilie C. *A Literary Tour Guide to the U.S.: Northeast*. New York: Morrow, 1978.

Hechtlinger, Adelaide. *Historic Homes and Sites of Revolutionary America*. Gretna, LA: Pelican, 1976.

Kull, Andrew. *New England Cemeteries*. Brattleboro, VT: Stephen Green, 1975.

Quinn, William P. *Shipwrecks Around Cape Cod*. Farmington, ME: Knowlton & McLeary, 1973.

Robinson, William F. *Abandoned New England, Its Hidden Ruins and Where to Find Them*. Boston: New York Graphic Society, 1978.

Scoville, Dorothy R. *Shipwrecks on Martha's Vineyard*. Oak Bluffs, MA: Martha's Vineyard Printing, 1977.
Skinner, Charles M. *Myths and Legends of Our Own Land*. Philadelphia: Lippincott, 1896.
Snow, Edward Rowe. *Tales of Sea and Shore*. New York: Dodd, Mead, 1934.
_____. *Great Storms and Famous Shipwrecks*. New York: Dodd, Mead, 1943.
_____. *New England Sea Tragedies*. New York: Dodd, Mead, 1960.
_____. *Mysterious Tales of the New England Coast*. New York: Dodd, Mead, 1961.
_____. *Tales of Terror and Tragedy*. New York: Dodd, Mead, 1979.
Stevens, Austin. *Mysterious New England*. Dublin, N.H: Yankee, 1971.
Yeadon, David. *Hidden Corners of New England*. New York: Funk & Wagnalls, 1976.

Natural History

Jorgenson, Neil. *A Guide to New England's Landscape*. Chester, CT: Globe Pequot, 1977.
Sterling, Dorothy. *The Outer Lands*. New York: Norton, 1978.
Zinn, Donald J. *The Handbook for Beach Strollers from Maine to Cape Hatteras*. Chester, CT: Globe Pequot, 1975.

Places to Visit

Bixby, William. *Connecticut: A New Guide*. New York: Scribner's, 1974.
Burroughs, Polly. *Nantucket: A Guide with Tours*. Chester, CT: Globe Pequot, 1974.
_____. *Guide to Martha's Vineyard*. Chester, CT: Globe Pequot, 1979.
Chesler, Bernice. *In and Out of Boston with (or without) Children*. 4th ed. Chester, CT: Globe Pequot, 1982.
Chesler, Bernice, and Evelyn Kaye. *The Family Guide to Cape Cod*. Barre, MA: Barre Publishing, 1976.

Clayton, Barbara, and Kathleen Whitley. *Exploring Coastal New England, Gloucester to Kennebunkport*. New York: Dodd, Mead, 1979.

_____. *Guide to New Bedford*. Chester, CT: Globe Pequot, 1979.

Doane, Doris. *Exploring Old Cape Cod*. Chatham, MA: Chatham Press, 1968.

Duncan, Roger F., and John P. Ware. *A Cruising Guide to the New England Coast*. New York, Dodd, Mead, 1972.

Henning, Alyson R., and Gwynne MacColl. *A Guide to Hartford*. Chester, CT: Globe Pequot, 1978.

Johnson, Stephanie L. *The Best of the Berkshires*. Chester, CT: Globe Pequot, 1979.

Moore, Marie. *Portrait of Essex*. Chester, CT: Globe Pequot, 1979.

Pratt, Dorothy, and Richard Pratt. *A Guide to Early American Homes, North and South*. New York: Bonanza, 1956.

Thollander, Earl. *Back Roads of New England*. New York: Crown, 1974.

Witteman, Betsy, and Nancy Webster. *Daytripping & Dining*. West Hartford, CT: Imprint Publications, 1979.

_____. *Weekending in New England*. West Hartford, CT: Imprint Publications, 1980.

Sports and Activities

Blaisdell, Paul H. *25 Walks in the Lakes Region of New Hampshire*. Somersworth, NH: New Hampshire Publishing, 1977.

Catlett, Cloe. *Fifty More Hikes in Maine*. Somersworth, NH: New Hampshire Publishing, 1980.

Doan, Daniel. *Fifty More Hikes in New Hampshire*. Somersworth, NH: New Hampshire Publishing, 1980.

Duncan, Roger F., and John P. Ware. *A Cruising Guide to the New England Coast*. New York: Dodd, Mead, 1979.

Fisher, Alan. *AMC Guide to Country Walks Near

Boston. Boston: Appalachian Mountain Club, 1976.

Freiden, John. *20 Bicycle Tours in Vermont*. Somersworth, NH: New Hampshire Publishing, 1979.

Hardy, Gerry, and Sue Hardy. *Fifty Hikes in Connecticut*. Somersworth, NH: New Hampshire Publishing, 1978.

Heavey, Tom, and Susan Heavey. *20 Bicycle Tours in New Hampshire*. Somersworth, NH: New Hampshire Publishing, 1979.

Pyle, Sara. *Canoeing and Rafting: The Complete Where-to-Go Guide to America's Best Tame and Wild Waters*. New York: Morrow, 1979.

Sadlier, Paul, and Ruth Sadlier. *Fifty Hikes in Vermont*. Somersworth, NH: New Hampshire Publishing, 1974.

_____. *Fifty Hikes in Massachusetts*. Somersworth, NH: New Hampshire Publishing, 1975.

Schweiker, Roioli. *Canoe Camping Vermont & New Hampshire Rivers*. Somersworth, NH: New Hampshire Publishing, 1977.

Weber, Ken. *Canoeing Massachusetts, Rhode Island & Connecticut*. Somersworth, NH: New Hampshire Publishing, 1980.

Winchester, Kenneth, and David Dunbar. *Walking Tours of New England*. Garden City, NY: Doubleday, 1980.

ITINERARY A

MYSTIC SEAPORT MUSEUM

ITINERARY A

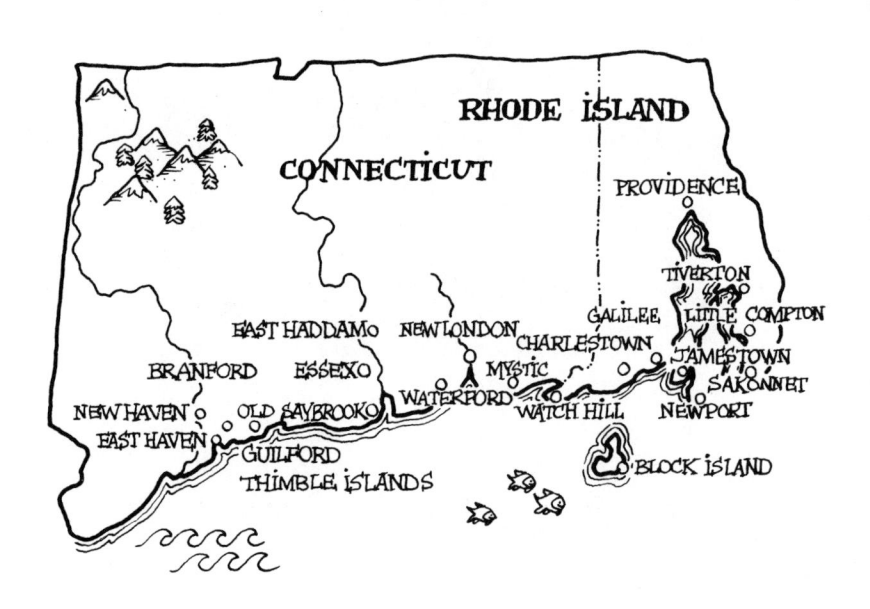

(Suggested Time: 5–7 days; 121 miles/194 kilometers)

The Southern Shore

New Haven	A·6
East Haven	A·8
Branford	A·8
Thimble Islands	A·9
Guilford	A·9
Essex	A·10
East Haddam	A·11
New London	A·12
Mystic	A·15
Stonington	A·20
Watch Hill	A·22
Charlestown	A·22
West Kingston	A·23
Galilee	A·23
Block Island	A·23
Point Judith	A·26
Narragansett Pier	A·26
Jamestown	A·27
Newport	A·28
Middletown	A·32
Tiverton	A·32
Little Compton	A·33

Blow, Ye Winds

'Tis advertised in Boston, New York, and Buffalo
Five hundred brave Americans a-whaling for to go.

>Blow, ye winds, in the morning,
>And blow, ye winds, high-O!
>Clear away your running gear,
>And blow, ye winds, high-O!

They send you to New Bedford, that famous whaling port,
And give you to some land-sharks for to board and fit you out.

They send you to a boarding house, there for a time to dwell,
The thieves they there are thicker than the other side of hell!

They tell you of the clipper ships a-going in and out,
And say you'll take five hundred sperm, before you're six months out.
Now we have got him turned up, we tow him alongside;
We over with our blubber-hooks and rob him of his hide.

Now the boat-steerer overside the tackle overhauls,
The Skipper's in the main-chains, so loudly he does bawl!

Next comes the stowing down, my boys; 'twill take both night and day,
And you'll all have fifty cents apiece on the hundred and ninetieth lay.

Now we are bound into Tonbas, that blasted whaling port,
And if you run away, my boys, you surely will get caught.

Now we are bound into Tuckoons, full more in their power,
Where the skippers can buy the Consul up for half a barrel of flour!

> But now that our old ship is full and we don't give
>   a damn,
> We'll bend on all our stuns'ls and sail for Yankee
>   land.
>
> When we get home, our ship made fast, and we get
>   through our sail,
> A winding glass around we'll pass and damn this
>   blubber whaling!

Southern New England is blessed with a magnificently varied coastline. Stretching across two states from New Haven to Little Compton are cities with major universities, river ports, historic towns, almost forgotten rural villages, and miles of nearly perfect ocean beach.

∽ Connecticut ∾

This itinerary begins in Connecticut, where features of the coast—a semiprotected sound, good harbors, and the mouth of a great river—made exploration and settlement inevitable. In 1614 Adriaen Block, a Dutch explorer and navigator, sailed through Long Island Sound, up into the lower reaches of the Connecticut River. Farther upstream the river separates the Berkshires from central Massachusetts, and Vermont from New Hampshire, linking north and south. Settlers used the river to reach Windsor, Hartford, and Wethersfield from their homes in Massachusetts as early as 1633.

Connecticut, originally named Quinnehtukqut from an Indian word meaning "beside the long tidal river," is called the Constitution State because it was the first colony to have a written constitution. More informally it's also called the Nutmeg State, for the peddlers who once traveled door to door selling spices. (Now and again customers would find little carved wooden pellets instead of the spices they had paid for.)

We suggest you start your exploration of the coast at New Haven, beyond the New York suburbs that fill the southwestern corner of the state, and move east along the water, with one excursion up the lower reaches of the Connecticut River. (For suggestions about places to visit in northern and western Connecticut, see itinerary F.)

New Haven

New Haven Chamber of Commerce
195 Church Street
New Haven
787-6735

Yale Information Office
341 College Street
New Haven
436-8330

Yale University Art Gallery
1111 Chapel Street
New Haven
436-0574

Yale Center for British Art
1080 Chapel Street
New Haven
432-4594

Sterling Memorial Library
120 High Street
New Haven
436-8335

Peabody Museum
170 Whitney Avenue
New Haven
436-0850

In 1638, Reverend John Davenport and Theophilus Eaton came from England to New Haven after a brief stay in what they felt was a too liberal Boston. The two established harsh laws to govern the settlement through the church. They interpreted the Bible strictly, and enforced its edicts rigidly.

Yale, founded in 1701 in Old Saybrook as the Collegiate School, moved to New Haven in 1716. Two years later the school was renamed for Elihu Yale, in appreciation for a 562-pound gift he made to the college. Tours of the university are available from Phelps Gateway off College Street, at the green. The **Yale Information Office** there provides maps and schedules.

The campus, with its separate enclosed colleges, is very much like Oxford University. A carillon in Gothic-style **Harkness Tower** fills the air with melody throughout the day. Inside, in the Memorial Room, you can follow the history of the college through a series of woodcarvings. From here, you can work your way through the many fine collections in the **Yale University Art Gallery**, the **Yale Center for British Art**, the **Sterling Memorial Library**, the **Beinecke Rare Book and Manuscript Library**, the **Yale Collection of Musical Instruments**, and the **Peabody Museum** (look for the dinosaur skeleton).

Bulldogs are everywhere in New Haven — on business signs, on clothing, even on gargoyled university buildings. It all began in 1892, when a bulldog named Handsome Dan was found in a local blacksmith's shop and was made the Yale mascot. The original Dan has been stuffed and is on display in a closely guarded glass box in the Payne Whitney Gymnasium. But his name lives on in each new bulldog, the living mascot.

The college green is like a European square, filled with people relaxing and talking with friends. It's also the site of two local celebrations. In late April or early May there's an historical reenactment of **Powder House Day**, the day Captain Benedict Arnold asked for the keys to the Powder House before he took his troops off to Boston to join the rebellion. The ceremony is complete with the Governor's Footguard in Revolutionary War uniforms. At the end of June, the **Mayor's Festival**, an ethnic fair, is celebrated here with crafts, dancing, food, and fireworks. Contact the chamber of commerce for more information.

From the green, head west out Whalley Avenue to **West Rock Park**. West Rock is part of a basalt ridge that rises from New Haven and continues north 20 miles to Southington. Geologists believe it was formed 200 million years ago as lava was forced up through a crack in the red sandstone crust. This left a "dike" several hundred feet thick (most are only a few feet wide). The trail along the ridge offers views of cliffs and harbors, tracks of prehistoric animals, and marks of glacial movement in the sedimentary rocks.

One stop along the trail is **Judges' Cave** — home for three months to two British regicides. In 1661 Edward Whalley and William Goffe, who had signed a warrant for the arrest and execution of King Charles I fourteen years earlier, fled for their lives when Charles II, the son of the beheaded king, offered a 100-pound reward for their capture. A plaque bolted to a nearby boulder tells the story:

> Here, May 15th 1661, and for some weeks thereafter, Edward Whalley and his son-in-law William Goffe, Members of Parliament, General Officers in the Army of the Commonwealth and signers of the death warrant of King Charles I, found shelter and concealment from the officers of the Crown after the Restoration. Opposition to tyrants is Obedience to God!

Regicides Trail, the path to Judges' Cave and out along West Rock, begins at the **West Rock Nature Recreation Center**. Just follow the blue markers along the trail for about three-quarters of

Yale Collection of
  Musical
  Instruments
15 Hillhouse Avenue
New Haven
436–4935

Beinecke Rare Book
  and Manuscript
  Library
Hall and High Streets
New Haven
436–8438

West Rock Park
New Haven
787–8016

THE SOUTHERN SHORE

a mile. The center itself has two museum buildings, pens filled with small native animals (bobcats, raccoons, red foxes, deer, and turkeys), and a picnic area.

When you leave the park, take Route 10 toward the city, and follow it to Long Wharf Drive. The **Long Wharf Theater** offers excellent theater—repertory and Broadway tryouts—in a converted warehouse building. Nearby, the **Liberty Belle**, a 250-passenger ship, makes short trips around the harbor.

Long Wharf Theater
New Haven
787-4282

Liberty Belle
Long Wharf
New Haven
562-4163

East Haven

From New Haven take Route 1 to East Haven. **Lighthouse Park Community Beach** is located right off Route 142. It's a wonderful beach for children: The surf is gentle and the drop-off is gradual. The sand is rocky with shells.

In town the **Branford Trolley Museum** contains ninety trolleys dating from 1878 to 1940. There are exhibits and guided tours, and you can ride back and forth to Short Beach at the end of the line, as often as you like.

Branford Trolley Museum
17 River Street
East Haven
467-6927

Branford

Continue on Route 1 to Branford, once a busy shipping center in its own right, now an industrial satellite and residential suburb of New Haven. The New Haven Colony purchased Totoket, as it was then called, from the Indians in 1638. It was later named Branford after Brentford, a town in England.

Bittersweet Farm (488-9161), on Route 1 between exits 56 and 57 off I-95, is a group of arts and crafts shops in redesigned poultry farm buildings. Here you'll find a seemingly unlimited array of wood carvings, jewelry, books, handwoven goods, stained glass, pottery, paintings, metal sculpture, ship models, leather, silk-screened products, and miniature furniture. And there's a cafe on the grounds. The **Bittersweet Farm Arts and Crafts Festival** is held here over the Fourth of July.

May through mid-October, you can take a cruise on the **Volsunga III**, from Branford to the Thimble Islands. There are 365 islands, 32 of them populated, in the group named by Stony Creek Indians for the thimbleberry (similar to the gooseberry). Indians used the islands' pink glacial deposit for arrowheads; later it was quarried to make foundations for the Statue of Liberty and the Brooklyn Bridge.

Captain Kidd used one of the islands, **High Island**, to hide from the colonists. Legend says he left gold in an underwater cave, perhaps on **Money Island**; treasure hunters are still searching for it.

The populated islands are all privately owned. But you might see the Jolly Roger flying and catch black motifs on homes, boats, and docks.

From Branford wind along Route 146 for about 8 miles, to Guilford. The town, named for lovely Guilford in Surrey, England, has a green surrounded by carefully preserved buildings dating from the early eighteenth to the late nineteenth century. Reverend Henry Whitfield, vicar of Ockley Parish, Saint Margaret's Church, in Surrey, led twenty-five young families from their homes in one of the most beautiful regions of England, and settled them here in 1639. He built his home of stone — in late medieval English style — the oldest stone house in New England. It has been restored and is open today as the **Henry Whitfield Museum**.

Two other early homes open for visits are **Hyland House**, a seventeenth-century home, restored and furnished; and the **Thomas Griswold House Museum**, with its costumes of the 1800s, historical exhibits, and period gardens.

The **Guilford Handcraft Center** (453-5947), on Route 77 just north of exit 58 off I-95, displays the products of two hundred artists and craftsmen. During the third week in July you can

Thimble Islands

Volsunga III
Stony Creek Public Dock
Branford
481-3345, 488-9978

Guilford

Henry Whitfield Museum
Old Whitfield Street
Guilford
453-2457

Hyland House
84 Boston Street
Guilford
453-9477

Thomas Griswold House Museum
171 Boston Street
Guilford
453-3176

Guilford Recreation Department
32 Church Street
Guilford
453-2763

see craftsmen at work at the **Guilford Handcraft Exposition and Sale** on the green.

The **Trails of the Guilford Westwoods** lead hikers through terrain that ranges from low and marshy to high and spectacular. Pick up a map from the **Guilford Recreation Department**. The park, with six hiking trails and a bridle path, is right off Boston Post Road (Route 1).

Friends recommend **Chello Oyster House** (453-2670) on Route 1. Here you can buy a clam chowder base that, when mixed with water or milk, is absolutely delicious—"almost as good as my mother's was!"

Essex

From Guilford take I-95, or more scenic Route 1, for 16 miles to Old Saybrook. Then continue on Route 9 to Essex. The area is a yachtsman's paradise, with beautiful harbors along the Connecticut River in Old Saybrook, Old Lyme, and Hamburg Cove.

Essex, on the west shore, has preserved the romance of its maritime and architectural past. The town became a shipbuilding center in the 1720s. The *Oliver Cromwell*, a twenty-four-gun vessel, was given to the patriots by the town during the Revolutionary War. In 1814 men from the British naval squadron blockading Long Island Sound arrived to destroy the shipping industry here. They burned twenty-two ships, among them the *Osage*, whose name now appears on the facade of a former inn on Main Street. Today the waterfront is bustling with sloops, ketches, schooners, and yawls.

Although shipping was the backbone of Essex's commercial growth, another industry was rooted here as well. At one time Essex was famous for its piano keys. In fact, Ivoryton, as it came to be called, was known to piano manufacturers around the world. Of course, there came a time when plastic keys replaced ivory ones, and yet another oldtime industry ended. Today the town thrives through its real estate, yachting facilities, and tourist attractions.

Walk along Main Street, past lovely colonials and Federal homes built during the early years of the nineteenth century. The **William Pratt House**, nearby, is even older. The original building, which dates from 1725, was one room. Later it was enlarged to four rooms with a gambrel roof. The house is filled with early American furnishings.

The **Griswold Inn** (767-0991), built in 1776, has a collection of Currier and Ives prints, marine oils, and firearms in the Gun Room, a nostalgic setting for lunch or dinner. Just across the street is the **Glass Basket** (267-2350), known for its pottery, quilts, jewelry, and miniature birds.

Essex sits near the base of the Connecticut Valley, the beautiful countryside bordering the Connecticut River. To see the area, take the **Valley Railroad** steam train from Essex Depot to Chester. There you can connect with a riverboat for a one- or two-hour cruise on the river.

William Pratt House
20 West Avenue
Essex
767-8987

Valley Railroad
Railroad Avenue
Essex
767-0103

From Essex follow Route 9A through Chester to Tylerville, to Route 82 into East Haddam. In town, the **Goodspeed Opera House**, which was built in the days of river steamboats, has been restored and now presents three musical shows each summer. Two presentations are revivals, one an original production.

If you're interested in weaving, don't miss a special treat nearby. For handwoven rugs, coats, ponchos, and yarn, visit **Finally Hand Weavers** (873-1111) on Mount Parnassus Road, off Route 82.

You stay on Mount Parnassus Road (Route 434) to get to **Devil's Hopyard State Park**. In the spectacular 860-acre park you'll find the turbulent **Eight Mile River**, the **Devil's Oven** (a small cave), groves of huge hemlocks, and **Chapman Falls** (a 60-foot waterfall). Legend says the devil sat high above the falls playing his violin while he directed

East Haddam

Goodspeed Opera
House
The Plaza
East Haddam
873-8664

Devil's Hopyard State
Park
Route 434
East Haddam
873-8566

THE SOUTHERN SHORE

Gillette Castle State Park
River Road
East Haddam
526-2336

the witches mixing hops into magic potions in the potholes below. Also here: 15 miles of hiking trails, and facilities for picnicking, fishing, and camping.

Follow Route 82 through East Haddam to Route 148, where you'll see signs to **Gillette Castle State Park**. William Gillette, an actor, built his medieval castle on a hilltop overlooking the river. It took five years to build. Its granite walls are 4 to 5 feet thick, and each of its twenty-four rooms is unique. Gillette designed, not only the structure, but also the heavy oak furniture. One piece, the dining room table, runs on a track. Also here: an art gallery and a collection of theater memorabilia (playbills, scrapbooks, magazine articles, even a stage set for a Sherlock Holmes play in which Gillette starred).

At one time there was a train that ran around the property to amuse the actor's guests. You can take a 2-mile hike beginning at "Grand Central Station," once the main terminal for Gillette's Seventh Sister Shortline. Follow the flagstone ramp to the sign reading "Loop Trail to River Vista, 0.5 mile." Turn left and walk through the woods. The trail follows the old railroad bed—sometimes crossing it, sometimes running parallel to it.

When you've finished exploring the park, you can follow Route 148 back to Chester; or, April through October, take the ferry from Hadlyme. Then pick up Route 9A south to Essex.

New London

After your excursion in the lower reaches of the Connecticut River, take I-95 from Old Saybrook to New London, a distance of 16 miles. The Thames River (*thaymes*, not *tems*) gives New London one of the best deep-water ports in New England. The harbor is large, fairly well protected, and busy with traffic from all kinds of vessels—navy and coast guard ships, submarines, fishing trawlers, ferries, and yachts.

In the seventeenth century, farmers used the river to ship their produce; a hundred years later,

CONNECTICUT

EAST HADDAM

The Goodspeed Opera House, built in 1876 and restored in 1963, offers performances of American musicals, a number of which go on to Broadway.

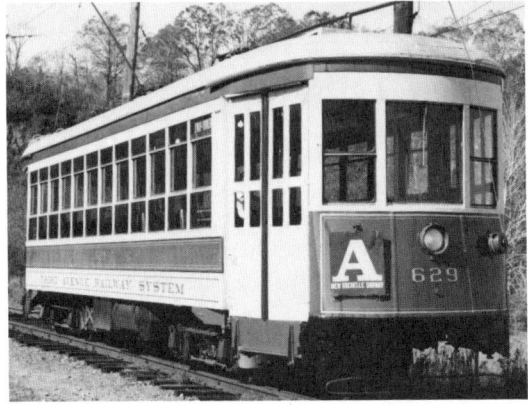

EAST HAVEN

Branford's #629N restored and operating at the Branford Trolley Museum.

NEW LONDON

The Hempstead House, built in 1678, is listed on the National Register of Historic Places. Joshua Hempstead's "kitchen" contains many rarities.

A•13

THE SOUTHERN SHORE

**U.S. Coast Guard
  Academy**
**Mohegan Avenue
New London
444-8611**

**Deshon-Allyn House
613 Williams Street
New London
443-2545**

**Lyman Allyn Museum
625 Williams Street
New London
443-2545**

**Hempstead House
11 Hempstead Street
New London
443-7949**

**Shaw Mansion
11 Blinman Street
New London
443-1209**

**Nathan Hale
  Schoolhouse
Captain's Walk
New London
443-1209**

whalers began bringing home their fortunes along it. During the Revolutionary War a number of New London vessels, privateers, raided British merchant ships. The devastating attack on the town in 1781 was retribution: Thirty-two British ships with seventeen hundred men, led by turncoat Benedict Arnold, destroyed the city.

In the 1860s almost eighty whaling ships called New London home; by 1900 the fleet was gone. Several New London whalers were in a group caught near Alaska by a Confederate warship during the Civil War; the rest of the fleet was gradually sold off or abandoned after the development of oil fields in Pennsylvania made whale oil less valuable. You can still see the hull of a schooner and the remains of other ships in the marine graveyard near the shipyard. (Take Route 32 north past the Coast Guard Academy, turn right onto Mohegan Avenue, then left on Naumkeag, and left again just before the shipyard.)

Today New London is still a marine center, home to the **U.S. Coast Guard Academy**. On the academy's grounds are a visitors' center and a museum. You can also tour the *Eagle*, a three-masted training bark, whenever it's in port (usually fall through spring). The *Eagle*, once a German sail-training ship, was confiscated as a war prize, restored, and then given its present name.

If you enjoy the Coast Guard Academy, try a visit to the **U.S. Naval Submarine Base** just across the river in Groton. (Follow the signs.) The one-hour bus tours – the only way to visit the base – stop at the submarine museum. Nearby, the *USS Croaker*, a submarine actually used in World War II, is open for tours. Call 448-1616 for information.

Red and white signs point the way to other tourist attractions. The **Deshon-Allyn House**, built in 1829 by a whaling captain, contains an impressive collection of original Federal furnishings. Right down the street, the **Lyman Allyn Museum** displays a charming collection of dolls, dollhouses,

A • 14

doll furniture, and toys. **Hempstead House**, built in 1678, is one of the few intact seventeenth-century houses still standing in Connecticut. On its grounds is the **Nathaniel Hempstead House**, built in 1759, one of two houses of mid-eighteenth-century cut-stone architecture in the state. The **Shaw Mansion**, a restored 1756 building, was used as Connecticut's naval office during the Revolutionary War. The **Nathan Hale Schoolhouse** is where Hale taught before he enlisted in the army.

Contact the chamber of commerce for more information and maps, and for current schedules for ferry service to Fishers Island, Block Island, and Orient Point on Long Island.

A few miles south of the city, off Route 213, is **Harkness Memorial State Park**. The beach here is sandy and clean, and there's gentle surf, no undertow, and a gradual drop-off. Nearby, the **Eugene O'Neill Memorial Theater Center** houses the National Playwriter's Conference, the National Critics Institute, the Barn Theater, Amphitheater and Instant Theater, the National Theater Institute, and O'Neill Media. Original plays are produced here during the summer season.

O'Neill's boyhood home, **Monte Cristo Cottage**, is now open regularly. The house was the setting for *Ah, Wilderness* and *Long Day's Journey into Night*, and some of the rooms were reconstructed as sets for the plays. You can feel the sadness of O'Neill's childhood and the unhappiness of his mother, Ella, a withdrawn woman who secluded herself when O'Neill and his brother needed her. The boys went to boarding school but spent summers here with their actor father, James.

From New London take Route 1, or I-95 and then Route 27, to Mystic, one of the oldest shipbuilding and whaling ports in New England. Mystic was settled in 1654, its name derived from the Pequot Indian's Mistuket. Modern Mystic Village is separated by the Mystic River: The

New London
 Chamber of
 Commerce
1 Whale Oil Row
New London
443-8332

Harkness Memorial
 State Park
Goshen Point
Waterford
443-5725

Eugene O'Neill
 Memorial Theater
 Center
305 Great Neck Road
Waterford
443-1238

Monte Cristo Cottage
325 Pequot Avenue
Waterford
443-0051

Mystic

THE SOUTHERN SHORE

village center and fine old homes lie on its west bank; the Seaport, aquarium, and Old Mystic Village, on the east bank.

There's an interesting shopping center on Route 27, at I-95, that houses forty shops in a recreated old New England village, nicely landscaped with a pond, a waterwheel, and ducks to feed. During the last weekend in June you can enjoy the craft exhibits here at the **Olde Mistick Village Art and Handcrafts Show** (874-5672).

Follow signs from the shopping area to **Mystic Marinelife Aquarium**. Here you can watch demonstrations with whales, dolphins, and sea lions; visit the touch-and-feel exhibit, where children can handle live specimens and the 8-foot-long water table; and look through microscopes. The aquarium runs a summer program for children, among its other educational programs.

Mystic Seaport is a place we love to explore, and we go back year after year. This 20-acre village imparts the living history of land and sea. You can smell the pine tar used on sailing ships, the fish; you can hear the gulls squawking and crying, a foghorn in the distance, someone singing sea chanteys.

Mystic Seaport sponsors many activities: movies, lectures, demonstrations, sailing courses for children, and educational programs for all ages. It also offers accredited monthlong or semester programs for college students. Students in the Williams Mystic program take courses in American maritime history, maritime literature, oceanography, marine ecology, and marine policy. They live in houses on the grounds, but spend several weeks on board the schooner *Westward*, a research vessel, gaining practical experience in living and working at sea.

The Seaport offers individual and family memberships at reasonable rates, and it's money well spent. Members receive free admission, mooring facilities at the Seaport, and a magazine

Mystic Marinelife Aquarium
Mystic
536-3323

Mystic Seaport
Route 27
Mystic
536-2631

filled with interesting maritime articles and schedules of special membership activities and weekends.

You'll want to spend a full day at the Seaport. Most visitors start with a tour of the ships. The *Charles W. Morgan*, a nineteenth-century wooden whaler, is usually moored at Chubb's Wharf. You can climb all over her, learn how whales were caught, and feel what it must have been like to live on board—the captain sleeping in a gimballed bed, the crew in the cramped, uncomfortable forecastle. The ship was built in 1841 in New Bedford, by Jethro and Zachariah Hillman. Over the next eighty years she completed thirty-seven whaling voyages. In 1941 she was towed to the Seaport for restoration. In recent years she's been refloated and extensively rebuilt at the shipyard on the grounds.

The *Joseph Conrad*, built in Copenhagen as a Danish sail-training ship in 1882, sailed under three flags before coming to Mystic in 1947. In 1905 she was rammed by a British freighter and sunk with the loss of twenty-two cadets. From 1934 to 1936 Alan Villiers and a group of students took the raised ship around the world on a 58,000-mile cruise. She is now permanently moored, a floating dormitory for visiting students. Look for demonstrations of sail setting and handling, and chantey singing, on board both the *Morgan* and the *Conrad*.

The third ship not to miss is the *L. A. Dunton*. She is the last Gloucester fisherman built primarily as a sailing vessel.

More than fifty other fishing vessels and yachts of specific historic types fill the Seaport's waterfront and boat sheds—it's a paradise for wooden boat aficionados. And, there are the shipyard and boat shop, too, where older methods of working in wood are still practiced. You'll leave with the scent of salt water, tar, and hemp, and perhaps a faint touch of the whale oil that permeated the being of whaling men.

The rest of the Seaport is a reconstructed village, with chapel, tavern, bank, general store, apothecary, and doctor's office to wander through. In the museum, along with several other magnificent exhibits, are "New England and the Sea," and the *Packard* exhibit, a reassembled salon and cabin section of a fine nineteenth-century sailing ship. And there are several buildings housing collections of ship figureheads, models, wheels, whaleboats, scrimshaw, paintings, even the toys of children who lived at sea. There are also excellent rotating exhibits in the new art gallery, and a scholar's collection of books and materials in the library. And the planetarium offers programs on navigation, meteorology, and astronomy.

Every day the shops along Seaport Street have staff members practicing and happy to talk about the crafts that were a necessary part of colonial life: weaving, printing, marine ironwork, barrel making, sail making, rope making, and open-hearth cooking. And there are special courses and programs throughout the year. Our favorites: the **Chantey Festival** in mid-June, which draws singers from all over the world; and the **Christmas Lantern Light Tours** in December.

Sea chanteys are part of the rich heritage of seafaring. Although they tell a musical story, they were not sung for pleasure. A chanteyman was hired to lead the ship's crew as they worked.

Chanteys are not all alike. There are four types, each varying in beat and tempo, that correspond with the work done on board sailing ships. The *capstan* (windlass) *chantey* was used to weigh anchor or to unload cargo. A story unfolded as the chanteyman sat on the capstan head and the sailors pushed on the capstan bars to the continuous rhythm of the song. The *halyard* (long-haul) *chantey* did not have a steady marching beat; instead it used two accented beats to time the pull of the men on the line, allowing them to rest in between pulls. The halyard chantey was used for heavy work (hoisting sails and yards). The *short-haul chantey* had a single accented beat for one

CONNECTICUT

MYSTIC SEAPORT MUSEUM

The Joseph Conrad, *one of the smallest full-rigged ships ever built, is the focal point of the Mystic waterfront.*

MYSTIC SEAPORT MUSEUM

Seaport Street, with its historic ships and buildings, attracts strolling visitors at the Museum.

MYSTIC SEAPORT MUSEUM

The Demonstration Squad describes the use of whaleboats and whaling implements.

A·19

pull, and was used for hauling sheets or furling sails. The *walkaway* (hand-over-hand) *chantey* was used for hoisting smaller sails or for scraping barnacles from the bottom of the ship.

From the Seaport dock you can board the **Sabino**, a 1908 coal-fired steamboat, for a cruise along the Mystic River. There are thirty-minute cruises during the day; a ninety-minute cruise, past Noank and Mason's Island toward Fishers Island, at six; and Dixieland jazz cruises every other Saturday during the summer. Several other charter vessels operate from Old Steamboat Wharf, and the **Mystic Whaler**, which runs weeklong cruises, has a wharf just north of the drawbridge.

Mystic Whaler
Holmes Street
Mystic
536-4218

Williams Beach, which is privately owned, is located off Route 1. The water is clean, with gentle surf and no undertow; there is a steep drop-off, but the area is roped.

On the other side of the Seaport, stop for lunch or dinner at the **Seamen's Inne** (536-9649), with its three dining rooms and oyster bar. The seafood is great, and the Sunday brunch is famous. On our last trip, we discovered the **Steamboat Cafe** (536-1975), on Old Steamboat Wharf. New owners have redecorated with nautical flair, and the schooners berthed not 6 feet from your chair offer a pleasant view.

Stonington

From Mystic take Route 1 east to Stonington, one of the most impressive old towns on the New England coast. As its name suggests, the land around Stonington was rocky, and settlers had a difficult time producing food. They also found it hard to keep wolves from necessarily shallow graves. Eventually they began to top each grave with a heavy stone slab. These **wolf stones** can still be seen in the cemetery near Wequetequock off Greenhaven Road, south of Route 1.

The compact town is laid out on a narrow peninsula, its fine captains' homes, many of them still in use, jammed together. This made Stonington particularly vulnerable during the War of 1812, when the British fleet shelled the town. (You can still see cannonballs in the beams of some of the old homes.)

For special seafood, try the **Harbor View Restaurant** (535-2720) on Water Street. Through the ornate wooden doors you step into a Victorian setting: dark paneled walls lined with antique plates, tiled fireplaces, and brass sconces. The cuisine is French and delicious, and served with a fine view of Stonington Harbor.

⁜ Rhode Island ⁜

Although the state of Rhode Island stretches only 37 miles between the borders of Connecticut and Massachusetts, it has 400 miles of shoreline. Wind and waves modulate the quiet coves, beaches, rugged cliffs, and ponds—a mecca for sailors and fishermen.

During the Ice Age a glacier ground southward until it came to a stop just beyond the coast, along a line running through Nantucket, Martha's Vineyard, Block Island, and Long Island. Accumulations of rock and gravel kept piling up in a ridge (called a *terminal moraine*) along the northern coast of Cape Cod (the Sandwich Moraine), along the west coast of Buzzards Bay (the Buzzards Bay Moraine), and through western Rhode Island (the Watch Hill Moraine). Several lakes scattered around Rhode Island are remnants of this glacier.

Rhode Island was discovered in 1524 by Giovanni da Verrazano, an Italian explorer, and was settled a century later by a bull-riding clergyman named Roger Williams. Williams had been banished by the Puritan leaders of the Massachusetts Bay Colony in 1635 for religious nonconformity; a year later he arrived by canoe with several followers in what is now Providence. In 1663 the Colony of Rhode Island and Providence Plantation was chartered by Charles II. The name came from the Greek island Rhodes; it's also called Aquidneck Island.

Williams was adept at keeping peace with the Narragansett Indians, as well as at acquiring land from them. Unfortunately the peace ended after the Wampanoag chief, Massasoit, died in 1674. Massasoit's son

Metacomet, or King Philip as the white men called him, knew the Indians were not being treated fairly. He convinced other chiefs to join him, and in 1675 went to war. During King Philip's War Indian warriors attacked towns in Connecticut, Massachusetts, and Rhode Island. Finally, in December, the colonists struck back at the Narragansett winter camp in a swamp near South Kingston, Rhode Island. They burned six hundred wigwams, killed a thousand Indians, and took hundreds of prisoners. Although Indians continued to ravage the countryside, this battle was the turning point in the war. In August 1676 King Philip's wife and son were captured and taken to Bermuda as slaves; Metacomet was killed in a swamp on Mount Hope Neck, and his head was placed on a stockade paling in Plymouth, where it stayed for twenty years.

Watch Hill

Misquamicut State Beach
Atlantic Avenue
Watch Hill
596-9097

Kimball Wildlife Refuge
Route 1
Charlestown
322-7103

Burlingame State Park
Cookestown Road
Charlestown
322-7994

From Stonington take Route 1 into Rhode Island to Westerly, and follow the signs to Watch Hill. One of the coast's oldest resorts, Watch Hill sits on a narrow peninsula between the Atlantic and the Pawcatuck River. The town is filled with lovely old colonial homes, and newer summer colonies spread out along the shore to the east. There are yachts in the harbor, a Coast Guard station, and a lighthouse.

For swimming, there are saltwater ponds and the ocean. **Misquamicut State Beach** is open to everyone. The surf is gentle (an occasional undertow); the drop-off, gradual.

Don't miss one of the oldest merry-go-rounds in the country, the **Flying Horse Carousel**, on Beach Street. When it was built, two white horses provided the power; they're gone, but the original red and black wooden horses are still here.

Charlestown

Royal Indian Burial Ground
Narrow Lane
Charlestown

From Watch Hill take Route 1A to Route 1. A few miles west of Charlestown you'll find the Audubon Society's **Kimball Wildlife Refuge**. It's located on the southern side of **Burlingame State Park**, a great spot for camping.

In town stop for information and a map at the booth on Route 1. Then walk through the **Royal Indian Burial Ground** for the sachems (great men) and their families of the Narragansett tribe.

The beaches here are beautiful. Take Charlestown Beach Road off Route 1 for the **Charlestown Community Beach**. **East Beach** is across the Charlestown Breachway in the Ninigret conservation area. There are several beaches, too, along the sound from Charlestown to Matunuck, among them **East Matunuck State Beach**, with its 8- to 10-foot waves. (Sorry. Surfing isn't allowed.)

East Matunuck State Beach
Succotash Road
East Matunuck
789-8585

From Charlestown take Route 2 north to West Kingston. Here you'll find **Indian Cedar Swamp**, now a 2,600-acre wildlife refuge, the scene of the Great Swamp Fight in December 1675. Every September there's an Indian pilgrimage to the granite shaft that marks the site of Indian fortifications during that decisive battle. For information about the refuge and the pilgrimage, contact the chamber of commerce.

West Kingston

Greater Westerly-
Pawcatuck-
Charlestown
Chamber of
Commerce
159 Main Street
596-7761

From Route 1 take the exit for Galilee and Point Judith. Galilee is known for the annual **Rhode Island Tuna Tournament**, held for three days in late August. Anyone with $5 and a boat can enter. The boats set out at dawn and come back between four and five each afternoon to crowds waving tuna flags and loudspeakers blaring out the latest results. In 1961 a 758¾-pound tuna broke the standing record.

A large fleet of charter and party fishing boats operates from Galilee, and the ferry for Block Island leaves from a pier in town.

Try **Georges** (783-2306) on Sand Hill Cove for great crabcakes to take out, and full lunches and dinners. Then head for **Roger Wheeler Memorial Beach** nearby. The sandy strip is protected from the surf by a jetty.

Galilee

Block Island, the "Bermuda of the North," was discovered in 1524 by Giovanni da Verrazano, but was named for Adriaen Block, the Dutch explorer who arrived in 1614. Actually the island has had

Block Island

a series of names: The Indians called it Manisses, Verrazano called it Claudia, and Dutch maps labeled it Adriaen's Eyland.

When Verrazano discovered the island, it was covered with trees; now it is almost barren. The **Mohegan Bluffs**, like the white cliffs of Dover, rise abruptly 200 feet above sea level. The cliffs spread along the southern coast for 5 miles, looking in spots like the profiles of Indians. They have long been a landfall for sailors.

The island has also been a mariner's nightmare, with at least two hundred wrecks remaining around it. The **Palatine Graves**, on the southwestern side, are relics of one of the most appalling. Whittier's poem tells the story of the ship that sailed from Rotterdam in 1732.

Although there are several versions of the story, some historians believe that polluted drinking water killed three hundred during the voyage; barely a hundred survived the crossing. Then, off Block Island, the ship foundered and caught fire. One woman stayed on board with her valuables, and legend says you can hear her screaming whenever the Palatine Lights appear, right before a storm.

Mooncussers may have played a part in the legendary wreck of the *Palatine*. These smugglers, pirates, and thieves would use lights to lure boats onto the rocks, and then would make off with their cargo. How did they come to be called mooncussers? That's easy. On moonlit nights—when ships couldn't be led onto the rocks—the thieves would cuss the moon.

Sailors now enjoy **New Harbor**, the well protected, large harbor in Great Salt Pond. Originally there was a piece of land separating the pond from the ocean, but this has been cut through by a channel 100 feet wide and 12 feet deep (at mean low water). With such excellent shelter, Block Island is a favorite haunt of yachtsmen and the scene of a fabulous collection of ocean-racing yachts every other June, during **Block Island Week**.

The Palatine
John Greenleaf Whittier

Old wives spinning their webs of tow,
Or rocking weirdly to and fro
In and out of the peat's full glow,

And old men mending their nets of twine,
Talk together of dream and sign,
Talk of the lost ship Palatine,—

The ship that, a hundred years before,
Freighted deep with its goodly store,
In the gales of the equinox went ashore.

The eager islanders one by one
Counted the shots of her signal gun,
And heard the crash when she drove right on!

Into the teeth of death she sped:
(May God forgive the hands that fed
The false lights over the rocky Head!)

O men and brothers! what sights were there!
White upturned faces, hands stretched in prayer!
Where waves had pity, could ye not spare?

Down swooped the wreckers, like birds of prey
Tearing the heart of the ship away,
And the dead had never a word to say.

And then, with ghastly shimmer and shine,
Over the rocks and the seething brine,
They burned the wreck of the Palatine.

In their cruel hearts, as they homeward sped,
"The sea and the rocks are dumb," they said:
"There'll be no reckoning with the dead."

But the year went round, and when once more
Along their foam-white curves of shore
They heard the line-storm rave and roar,

Behold! again, with shimmer and shine,
Over the rocks and the seething brine,
The flaming wreck of the Palatine!

THE SOUTHERN SHORE

Block Island State Beach
Water Street
Block Island
466-2130

Interstate Navigation
Galilee State Pier
Point Judith
783-4613

Point Judith

Narragansett Pier

Scarborough State Beach
Ocean Road
Narragansett Pier
783-1010

The island has something for everyone. For fishermen there are giant bluefin tuna, school tuna, swordfish, marlin, striped bass, and flounder in the waters off the island. For cyclists there are uncluttered roads with gradual inclines and beautiful views. And for swimmers there are superb beaches everywhere. The ones on the east side are better for swimming when the afternoon southwesterly is blowing hard. Try **Block Island State Beach**, which is in walking distance of the ferry. The surf is gentle, and the drop-off is gradual.

Block Island is 12 miles off the mainland, a short ferry ride from Galilee. (Ferries also make the longer runs from New London and Providence.) For a schedule contact **Interstate Navigation**. If you want to take your car, you must send a deposit ($5 one way) and be on the pier a half hour before sailing.

Follow the road from Galilee to Point Judith. During the Revolution a Coast Guard station and tower beacon were located here, but the original wooden lighthouse was destroyed in the hurricane of September 1815. In its place the town built an octagonal brick lighthouse that's still standing. (That storm of 1815 devastated Providence, where large vessels, torn from their moorings, crashed into the bridge, rammed through buildings, and blocked streets. In Narragansett Bay the tide rose 11 feet 9 inches above mean high water.)

Narragansett Pier, a few miles north of Point Judith, was once the site of Stanford White's Narragansett Casino. Only the Gothic twin towers remain; a storm in 1886 destroyed the rest of the pavilion.

Today beautiful homes and clubs line the shore, and there's a lovely sand beach in the center of town. **Scarborough State Beach**, a youth beach complete with jukebox, is just south of the town.

From Narragansett Pier take Route 1A to Route 138, to Jamestown, or Conanicut Island, in Narragansett Bay. The island is connected to the mainland on the west by a free bridge; to Newport on the east by a high toll bridge with spectacular views.

Originally named for King James I, the island is rich in Revolutionary War history. In 1775 the British burned most of the town, but a few old houses are still standing. Captain John Eldred, who died in 1784, would harass the Redcoats from a spot on the eastern side of the island—his one gun sounding like a whole company. Much later, after the Civil War, during the "cottage" period, fashionable people from Philadelphia, New York, Washington, and Saint Louis would spend their summers here.

In the **Old Friends Burial Ground**, on Route 138, half a mile west of North Main Road, are the graves of early settlers and Revolutionary War soldiers. In the **Jamestown Museum** the historical society has created several interesting exhibits about old Jamestown, and a display on a succession of island ferries. The society has also put an old windmill in working order on North Road, off Route 138.

When you've finished walking around the town, drive out Fort Getty Road past Mackeral Cove and an interesting old farm complex with weathered cedar-shake buildings. At the end of Fort Getty Road, at the southernmost tip of the island, you come to one of the treasures of this part of the world—the **Beaver Tail Lighthouse** area. Terraced rock faces shot through with quartz receive the brunt of ocean waves as they crash over and over, sweeping and swirling down and back to sea. You can actually see the wind as the fog blows in.

The first lighthouse here was built in 1749; its foundation was uncovered by the hurricane of

Jamestown

Old Friends Burial Ground
Eldred Avenue
Jamestown

Jamestown Museum
Narragansett Avenue
Jamestown
423-0784

Beaver Tail Lighthouse
Beaver Tail Road
Jamestown

Newport

Newport Chamber of Commerce
10 America's Cup Avenue
Newport
847-1600

Old Colony House
Washington Square
Newport
847-6992

Wanton-Lyman-Hazard House
17 Broadway
Newport
846-3622

Trinity Church
Queen Anne Square
Newport
846-0660

Hunter House
54 Washington Street
Newport
847-1000

Touro Synagogue
84 Touro Street
Newport
847-4794

1938. The present lighthouse was built next to the original in 1856.

As you head back to town along Beaver Tail Road, look on the right at the lovely weathered shingle homes facing Newport—our next stop.

Newport has enjoyed two major periods of prominence: as a center for world trade during colonial times, and as a fashionable resort during the Golden Age of the late nineteenth century. Over the last several decades the city has come alive again as the premier yachting center in New England—the site of the **America's Cup** races, the starting point for the **Bermuda Race** and many other class championships, and home of the **Newport Sailboat Show**, the largest in-water show in the country. And the city is also a center for various music festivals, starting with the **Newport Jazz Festival** over the Fourth of July.

From Jamestown cross the high bridge into Newport, and take Farewell Street to the center of town. Your first stop should be the chamber of commerce, where you can get maps for self-guided tours, and arrange bus tours and boat trips. Downtown highlights: **Hunter House** and its exhibits of original Goddard and Townsend furniture, silver, and portraits; **Old Colony House**, the colonial capital as well as a barracks, hospital, and jail; the **Wanton-Lyman-Hazard House**, a 1675 Jacobean house, the oldest in Newport; the **Touro Synagogue**, built in 1759, the first synagogue in the country; and **Trinity Church**, with its unusual wineglass pulpit set on three levels.

Around the corner from Trinity Church is the mysterious **Old Stone Tower**, its origins clouded in legend. Some say both the tower and a skeleton discovered in New Bedford in 1831 were the remains of Viking explorations here between the tenth and twelfth centuries. And Longfellow agreed. In his poem "The Skeleton in Armor," the

RHODE ISLAND

WATCH HILL

The Coast Guard Light Station is located on a point on the north side of the east entrance to Fishers Island Sound.

NEWPORT

The dining room at The Elms. Built in 1901 for Philadelphia coal baron, Edward J. Berwind, this French-style chateau is the best furnished of the society houses.

NEWPORT

The Marble House cost, including furnishings, a total of $11-million when it was built in 1892.

A·29

THE SOUTHERN SHORE

Old Stone Tower
Mill Street
Newport
846-9600

**Preservation Society
  of Newport County**
118 Mill Street
Newport
847-1000

The Breakers
Ochre Point
Newport
847-6543

The Elms
Bellevue Avenue
Newport
847-0478

Château-sur-Mer
Bellevue Avenue
Newport
847-0037

Rosecliff
Bellevue Avenue
Newport
847-5793

Viking tells of building "the lofty tower, which, to this very hour, stands looking seaward."

In the reconstructed wharf area of the old town are dozens of spots that invite leisurely strolling and shopping, including **Bowen's Wharf**, **Bannister's Wharf**, and the **Brick Market**. The **Armchair Sailor Bookstore** (847-4252), on Bannister's Wharf, has a fine collection of Newport books as well as new and used marine books, and a catalog of available marine works.

In a bustling tourist town like this one, there are many places for lunch, some on the water. Locals and sailors go to **Salas' Dining Room** (846-8772) on Thames Street for oriental and Italian dishes, and clams and lobster. (Orders-to-go too.) The **Black Pearl** (846-5264) on Bowen's Wharf is the "in" place to eat if you're willing to put up with a long wait. Or enjoy chowder and a lobster roll under an umbrella at any one of a number of places along the water.

There are few visitors to Newport who aren't fascinated by the fabled mansions of Bellevue Avenue, those elegant monuments to high society in one of America's most ebullient moments. The mansions that are open to the public are maintained by the **Preservation Society of Newport County**, where you can buy tickets for one or all, either by bus tour or on your own. Be prepared for long lines if you go during high season or on holiday weekends.

The Breakers, built by Cornelius Vanderbilt in 1895, is the most magnificent of the homes. Look for the stained-glass ceiling in the Great Hall. **The Elms**, built by E. J. Berwind, a Philadelphia coal magnate, is modeled after an eighteenth-century château in France. On the grounds are marble tea houses, fountains, and a sunken garden. **Château-sur-Mer**, an elegant Victorian mansion, was owned by William S. Wetmore, who made a fortune in trade with China. **Rosecliff**, designed by Stanford White and built in 1902 for Herman

Oelrichs, has the largest ballroom in Newport. The party in *The Great Gatsby* was filmed here. **Marble House** is a French palace built for William K. Vanderbilt in 1892. **Belcourt Castle**, designed in the style of Louis XIII for Oliver Belmont, contains fine collections of armor and stained-glass antiques, and a gold coronation coach. **Hammersmith Farm**, built by John W. Auchincloss in 1887, and once the home of Jacqueline Bouvier Kennedy Onassis, now is open to the public. Frederick Law Olmsted designed the lovely gardens.

For a view of both the mansions and the breakers below, follow **Cliff Walk** along the shore. The 3-mile path begins just west of Newport Beach, at Memorial Boulevard, and ends on a side street off Bellevue Avenue. This elegant walk was designated a national recreation trail in 1975.

There are a number of cemeteries in Newport, some with fine collections of eighteenth-century stonecutting. The **Common Burying Ground** is one of the most interesting, and the churchyard at **Trinity Church** (page 28) has a collection of carved stones laid flat on the ground.

The **America's Cup races** are one remnant of Newport's grand era. They were revived thirteen years after World War II ended, in 1958. Since then the challenge races have been held every three years in Rhode Island Sound off Newport, and will remain a fixture here as long as there are foreign challenges and a successful American defense. (In recent years crews from Britain, Australia, Sweden, Canada, and France have all tried to break the American winning streak.)

Financing an entry is not an easy job. Usually a syndicate pools capital for a season's campaign, which can cost anywhere from $750,000 to over $1,000,000 – and that doesn't include the boat! The cup, worth 100 guineas in 1851, today is prized more than any other trophy in the sailing world.

Trials begin in June and continue throughout the summer, with the best-of-seven series taking

Marble House
Bellevue Avenue
Newport
847-2445

Belcourt Castle
Bellevue Avenue
Newport
846-0669

Hammersmith Farm
Ocean Drive
Newport
846-7346

Common Burying
 Ground
Farewell Street
Newport

THE SOUTHERN SHORE

place in September. Although the competition is often keener during the trials than in the final series, the fun comes from watching the huge spectator fleet maneuvering through the harbor and from taking part in the general celebrations. You can stand on the sea wall at Fort Adams State Park, near the mouth of the harbor, to watch the fleet head out and back. Or have a closer look from one of the many vessels in the harbor. Check with the chamber of commerce (page 28) for details, and book your place six months in advance to be sure you get somewhere near the course.

Middletown

Norman Bird Sanctuary
Third Beach Road
Middletown
846-2577

Second Beach
Sachuest Point Road
Middletown

Third Beach
Sachuest Point Road
Middletown

From Newport follow Memorial Boulevard into Middletown. The **Norman Bird Sanctuary** is one of the best birding areas in New England. (Over 250 species are recorded.) The 450-acre refuge, in the nineteenth century a farm belonging to the Norman family, has over 10 miles of trails. There's a wonderful view of Second Beach and the sea from 50-foot-high **Hanging Rock**. Stop at the museum for a guide to the ecology trail and for the *Norman Bird Flyer*, a magazine filled with interesting articles about wildlife and schedules of events.

After your hike, head for a swim, at **Second Beach**, which has rolling surf and a gentle drop-off. The water at **Third Beach** (it's also called Navy Beach or Peabody's) is clean, but there's a steep drop-off in some areas.

Tiverton

From Middletown take Route 138 to Tiverton, and then drive the back roads through the lovely farm country and quiet beach settlements that lie south of Fall River and New Bedford. (Or, if time's a problem, you can head directly north to I-195 and New Bedford.) We've tried a number of routes, amused by the lack of either numbers or road names, and have created our own rule of thumb for coping with junctions: When in doubt, follow the yellow lined road that seems to bend in the right general direction.

Little Compton

From Tiverton follow Route 77 south through Tiverton Four Corners. Watch for the road on the left to **Little Compton**. There are fine stones from early colonial days in the graveyard on the commons, and great chowder, pies, and quiche at **Commons Lunch** (635-4388).

More meandering? Head back to Route 77 and go south to Sakonnet on the point. Or take the back roads up to Adamsville to visit **Stonebridge Dishes** (635-9500), a shop that carries imports at discount prices, and a 225-year-old gristmill that's still grinding corn for johnnycake meal. From here follow the signs to Westport Point and the start of the next itinerary.

You're in a backwater of modern civilization just a dozen miles south of the major highway that connects New Bedford and the Cape with Providence and New York. Yet, in Sakonnet or nearby Westport, you're off the track in a rural world not unlike the English countryside. Enjoy!

ITINERARY B

CAPE COD NATIONAL SEASHORE

ITINERARY B

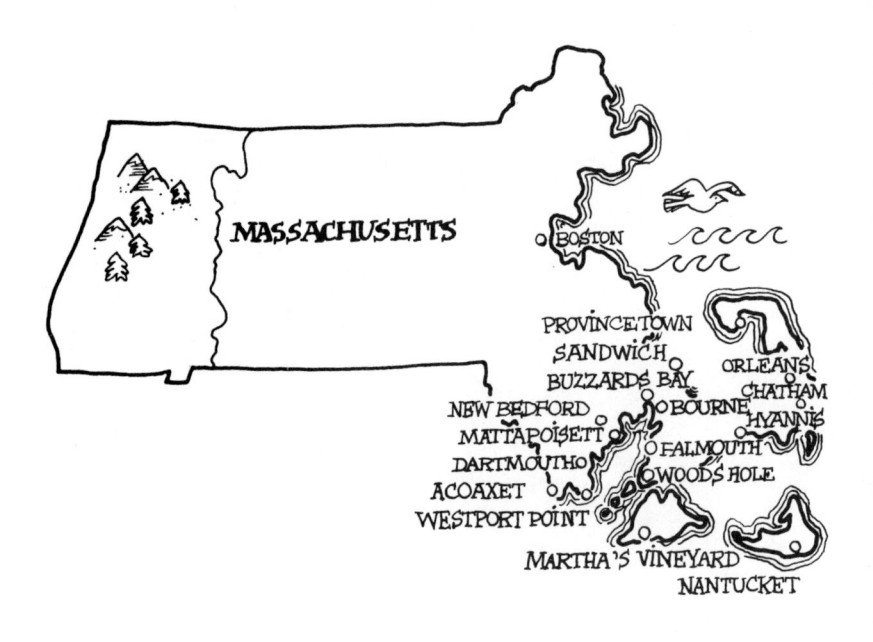

(Suggested Time: 7–9 days; 195 miles/312 kilometers)

The Cape and the Islands

Westport Point	B·39
South Dartmouth	B·40
New Bedford	B·41
Falmouth	B·46
Woods Hole	B·47
Martha's Vineyard	B·48
Vineyard Haven	B·51
Oak Bluffs	B·51
Edgartown	B·51
Chappaquiddick	B·52
Gay Head	B·53
Menemsha	B·53
Nantucket	B·54
Hyannis	B·57
Chatham	B·57
Monomoy Island	B·59
Orleans	B·63
Eastham	B·64
Cape Cod National Seashore	B·66
Nauset Area	B·66
Mac. Station	B·66
Pilgrim	B·67
Province	B·67
Provincetown	B·67
Brewster	B·68
Dennis	B·69
Barnstable	B·69
Sandwich	B·69

Cape Cod Chantey

Oh, Cape Cod girls they have no combs,
Heave away, heave away!
They comb their hair with codfish bones,
Heave away, heave away!

Heave away, you bully, bully boys!
Heave away, heave away!
Heave away, and don't you make a noise,
For we're bound for Australia!

Oh, Cape Cod boys they have no sleds,
They slide down hill on codfish heads.

Oh, Cape Cod cats they have no tails,
They blew away in heavy gales.

From the end of the Revolution to the turn of the century Massachusetts developed both its shipping and whaling industries. Ports along the coast were booming with activity, creating individual fortunes and general prosperity. Although the War of 1812 disrupted that prosperity, for a time, shipbuilding, coastwise and long-distance trade, and whaling continued to generate wealth in ports like New Bedford and Salem throughout the first half of the century. But land-based industry—in the textile and manufacturing mills of Fall River and Lowell—was beginning to create an alternative base for the state's financial development. The Civil War and the hordes of immigrant workers who arrived after it, hurried the transition from sea to land. And by the end of the nineteenth century, Massachusetts dominated New England's industrial community.

The terrain in Massachusetts tilts from west to east, with high land from the Berkshire Mountains to the Connecticut River, and a gradual slope toward the shoals and rich fishing banks of the continental shelf in the eastern two-thirds of the state. Along that slope are forests, glacial lakes and ponds, the curiously shaped tail of Cape Cod, and such outposts as Nantucket, Martha's Vineyard, and the Elizabeth Islands.

The Southern Shore

This itinerary begins at the Rhode Island border, on the road from Adamsville to Westport Point. From here you can continue on the back roads working your way through untouched rural land and quiet shore settlements, or head directly north on Route 88 to I-195 east, to New Bedford.

Westport Point

Westport Point sits across the Westport River from Acoaxet. Be sure to stop at **Moby Dick Wharf** (636–4465) at the south end of the bridge. This friendly restaurant overlooking the harbor offers delectable quahog chowder, a full seafood menu, and a special Sunday brunch. We learned from the menu that this area used to be called the Devil's Pocketbook because "the illusion of an unbroken coastline from the open sea made this harbor a haven for early smugglers and Revolutionists." It seems rum-running was a popular sport here at different times in history!

Friends recommend a small homey restaurant called **Ellie's Place** (636-5590), on the Main Road, about 3 miles north of the bridge. There are daily specials (corned beef and cabbage on Thursdays) and delicious home-baked desserts. **Carols** (636-1287), on Charlotte White Road, is the place for terrific clams.

From Westport Point follow the signs to **Horseneck State Beach**. The dune-lined beach is 2 miles long. The water is clean and warm (about 70 degrees in summer), but the surf can be strong.

Horseneck State Beach
Route 88
Westport
636-8816

From the beach follow the coast road to East Beach Road for about a mile. Turn north on Old Horseneck Road, where you'll find the **Bayside Restaurant** (636-5882). Stop for quiche, homemade carrot cake, Indian pudding, and huge seafood platters.

South Dartmouth

Continue jogging through the countryside, past rock walls and farms, on Old Horseneck Road, Russell's Road, Mills Road, and Gulf Road, to South Dartmouth. There are several interesting shops on Elm Street. We keep our family supplied in duffle bags and sailcloth ends at **Manchester Sail Makers** (992-6322). The **Packet** (994-0759) caters to yachtsmen, stocking everything from charts to sports clothes.

The **Sail Loft** (994-4542) has seafood meals and a great Sunday brunch. It's here we learned the story of Padanarum, the town's local name. It seems in the early eighteenth century Laban Thatcher, a well-to-do settler, saw similarities between his own life and fortunes and those of the Biblical Laban who lived in Paddan-Aram. So he named the area Padanarum. Unhappily, that later Laban "threw his weight around too much and the council of ministers, not to be discomfited by any mere mundane pressure, decided Laban had had it and brought against him 'eleven serious and grievous charges.'... Laban Thatcher was summarily excommunicated and, together with a few of his sympathizers, was packed off to Little Compton, Rhode Island."

From Padanarum, drive a few miles north on Dartmouth Street to New Bedford, one of the most interesting cities in New England because its history reflects the major stages of economic development and decline in the region.

Bartholomew Gosnold, a British explorer, sailed the *Concord* in 1602 to Cape Cod and Cuttyhunk Island, and finally landed near the mouth of the Acushnet River. In 1652 settlers bought the land from the Wampanoag Indians that included the area from Westport to New Bedford. That purchase didn't mean peace, though: Over a number of years the Wampanoags continued to murder settlers and devastate their lands.

Joseph Russell III founded Bedford Village (now New Bedford to the west and Fairhaven to the east of the Acushnet River) in the 1740s, and, more significantly, started up the whaling industry here. In 1778 the British destroyed the village, leaving the whaling industry at a standstill for a number of years. Finally, in 1787, the rebuilt town to the west of the river became New Bedford.

The town prospered, and by the middle of the nineteenth century, was one of the most successful and powerful whaling ports in the world. But that prosperity waned as whales grew scarce and whaling voyages grew longer, and as the lure of easy fortunes led many sailors to strike out for California. During one disastrous cruise in 1871, thirty-three New Bedford ships were locked in Arctic ice. Their twelve hundred sailors survived, but the financial loss to shareholders was irreparable.

With the decline of whaling and the increase of industrial development, New Bedford turned to textile mills, which created a booming economy from the 1880s through the late 1920s. But with the depression, industrial development turned elsewhere.

New Bedford

New Bedford
  Chamber
  of Commerce
227 Union Street
New Bedford
999-5231

New Bedford Whaling
  Museum
Johnny Cake Hill
New Bedford
676-1026

Seamen's Bethel
15 Johnny Cake Hill
New Bedford

Today New Bedford is rehabilitating its downtown section. The area is lit with gas lamps, and the roads have been repaved with cobblestones (Wear comfortable shoes!). To begin your self-guided walking tour of the **Waterfront Historic District**—an area filled with marine shops and restored nineteenth-century architecture—visit the chamber of commerce. Here you'll find information about the **Moby Dick Trail** and other attractions in the area.

New Bedford and whaling are irrevocably associated with Herman Melville's *Moby Dick*. The story is told in the **New Bedford Whaling Museum**. Among the exhibits are an 8½-foot-high panorama of a worldwide whaling voyage that stretches around the room (it was painted in 1848); an authentic replica of a square-rigged whaler, an 89-foot-long half-model that you can climb aboard and explore; whaling relics and scrimshaw; and replicas of a rigging loft, sail loft, and cooperage shop. The museum also schedules whale-watching trips.

Across the street from the museum you'll find the **Seamen's Bethel**, filled with nautical memorabilia. Here is a photograph of Melville and the story of his voyages to the South Seas, where he "discerned the primordial beauty and terror of this world and the danger-ridden labors of whaling" that he later put into "the immortal saga of *Moby Dick*." The chapel, with boat-shaped pulpit, was built for sailors in need of a place for worship and rest; and Melville used it in *Moby Dick*, as the site of Father Mapple's sermon. Legend says that Enoch Mudge, a preacher in the 1840s, once took the bethel's organ, perched in a wheelbarrow, down to the docks to perform a last-minute service for departing seamen.

Next door is the **Mariner's Home**, bearing a characteristic plaque: "Latitude 41°–35°,

Longitude 70°–55°." At night red and green port-and-starboard lanterns light up on either side of the door.

At the foot of Union Street, at **State Pier**, sits the lightship **New Bedford**. The 133-foot ship, painted bright red, once marked a welcome landfall for ships returning from all over the world. During the summer you can go aboard and explore the vessel, imagining what life must have been like for the men who lived on her through the gales of winter. State Pier is also home to the **Blessing of the Fleet**, a ceremony held every August. A "dressed" fishing fleet passes in review, and prizes are awarded for the best decorations. New Bedford is now the fifth largest fishing port on the East Coast. You can watch the scallop auction at seven every weekday morning (the fish auction is at eight) at the Wharfinger Building on the waterfront.

The New Bedford–Fall River area is a shopper's paradise. There are thirty-nine factory outlets here, all listed in a booklet that's available at tourist offices and some stores. Two of the best are the **Revereware Factory Store** (999-5601) on North Front Street in New Bedford, and **Fall River Knitting Mills** (678-7553) on Alden Street in Fall River.

From New Bedford you can take I-195 directly into the village of Buzzards Bay, or older Route 6 through Fairhaven, Mattapoisett, and Wareham. If you're hungry, stop en route for authentic Italian food at the **Pasta House** (993-9913) on Alden Road in Fairhaven. The owner, who's from Italy, makes all the pasta, and you can buy some to take along if you want. Or stop for lunch or dinner at one of the oldest seaside inns in the country. The **Mattapoisett Inn** (758-4922) is on Water Street in Mattapoisett, right on the harbor between Shipyard Park and Barstow's Wharf.

Mariner's Home
Johnny Cake Hill
New Bedford
992-3295

New Bedford
State Pier
New Bedford
999-1646

Cape Cod

During the Ice Age, as the sun melted the glacier advancing from the north, the power of the moving ice dissipated south of mainland New England. Rock continued to pile up with glacial momentum from the north, leaving a ridge (a terminal moraine) along Cape Cod, the Elizabeth Islands, Nantucket, and Martha's Vineyard. The islands developed as the ice moved in lobes—two lobes coming together, piling up rocks and gravel, to form each island.

The melting ice carried off any rich soil, and the residual sandy soil does not hold enough moisture to nourish most plants. The scrub pine is everywhere, and heath foliage—huckleberry, sheep laurel, blueberry, and bearberry—grows where nothing else will. In low areas cranberry flourishes, providing an important seasonal industry for the region. And azalea, rhododendron, and holly, which were planted later, add color to the landscape.

Some historians believe the Cape was discovered in 1004 A.D. by Thorvald the Viking. We know that Bartholomew Gosnold arrived in his ship, the *Concord*, in 1602. He caught many codfish while anchored here, and the name *Cape Cod* may have been derived from entries in his log. It's also probable that the Pilgrims made a stop at the end of the Cape before landing in Plymouth—a controversy yet to be resolved between Plymouth and Provincetown.

The seafaring heritage of the Cape began in the seventeenth century, when many towns became whaling centers and home ports for the square-riggers that set out to bring native products to the world. A sense of daily life during the seventeenth and eighteenth centuries has been preserved for us in the stately mansions owned by sea captains, in the cottages patterned after the homes settlers had left behind in Devon and Cornwall, in churches and windmills, and in the recorded heritage of journals, logs, and letters.

The weather on Cape Cod is mild for much of the year. Although you may find heat and humidity in July and August, sea breezes usually cool the land. In summer the average high temperature is in the 70s; the low, around 60.

The Cape and the islands are ringed with magnificent beaches. Those along the south coast enjoy warmer water (influenced by the Gulf Stream);

those on the north side, along Cape Cod Bay, are cooler, sometimes even cold. In the National Seashore area on the Atlantic you'll find heavy surf and an occasional undertow.

Today visitors can hike along sand dunes; swim, fish, or boat on the ocean, bays, and interior lakes; and explore the lighthouses and coves, rich with the legends and lore of shipwrecks.

Before you go, write for maps and information to the Cape and island chambers of commerce. Specific information about tours is available from the **Cape Cod National Seashore** and the **Massachusetts Audubon Society**. For a calendar of current events, "Happenings Along the Americana Trail," contact the **Bristol County Development Council**.

You'll find summer theater in Chatham, Dennis, Falmouth, Harwich, Hyannis, Orleans, and Provincetown. For performance schedules, write to the Cape Cod Chamber of Commerce or to the tourist information office in the individual town. These are also your sources for the *Sportsman's Guide to Cape Cod*, a pamphlet that lists information about deep-sea fishing, surfing, surfcasting, sailing, scuba diving, swimming, bicycling, hiking, tennis, and golf.

There are three information booths for on-site visits: at the Bourne traffic circle in Buzzards Bay (759-3814), at the Sagamore rotary (888-2438), and on the Mid-Cape Highway at the junction of Routes 6 and 132 (362-3225). These centers can advise you on nearby campgrounds as well as other tourist accommodations.

Our route begins with Falmouth and the islands, and then moves from Hyannis out to Provincetown and back to the Sagamore Bridge. Each leg can be covered separately in several days, or together in a week.

Route 28 takes you from Bourne through the populated south coast to Orleans. Route 6A follows the north coast through marshy, less developed land. Both routes are narrow and winding in places, often congested, and fun to poke along.

Cape Cod Chamber
  of Commerce
Mid-Cape Highway
Hyannis
362-3225

Cape Cod National
  Seashore
South Wellfleet
349-3785

Massachusetts
  Audubon Society
Ashumet Road
Hatchville
563-6390

Bristol County
  Development
  Council
Box 831
Fall River
676-1026

Falmouth

Falmouth Historical Society
Palmer Avenue
Falmouth
548-4857

First Congregational Church
Main Street
Falmouth
548-3700

Ashumet Holly Reservation
Route 151
East Falmouth
563-6390

From Orleans to Provincetown there's only one major highway, Route 6 (the Mid-Cape Highway) — the central artery through the Cape. Total mileage around Cape Cod is a comfortable 157 miles (253 kilometers), but travel can be exasperatingly slow on summer weekends.

From the Bourne Bridge follow Route 28 south to Falmouth, once a major whaling and fishing port. Surrounding the village green are the stately foursquare homes of sea captains, whose wives watched for their return from widow's walks atop the roofs. The **Falmouth Historical Society** has a widow's walk; collections of Sandwich glass, period furniture, and whaling memorabilia; and a colonial garden. In the **First Congregational Church** hangs an original Paul Revere bell, one of the few still being used.

Nearby, the **Market Bookshop** (578-5636) has a fine collection of books about the Cape. Behind the bookstore is the **Market Barn Gallery** (540-0480), which is open from June through September. Here you'll find unusual and distinctive oils, watercolors, sculpture, jewelry, and prints.

Falmouth has twenty-five public parks, many beaches, and several bicycle paths, including the **Shining Sea Bikeway**, a 3-mile track over an abandoned railroad bed from the Falmouth Station to the ferry terminal in Woods Hole. We especially enjoy the **Nobska Lighthouse** area and **Quisset Harbor**. The former has a good beach; the latter, both a beach and bird refuge.

In East Falmouth the Massachusetts Audubon Society maintains the **Ashumet Holly Reservation**. This 45-acre park was given to the society to preserve the famed holly collection of Wilfred Wheeler. Besides holly you'll see dogwood, magnolias, viburnums, rhododendrons, and wild flowers in spring; oriental lotus blossoms in summer; and Franklinia blooms, an unusual fall-flowering shrub, in autumn. There are several nature trails through the groves of trees and shrubs.

Food in Falmouth? There are lots of good restaurants in the area. The **Regatta** (548-5400), near the marina, is a special place for dinner. And so is the **Coonamesset Inn** (548-2300) on Jones Road. Less formal, but equally delicious, is the **Chart Room** (563-5350) in nearby Cataumet.

A trip to Cape Cod means beaches, and beaches mean beachcombing. Shells, beach or sea glass, driftwood, and interesting stones are all here for the taking. Or you can join an ecologist at work on the sand. We spent a few days at a conference on Martha's Vineyard where one of the sessions was held on the beach in a pouring rain. The professor who led us there had us entranced with the different life forms at different levels under the sand. And we learned about the composition of the sand, worn from crushed quartz, feldspar, and garnets; the effects of tide and wind; the single-celled plankton, food for larger sea beings; jellyfish, sand hoppers (or beach fleas), clams, snails, oysters, mussels, scallops, starfish, and mole crabs; and the plant life—the seaweed, eelgrass, moss, kelp, and flotsam and jetsam that appear with each tide. Sound interesting? Two excellent books by Dorothy Sterling and Donald Zinn about the hidden life of beaches are listed in the Readings.

Continue for several miles along Route 28 to Woods Hole. A principal port of the Cape, the town is the base for ferry service to Martha's Vineyard and Nantucket. It is also a major center for marine research, home to the **Marine Biological Laboratory** and the **Woods Hole Oceanographic Institute**. The institute, founded in 1930 as a private nonprofit organization for ocean research, is now a world center for oceanography. If you want to know more about the work done here, contact the public information office for a tour of the facilities and research vessels in port. That office is also the place to pick up a weekly calendar of maritime lectures and other scientific programs at the institute.

Woods Hole

Marine Biological
Laboratory
167 Water Street
Woods Hole
548-3705

Woods Hole
Oceanographic
Institute
Water Street
Woods Hole
548-1400

National Marine
Fisheries Service
Albatross Street
Woods Hole
548-7684

The aquarium of the **National Marine Fisheries Service** is part of a research project to study fish and invertebrates. It's well organized, and worth a tour both for adults and for children. The service also offers lectures and programs by scientists and technicians from its research groups.

Woods Hole is also the home of the **Sea Education Association**, a year-round school offering students college credit for a twelve-week program that includes classes on shore and then a voyage aboard the sailing research vessel *Westward*, a 100-foot schooner.

Imagine yourself, a seabag on your shoulder, embarking on a beautiful sunny day. Watch your head as you clamber down the almost-vertical gangway. You share your cabin with anywhere from two to four shipmates; but you might be lucky enough to have a bunk built into the curve of the ship's topsides, with the privacy of a curtain, a shelf for books, and your own porthole! You've brought a minimum of clothing (most of it warm) but remembered your foul-weather gear and sea boots; and all of this resides in your bunk with you.

Research activity goes on day and night, and everyone's eager to share his or her findings. Faculty, students, and ship's officers get to know each other well, eating together, hoisting and striking sails, sharing thoughts through long four-hour watches at night, and working together on research projects. Life at sea replaces your normal routine with a new one that focuses on the needs of the ship and the shipmates who share this tiny society in the midst of a restless sea.

Martha's Vineyard

Take the ferry to Martha's Vineyard. The **Steamship Authority** offers year-round service—for cars too—from Woods Hole. (During summer months, make reservations for your car well in advance.) The **Island Commuter Corporation** leaves from Falmouth; **Hy-Line**, from Hyannis. All offer day trips.

CAPE COD

The draggers still come in with their great nets and the lobstermen land their catches at Menemsha on Martha's Vineyard.

MENEMSHA

Oriental Lotus blossoms from mid-July to mid-September at the Mass. Audubon Society's reservation.

ASHUMET HOLLY RESERVATION

The Jethro Coffin House, built in 1686, is the oldest house on the island.

NANTUCKET

Steamship Authority
Box 284
Woods Hole
540-2022,
   800-352-7104 (from Massachusetts only)

Island Commuter Corporation
Falmouth Heights Road
Falmouth
548-4800

Hy-Line Hyannis Harbor Tours
Ocean Street Dock
Hyannis
775-7185

Island Voyage
Box 57
Hyannis
771-7211

Martha's Vineyard Chamber of Commerce
Beach Road
Vineyard Haven
693-0085

The island, barely 20 miles long and 10 miles wide, attracts thousands of visitors each year to its splendid colored cliffs, beaches, coves, dunes, rolling moors, and salt marshes. The sea spreads its scent everywhere.

You can explore the island in your car, or on one of **Island Voyage**'s bus tours, or on a bike (rent one or bring your own). During the past ten years over 20 miles of bike paths leading all over the island have been developed. There's a booth at the intersection of the Edgartown–Oak Bluffs road with the Edgartown–Vineyard Haven road where you can get information about cycling, and beaches and tourist sites on the Vineyard.

The Vineyard's roads wind through all kinds of terrain—some flat areas, some hilly ones. Here's a list for cyclists of several routes to follow, with descriptions and mileage, adapted from Polly Burroughs' *Guide to Martha's Vineyard*.

Vineyard Haven to Oak Bluffs to Edgartown along the shore road: flat, about 8 miles.

Edgartown to Felix Neck Wildlife Sanctuary: hilly, 2 miles.

Chappaquiddick ferry dock to Dyke Bridge: one hill, 3 miles.

Edgartown to South Beach at Katama: flat, about 3 miles.

Edgartown to West Tisbury: hilly, 9 miles.

West Tisbury to Beetlebung Corner, Chilmark: hilly, 5 miles.

Beetlebung Corner to Gay Head: very steep hills, 6 miles.

Menemsha to North Tisbury on North Road: hilly, 5½ miles.

North Tisbury to Vineyard Haven: flat, 5 miles.

Lambert's Cove Road: hilly, 4½ miles.

Vineyard Haven to Edgartown on the inland road: hilly, 6½ miles.

Edgartown to the airport: hilly, 4½ miles.

Oak Bluffs to the airport: partly hilly, 7 miles.

Vineyard Haven to the airport: partly hilly, 5 miles.

Vineyard Haven

Much of Vineyard Haven was destroyed by the Great Fire of 1883. The rebuilt town is the main port of the island (the ferry from Woods Hole docks here), and houses a substantial winter community. There are shops along Main Street, including the **Bunch of Grapes** bookstore (693-2291) and several bike rental stores.

Oak Bluffs

The ferries from Falmouth and Hyannis (summers only) land at Oak Bluffs, a cluster of Victorian cottages with gingerbread scrollwork. The cottages were built on lent sites, with each family trying to outdo the next in color and ornateness. The town was settled in 1642, but didn't become popular until 1835, when it was first used for a Methodist camp meeting by "Reformation" John Adams, whose passionate sermons and tearful praying won converts away from the Congregationalists on the island. The conical open Tabernacle, with its lovely stained-glass windows, was built in 1870.

In the center of town, kids have a chance to catch the brass ring for a free ride on one of the oldest carousels in the country. And in July there's a craft fair at **Wesley House**.

Wesley House
Lake Avenue
Oak Bluffs
693-0135

Edgartown

Edgartown is one of our favorite places. A famous whaling port, the town retains its colonial charm with the elegant homes built from whale oil fortunes. The harbor is nearly always packed with visiting yachts, but it's especially busy one week in July, during the **Edgartown Regatta**.

The **Thomas Cooke House** has an extensive collection of scrimshaw, ship models, whaling gear, costumes, and antique furniture.

Stop for lunch at **Martha's Restaurant** (627-8316) on Main Street. On the menu: all sorts of special sandwiches, quiches, soups, hamburgers, eggs Benedict, and interesting salads. The **Kelley House** (627-4394), an Edgartown tradition since 1742, has kept the cozy atmosphere of colonial times. Try a meal in the attractive dining room. **Navigator Restaurant** (627-4321), right on the water, features nautical decor and seafood.

Fishermen call it the World Series of Fishing. What is it? It's the annual **Striped Bass and Bluefish Derby**, and it's held in Edgartown between September 15 and October 15. Fishermen from all over the country look on the derby as a test of skill, endurance, and know-how. Although at least a thousand people enter the contest each year, only a small number of them—the hard-core group—spend every waking hour fishing. These are the people who can "smell" the fish; who know to look for an oil slick on the water (a sign of fish secretions). These are the people who suffer long hours of cold, wet, and dark as they watch through the night for striped bass; or who get up in the middle of the night to fish just before high tide, when the fish are running. And these are the people who zealously guard the best fishing spots, passing down secret locations from father to son.

We happened to walk by the headquarters and weigh-in station in the harbor, and were entranced by the excitement, activity, and camaraderie among the participants, their families, their friends, and anyone who just came along to check on the latest news.

For derby details—regulations, weigh-in procedures, and the long list of awards—write to the Vineyard's chamber of commerce (page 45).

Chappaquiddick

Chappaquiddick is steeped in the lore of shipwrecks. A terrible one took place in January 1866, during the worst blizzard in many years, when the *Christina*, a two-masted schooner, ran aground on

Hawes Shoal. The lighthousekeeper saw the wreck, but couldn't rescue the crew until the storm ended. He watched as the vessel settled lower and lower in the water, the men clinging to the rigging. One by one they froze, until just a single man was left alive; he was eventually rescued by a whaleboat from Edgartown.

Gay Head

Gay Head, on the southwest tip of the island, is marked by varicolored cliffs, a national monument. Each colored layer records a part of history that took place before the Ice Age. The layer of black at the bottom indicates buried forests; red and yellow layers are clay; a layer of green sand that turns red when exposed to the air contains fossils of crabs and clams; the gravellike layers contain sharks' teeth, whale bones, and animal skeletons. Sorry, no climbing on the cliffs. Erosion is doing enough damage without visitors' help. The cliffs are just one of Gay Head's claims to fame; its harpooners are another. In *Moby Dick*, Melville wrote that Gay Head had produced the most daring harpooners in the world. (Moby Dick was patterned after a ferocious white whale, Mocha Dick, who caused the death of thirty men before he was killed in 1859.)

Many of the inhabitants of Gay Head are of Indian descent. In September 1981, after four years of negotiations, the town agreed to return 238 acres of shorefront property to the three hundred-member Wampanoag tribe. The land, which is worth close to $3 million, will be kept in its natural state. Part of the agreement allows the Indians to apply for federal funds to buy 175 acres of land to use for housing.

Menemsha

Menemsha's harbor—you'll recognize it if you've seen the movie *Jaws*—is popular with fishermen (bluefish and striped bass) and yachtsmen. Menemsha Pond is a beautiful anchorage, but be careful: The entrance is

Nantucket

Nantucket Island Chamber of Commerce
Pacific Club Building
Nantucket
228-1700

Nantucket Information Bureau
22 Federal Street
Nantucket
228-0925

Nantucket Historical Association
Union Street
Nantucket
228-1894

Whaling Museum
Broad Street
Nantucket
228-1736

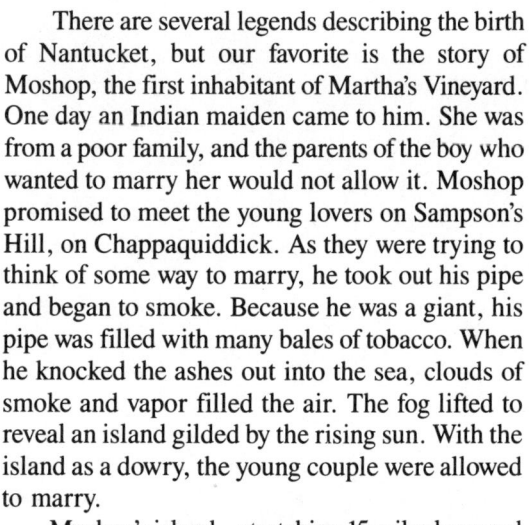

constantly shoaling up and being dredged so the underwater terrain may not be what your chart indicates.

There are several legends describing the birth of Nantucket, but our favorite is the story of Moshop, the first inhabitant of Martha's Vineyard. One day an Indian maiden came to him. She was from a poor family, and the parents of the boy who wanted to marry her would not allow it. Moshop promised to meet the young lovers on Sampson's Hill, on Chappaquiddick. As they were trying to think of some way to marry, he took out his pipe and began to smoke. Because he was a giant, his pipe was filled with many bales of tobacco. When he knocked the ashes out into the sea, clouds of smoke and vapor filled the air. The fog lifted to reveal an island gilded by the rising sun. With the island as a dowry, the young couple were allowed to marry.

Moshop's island—stretching 15 miles long and 4 miles wide—sits 30 miles off the mainland. You can get here by ferry from Martha's Vineyard and Woods Hole (Steamship Authority, page 50), and from Hyannis (Hy-Line, page 50).

For information about the island's historical sites and a season pass for most of them, contact the **Nantucket Historical Association**.

The old town is much the same as it was in the early nineteenth century, with beautiful homes built from the proceeds of whaling. Begin your tour at the **Whaling Museum**, up the street from Steamboat Wharf, where the ferries dock. Here you'll find an outstanding collection of whaling gear, a whaleboat, and some fine examples of scrimshaw. You'll also learn about the "Nantucket sleigh ride"—the endurance contest between whale and men in the whaleboat as the whale dove and plunged madly after being harpooned, towing the whaleboat behind it. Our guide related the tale of one such trip: While traveling rapidly to leeward on a "sleigh ride" the crew looked back and saw an empty whaleboat following in their wake. A wave eventually smashed her to pieces, but the crew was still curious, wondering where she had come from. When they arrived back on board their ship and hoisted up their own whaleboat, the mystery was solved. The whale they'd been chasing had traveled so fast that the paint stripped off the whaleboat. What they had seen was their own shell of paint following them!

Head up Broad Street, turn right on Centre Street, and follow it to **Oldest House**, the home of Jethro Coffin. It was built in 1686. Look for the secret hiding place in the closet, and the horseshoe chimney. Follow Centre Street back to Main Street, turn right to the **Hadwen House-Satler Memorial**, a large, comfortable home built in 1845 for a wealthy whale oil merchant. Turn left on Pleasant to Mill Street, to the **1800 House**, which is furnished as a Nantucket home during the great whaling era. Continue on Pleasant Street to South Mill Street, and the **Old Mill**, which is made of wood salvaged from shipwrecks.

At the waterfront, on **Straight Wharf**, sits the **Lightship Nantucket**, which once guarded the South Shoals. This entire area has been restored, the new cobblestone paths leading past displays of weaving, scrimshaw, jewelry, pottery, leather goods, wood carvings, lightship baskets, and a sidewalk art show in August. Before you leave, stop at Al Hartig's kite shop, **Nantucket Kiteman** (228-2297). Al is an expert kite builder and flyer, and he's always willing to share his know-how. And for real aficionados, there's a kite-flying contest at the **Miacomet Fair**, in late July.

The **Maria Mitchell Association** operates an aquarium, an observatory, and a natural science museum, and offers a wonderful series of lectures on astronomy.

The **Jared Coffin House** (228-2400), an inn built in 1845 by a successful ship owner, features

Oldest House
Sunset Hill
Nantucket

Hadwen House-Satler
Memorial
Main Street
Nantucket

1800 House
Mill Street
Nantucket

Old Mill
South Mill and South
Prospect Streets
Nantucket

Lightship Nantucket
Straight Wharf
Nantucket

Maria Mitchell
Association
1 Vestal Street
Nantucket
228-2896

antiques in the living room and library, and canopy beds in some of the guest rooms. Come for the night or just a meal. Lunch is served in the cosy taproom or on the patio.

From town there are several beaches you can bike to, including two excellent beaches for surfing: **Surfside** (out Atlantic Avenue to the south) and **Siasconset** (out Milestone Road to the east). Notice the wind direction as you set out. The afternoon southwesterly often reaches 25 miles an hour by three or four, just about the time you'll be heading back. Nonbikers can cover the distance by bus — either on a shuttle bus from point to point or on a tour.

Scuba divers have discovered the remains of some 750 wrecks around the island. In the blizzard of 1886 the 117-foot three-masted schooner *T. B. Witherspoon* crashed into Little Mioxe Rip Shoal. As the waves hurtled through portholes flooding the cabin, the sailors took to the ratlines. The mate, his wife, and his five-year-old son, who cried "Papa, won't God save us?" remained in the cabin. Only after the boy and his mother died, did the mate leave them to find all but one of the sailors who had climbed aloft frozen or drowned. He helped rescuers save the surviving sailor, and remained the last man on board who lived to tell the story.

In 1918 the lightship *Cross Rip*, anchored off the northern shore of the island, disappeared in the midst of an ice floe. She drifted away from Nantucket, and was found thirty-nine years later near West Dennis. Scientists used an alarm clock on board to establish her age and identity.

Linguists are fascinated by the speech patterns of native Nantucketers, the heritage of their strong sea background. You "see if the coast is clear," "keep your weather eye peeled," "look out for squalls," and "keep an eye to the windward." If you're reckless you're "sailing too close to the wind." If you get the better of someone you've "taken the wind out of his sails." If you're ready you're "on deck." And if you're experienced you "know the ropes."

When you've finished exploring the island, take the ferry back to the mainland, where the itinerary continues in Hyannis.

Hyannis is the center of transportation, shopping, and vacation facilities for the south shore of the Cape. It's often very crowded in summer, but you can find almost anything you need here. On a rainy day, visit **Colonial Candleshop of Cape Cod** (771-3916), on Main Street just south of Route 28. There are tours, a gift shop, and a seconds outlet. Nearby, on Route 28, you'll find sweaters at factory prices at the **Fall River Knitting Mills** (775-2037).

Hyannisport was the summer home of President Kennedy. The **John Fitzgerald Kennedy Memorial**, a 12-foot fieldstone wall with the presidential seal, a fountain, and a pool, is next to the town park. Come for a fine view of the outer harbor.

From Hyannis drive east on Route 28 through West Yarmouth, West Dennis, Dennis Port, and Harwich Port, to Chatham. Located on the elbow of the Cape, Chatham is surrounded on three sides by the sea. Once busy with shipbuilding, whaling, saltworks, and shoemaking, residents now support themselves with fishing and tourism. Yet the town has retained the lovely colonial homes and charm of the past. Harwich and Chatham, though geographically close, have had a running rivalry for years. One tall tale about a Harwich ship that foundered says the crew paddled toward shore on planks and hatch-covers. As they got near land, one of them asked the crowd on shore where they were. When someone yelled, "Chatham," the sailor turned around and headed back out to sea.

Hyannis

John Fitzgerald Kennedy Memorial
Ocean Street
Hyannis

Chatham

Old Atwood House
Stage Harbor Road
Chatham
945-2493

Old Grist Mill
Shattuck Place
Chatham
945-0342

Chatham Lighthouse
Shore Road
Chatham

Chatham Railroad Museum
Depot Road
Chatham
945-3132

Sylvan Gardens
Old Main Road
Chatham

Chatham Chamber of Commerce
Main Street
Chatham
945-0342

The **Old Atwood House** was built before the Revolution by Joseph C. Atwood, a sea captain. The Chatham Historical Society maintains the house and has its offices here. Rooms are furnished with period pieces, and there are collections of Sandwich glass, seashells, and china. From the front lawn look for the turret of an old Chatham lighthouse.

The windmill at the **Old Grist Mill** still grinds corn when there's enough wind. Bring a picnic to eat here or at nearby **Chase Park**.

Chatham Lighthouse is open to visitors, and offers a fine view of the coast. A restored train depot houses the **Chatham Railroad Museum**. On display are photographs, models, and a 1910 caboose. **Sylvan Gardens**, a horticulturist's private garden, is a delight. Come enjoy the plantings and the fine view of the sea—all free.

Summer Fridays at 7:30 the Chatham Band gives a concert at **Kate Gould Park** on Main Street. Families can sing together, and children can buy balloons from American Field Service students.

Chowderworks (945-2019) on Main Street serves great quahog and seafood chowders, and lobster salad. Or make it yourself with fresh seafood from the **Chatham Cooperative Seafood Fish Market** (945-1403) on Crowell Road. The store's open seven days a week.

For information about the town stop at the chamber of commerce information booth on Main Street, next to the town offices. The booth is also the place for information about gravestone rubbing at **Union Cemetery** and **Old Cemetery**. Gravestone rubbing, in Europe a hobby for years, is growing more and more popular here. Your best source of information about permits and stones is usually town hall; for supplies (rice or tableau paper, hard wax, masking tape, scissors, and an eraser) try a rubbing center or an art store.

With permit and materials in hand, head for the cemetery. Choose a stone that has a flat raised design. Slate is usually smooth; sandstone, rough. Once you've looked over the stone, keeping pattern and indentations in mind, place your paper over it, tape it securely on all sides to the back of the stone, trace the edges with your fingers, color the boundaries lightly, and finally rub with more pressure. Use short strokes in the same direction, and darken the paper evenly. Polish the rubbing, while it's still taped, with a piece of nylon stocking. You can leave the rubbing just as it is, with weather cracks and chips showing, or you can touch up these marks by laying the paper on a flat surface. When you leave be sure to take all scraps of tape, paper, and crayons with you. At home, glue a small dowel at the top and bottom of your masterpiece and hang it with a cord, or frame it. Happy rubbing!

Monomoy Island

Monomoy Island, off the coast of Chatham, is now part of a national wildlife refuge (page 45). The long sandspit stretches 10 miles to the south, creating problems for mariners. Pollock Rip Passage off Monomoy Point, tricky with riptides and shoals, is the only way to get into Nantucket Sound from the east. A *Cruising Guide to the New England Coast* recommends navigating with extreme caution when the weather is foggy. Even with today's accurate charts and instruments, sailors continue to run aground. In fact, the Coast Guard advises that the direction and velocity of the current cannot be predicted accurately off Monomoy.

The island's treacherous shoals have played a part in the history of our country, forcing the *Mayflower* to change course. A sign at Chatham Lighthouse (page 58) reads:

> About nine miles SE of this place are the shoals of Pollock Rip which turned the Mayflower back to Provincetown Harbor and

caused the Pilgrim Fathers to settle in Plymouth instead of on the Jersey Coast, their original destination.

In October 1770 a number of ships foundered during a violent storm: A sloop returning from a whaling trip was wrecked near Eastham, another at Race Point; and a whaling schooner foundered in Chatham.

In 1778 the *Somerset*, a sixty-four-gun British man-of-war, was caught in the area between the Highlands in Chatham and Pollock Rip Shoals, and crashed onto a reef. (Longfellow wrote about the *Somerset* and her captain, George Curry, in the third verse of "Paul Revere's Ride.") The captain surrendered himself and his crew to men from Provincetown who had come to salvage the wreck. Revolutionary history recalls the winterlong march of the five hundred prisoners across the Cape to Boston. Over a hundred years later the *Somerset*'s timbers appeared in the sands of Peaked Hill Bars in Provincetown. And in June 1973 her bones appeared again.

The outer beaches of the Cape between Monomoy and Provincetown—great for swimming and surfing on fine summer days—have been one of the Atlantic's most fearsome graveyards. In 1898 a side-wheeler, the *Portland*, sank with close to two hundred people on board, 7 miles northeast of Highland Lighthouse. The same storm sank ten large vessels and several smaller ones, and blew down nine wharves and twenty-one buildings. Oldtimers claimed this particular storm was the most vicious they'd ever experienced. The keeper of the Wood End Light and several other men were able to save survivors from one of two sinking schooners. The men on the *Jordan L. Mott* clung to the rigging for fifteen hours before help came; the men on the *Lester A. Lewis*, also standing in the rigging, were not as lucky.

The dramatic shipwrecks off Monomoy gave rise to dramatic rescues. A local favorite starred a man called "Crazy George" (he was the only one crazy enough to attempt hazardous rescues). It happened on November 1815, in a gale off the island. On his third try—his first two rescue boats were smashed on the rocks—George carefully rode the crest of each wave, jumped over the bar between the inner and outer beach, and then made two passes alongside the stranded ship to pick up survivors!

There was a lifesaving service in operation, even in Crazy George's time. In 1786 the Massachusetts Humane Society had been formed to help seamen in distress. By 1850 the government had begun building lifeboat stations, and the United States Life Saving Service was created by Congress in 1871.

There were thirteen lifesaving stations along the perilous section of Atlantic coast from Wood End and Race Point, at the tip of the Cape, to Monomoy Point. During bad weather this long stretch of beach was patrolled night and day. Each patrol walked anywhere from 2 to 4 miles to a halfway house, where he met the patrol from the next station, and then turned back to his home station. Red flares were used to warn ships away from shoals and to signal that help was on the way. Rescue operations included firing a line to the stricken vessel and sending a breeches buoy to transport the crew to shore. The last time a breeches buoy was used was in January 1962 to save men from the *Margaret Rose*; now helicopters perform the same function.

Although weather and shoals claimed many ships, local history tells too of the mooncussers—salvage pirates who would lead ships to their doom with false lights.

You can visit Monomoy on a wilderness tour that begins at the coast guard station at Chatham Light (page 58). The daylong excursion includes a 4½-mile boat trip and guided walks around the island.

Mooncussers

Would you walk with me there over hallowed soil,
   Would you tread the shores that the Pilgrim
     has trod,
Would you dwell on the way-worn veteran's toil,
   Then haste to the highlands of stormy Cape Cod.

For I've heard there the moon-cusser telling his story
   To the foam of the billows that rolled on the shore,
And I knew as he mumbled the deeds of his glory
   That he thought of the friends that would meet
     no more.

And at last when he finished these sayings of wonder,
   While the winds and the waves were repeating
     the tale,
He exclaimed in a voice that seemed louder
     than thunder,
   "I see in the distance my fortune — a sail!"

Then he lighted his lantern and rapidly flew to
     the beach,
   To the beach that was white with the mariner's
     bones,
But the air that was wet with the evening dew
   Had too often echoed the sufferer's groans.

And the sailor steered boldly his bark o'er the ocean,
   For he well knew the spot where the traveller stood,
And he saw from the dim lamp's tremulous motion
   It was not a light-house of dreary Cape Cod.

But as lately I wandered along on its banks
   And the rough rocks ascended to breathe the sea air,
Oh my heart beat to heaven a tribute of thanks,
   For the robber of midnight no longer was there.

For no more shall be seen there the moon-cusser's
     light;
   No longer to plunder the shores shall he roam,
For the horse and the rider have taken their flight,
   And the lantern they carried shall lighten
     them home.

> But I saw in the darkness a white form walking
> Around on the sand of the sea-beaten shore,
> And he seemed with the spirits of H--l to be talking
> And telling the stories of days gone o'er.

Orleans

A dozen miles north of Chatham on Route 28 is Orleans. Stop at the **Orleans Information Center** or the **Orleans Historical Society** for information about the town.

Orleans is the only town on the Cape with a French name (for Louis-Phillipe de Bourbon, Duke of Orleans, who visited in the 1790s); the others all have English or Indian names. In 1717 the first Cape Cod Canal was dug here. It was large enough to accommodate whaleboats, and its ruins are still visible on Bridge Street. Nearby **Rock Harbor** is a center for fishing boats of all kinds.

Off Orleans, in Cape Cod Bay, sits the **"Target Ship"** – its hull a mass of holes. The *James Longstreet*, a Liberty ship built during World War II, ran aground in a storm. Repairs would have been very expensive, so the ship was towed to her present location, and has been used for target practice ever since. (Each attack provides fireworks for miles around.) Sailors take note: Stay clear. There are unexploded shells in the area.

In early July and again in early August the town hosts the **Artists and Craftsmen's Guild Art and Craft Shows** at Nauset Regional Middle School. The school is also the site of the **Antique Exposition** in mid-August. **Peacock Alley**, on Route 28 in the former home of Peter Hunt, houses an interesting potpourri of shops that sell yarn, leather goods, sweaters, stained glass, paintings, and antiques. For beautiful fabrics and clothing, try **Lilly Pulitzer** (255-2630) (there are branches in Osterville and Edgartown too).

Love seafood? You'll love the **Lobster Claw** (255-1800) on Route 6. The informal atmosphere,

Orleans Information Center
Route 6A and Eldredge Parkway
Orleans
255-1386

Orleans Historical Society
River and School Roads
Orleans

complete with fishnets, makes this a great place for lunch. For more formal fare try the **Captain Linnell House** (255–3400) on Skaket Road. The house, built in 1840, was once a sea captain's mansion. Today the restaurant specializes in seafood and continental cuisine.

Eastham

Eastham is the gateway to the National Seashore. The ocean beaches here are among the finest in New England, and aficionados of surfing gather at **Nauset Light Beach** off Route 6 for some of the best conditions in the Northeast. The five beaches on the bay offer warmer water, and may appeal more to families with young children. The whole area abounds with sand dunes, lightly traveled roads (good for cycling), and nature trails. Thoreau's walking tour of the Cape began in Eastham. He described the breakers as "wild horses of Neptune" on an ocean where "man's works are wrecks."

Henry Beston, the author of *The Outermost House*, lived on the beach in Fo'castle, once the only house south of Nauset Light. Fo'castle was moved twice when erosion threatened it, and finally was placed on the other side of the dunes for protection from the surf. In the blizzard of February 1978, wild seas destroyed the house, and now even the land on which it stood is under water.

The pride and joy of Eastham, a three hundred-year-old windmill, is the spark each fall for **Windmill Weekend**. Come for kite flying, family volleyball, children's games, a 3- and a 5½-mile road race, square dancing, a parade, a band concert, and a cookout. The windmill is located on Samoset Road and Route 6. Although it isn't operating any longer, you can still see the old hand-made machinery—wooden gears, a 7-foot peg wheel, and a full set of sails. And a guide is on hand to give you a full description and answer questions.

Stop at the **Eastern Historical Society** for information about other sites in town.

Eastham Historical
 Society
Nauset Road
Eastham
255–0788

CAPE COD

NANTUCKET

The center of town is full of visitors all summer long who travel by path and cobbled lane enjoying all the island has to offer.

EASTHAM

The gray-shingled octagonal windmill which once ground grain for the residents of this Cape Cod community, was restored by the Works Progress Administration in 1936.

HERITAGE PLANTATION

A diversified museum of Americana including exhibits of military history, horticulture, antique autos, and folk art.

B·65

Before you leave enjoy a lobster roll, filled with large luscious chunks of meat, at the **Eastham Lobster Pool** (255-9706) on Route 6 in North Eastham. You know it's fresh because the pool and the restaurant are in the same building.

Cape Cod National Seashore

The Cape Cod National Seashore was developed in 1961 and is managed by the National Park Service. The 27,000-acre preserve is separated into four major areas.

Nauset Area

Salt Pond Visitor Center
Route 6
Eastham
235-3421

At the **Salt Pond Visitor Center** you'll find exhibits on the natural history of the area; a ten-minute orientation film; descriptions of walks, beaches, and picnic areas; and a schedule of evening programs in the amphitheater.

The **Fort Hill Trail** is a 1½-mile self-guided walk that begins a mile south of the visitors' center at the lovely mansard-roofed home built on Fort Hill by whaleship captain Edward Penniman in 1867. The **Buttonbush Trail** is a mile long with a guide rope for the blind. Signs, signaled by plastic disks along the rope, are written in braille and large print.

Marconi Station Area

Wellfleet Bay Wildlife Sanctuary
South Wellfleet
349-2615

In 1903 the first wireless message was sent to Europe from this station in South Wellfleet. The site is marked by an interpretive shelter with exhibits about Marconi Station. The **Atlantic White Cedar Swamp Trail**, a 1-mile inland walk, begins here. The trail winds through thick bushes and tall cedars, and into a swamp, a remnant of a glacier. (Part of the trail is on a boardwalk through the swamp, so bring insect repellent.)

The **Wellfleet Bay Wildlife Sanctuary** is located nearby. The 600 acres of beach, woods, moor, and salt marsh are maintained by the Massachusetts Audubon Society. The wildlife tour—in a beach buggy—takes at least an hour.

Pilgrim Heights Area

The interpretive shelter in North Truro has exhibits on Indians and Pilgrims. The **Pilgrim Spring Trail** (to a spring where the Pilgrims first drank water) and the **Small Swamp Trail** (a look at the effects of glaciers on the area), each a half mile long, begin here. Nearby **Highland Light** has a collection of materials on shipwrecks, and other historical information.

Province Lands Area

The **Province Lands Visitor Center** has exhibits and an orientation program on the natural history of the area. And you can pick up information on activities and schedules for evening programs in the amphitheater. The **Beech Forest Nature Trail** begins a mile from the visitors' center, and provides water views of inland ponds and a walk through a beech forest.

Province Lands
  Visitor Center
Race Point Road
Provincetown
487-1256

Part of the function of the National Seashore is to preserve the land. The Cape is vulnerable to erosion by wind-swept sand and to damage by salt spray. A survey several years ago showed a loss of 105 feet of coastline in just one area since 1973. The staff is constantly struggling to determine the probable course of erosion and to guard against it. At times sand dunes are allowed to shift or migrate in order to form a shield; at others beach-grass is planted to stabilize them.

Provincetown

Provincetown has long been a summer colony for painters and writers; exhibits and theater are available all summer. Eugene O'Neill did much of his early experimental work here with the Provincetown Players.

"P-town" is a walking town, with narrow interesting streets. Come early and park your car at **MacMillan Wharf**; then tackle the town on foot.

The waterfront has its own fascination: A large fishing fleet and visiting yachts keep the harbor busy all summer long. Come the last Sunday in

THE CAPE AND THE ISLANDS

Pilgrim Memorial Monument
Monument Hill
Provincetown

Provincetown Museum
Monument Hill
Provincetown
487-1310

Provincetown Chamber of Commerce
MacMillan Wharf
Provincetown
487-3424

June for the **Blessing of the Fleet**—a colorful local ceremony right on MacMillan Wharf.

On Commercial Street, near the wharf, you can buy a loaf of Portuguese bread, or stop for lunch at **Cookies** (487-1800), famous for authentic Portuguese dishes. **Pepe's Wharf** (487-0989), up the street, offers seafood and Portuguese specialties with the view, in a building that's partially over the water.

Off Bradford Street, which runs parallel to Commercial, is the **Pilgrim Memorial Monument**. The 255-foot granite tower was built in 1910. From the top there's a marvelous view of the area. The **Provincetown Museum**, right next to the monument, displays early firefighting equipment, a dollhouse, and a collection of ship figureheads.

Head out Conwell Street to **Race Point Beach**. Here you can try your hand at hang gliding from the dunes, keep your eyes peeled for whales (they come quite close to the beach), or just enjoy the beautiful clear water.

For more information about the town and local activities, contact the chamber of commerce.

Brewster

New England Fire and History Museum
Route 6A
Brewster
896-5700

Cape Cod Museum of Natural History
Main Street
Brewster
896-3867

Drummer Boy Museum
Route 6A
Brewster
896-3823

When you leave Provincetown follow Route 6A and then Route 6 back through North Truro (where you can check in the town hall about gravestone rubbing in **North Cemetery**), Wellfleet, Eastham, and Orleans, to Brewster, once home to many sea captains.

Here, start your explorations at the **New England Fire and History Museum**, the **Cape Cod Museum of Natural History**, and the **Drummer Boy Museum** (twenty-one life-size scenes of the American Revolution). Then, farther up Route 6A, stop at **Sealand of Cape Cod**, where you can watch a forty-minute dolphin show, and then stroll through the other buildings to see all sorts of fish and a large loggerhead turtle. Outside there are ducks, penguins, seals, and otters.

Stony Brook Mill, a working gristmill originally built in 1663, was rebuilt in 1873. It's located in an area called Factory Village, where a tannery and cloth mill once stood. If you come in the spring, walk along Stony Brook and watch the herring (or alewives) swim upstream to spawn.

Sealand of Cape Cod
Route 6A
Brewster
385-9252

Farther west on Route 6A is Dennis, a group of villages made up of Dennis Port, East Dennis, South Dennis, and West Dennis. Henry Hall began the first commercial farming of cranberries here in 1816.

Climb **Scargo Hill Tower** for a fine view of the ocean and bay; on a clear day you see the monument in Provincetown. Gravestone rubbing is allowed behind the town offices (485 Main Street) in South Dennis.

Dennis

Scargo Hill Tower
Scargo Hill Road
Dennis

Stay on Route 6A heading west, to Barnstable, where the Society for the Preservation of New England Antiquities maintains the **Old Crocker Tavern**. Once known as Aunt Lydia's Tavern, then Sturgis Tavern, it was built in 1754 by Cornelius Crocker; Lydia Sturgis was his daughter. The house contains eighteenth-century furnishings and exhibits. Sturgis Library, nearby, is the oldest library in the United States. The rooms in the front are furnished as nineteenth-century sitting rooms, and contain old books and records. The rest of the library is modern. Ask about the lectures on Cape Cod. The **Donald G. Trayser Museum** in the old brick Custom House displays Indian relics, old records from the post office, dolls, toys, silver, period furniture, and carriages.

Barnstable

Old Crocker Tavern
Route 6A
Barnstable

Sturgis Library
Route 6A
Barnstable
362-6636

Donald G. Trayser
  Museum
Route 6A
Barnstable
362-2092

Continue west on Route 6A past Barnstable Harbor and Sandy Neck Beach, to Sandwich. Settled in 1639, it's the oldest town on the Cape. From 1825 to 1888, until a strike forced the factory's closing, it was the home of the Sandwich Glass Company. Many think the factory was built here

Sandwich

for the supply of sand needed in processing glass, but the sand used was brought in from the Berkshires. Actually the factory was located in Sandwich because the local scrub pine forests provided cheap fuel for the furnaces.

During the nineteenth century pressed table glassware was inexpensive, and there were dozens of patterns available. But some Sandwich glass is rare and very valuable. The glassmakers often created special designs and blew unusual pieces, many of which are in the superb collection at the **Sandwich Glass Museum**.

If Sandwich whets your appetite for the glassblower's skill, you'll enjoy a visit to **Pairpoint Glass Works** on Sandwich Road in nearby Sagamore. Here you'll see modern-day craftsmen at work.

Other highlights in town: **Dexter's Grist Mill**, built in 1654, has been restored and is working, grinding corn. **Hoxie House**, a restored saltbox overlooking Shawme Lake, dates from 1637, and contains period furnishings. **Heritage Plantation** has a collection of antique automobiles, a military museum, a working windmill, a carousel, Currier and Ives prints, and a collection of folk art. The grounds—76 acres—are a horticulturist's dream. Come in July when the **Arts and Crafts Fair** is held. **Yesteryear's Museum** is filled with dolls and dollhouses from all over the world—a treat for kids of all ages.

Before you leave town, make a stop at **Quail Hollow Farm** (888-0438) on Route 130 for delectable blueberry and lemon breads, jams, and turkeys.

Continue along Route 6A to the **Sagamore Bridge**, at the east end of the canal. In 1918 the war department bought the Cape Cod Canal from August Belmont, who had built a narrow canal that would not handle freighters. After reconstruction the canal became a major artery for marine traffic.

Sandwich Glass
  Museum
Town Hall Square
Sandwich
888-0251

Hoxie House
Water Street
Sandwich

Heritage Plantation
Pine and Grove
  Streets
Sandwich
888-3300

Dexter's Grist Mill
Town Hall Square
Sandwich

Yesteryear's Museum
Main and River
  Streets
Sandwich
888-1711

Sailors beware: There are very strong currents running through the canal (sailboats must use auxiliary power), and extreme wind shifts from one end of the canal to the other. (A strong afternoon southwesterly against the current can kick up one of the nastiest seas imaginable at the Buzzards Bay entrance.)

After you cross the bridge, follow the west (land) side of the canal on Route 6 and stop at the **Herring Run Diner** (888-0084) for one last lobster roll. Then it's in to Boston town by way of Plymouth and the towns along the South Shore.

ITINERARY C

OLD NORTH CHURCH

ITINERARY C

(Suggested Time: 7–10 days; 150 miles/240 kilometers)

Historic Boston and the Bay Colonies

Plymouth	C·78
Duxbury	C·80
Scituate	C·80
Cohasset	C·82
Hingham	C·83
Quincy	C·83
Boston	C·84
The Freedom Trail	C·86
Off the Trail	C·93
Boston Harbor Islands	C·96
Cambridge	C·97
Sharon	C·98
Lowell	C·99
Lexington	C·100
Concord	C·101
Sudbury	C·105
Marblehead	C·107
Salem	C·109
Cape Ann	C·115
Gloucester	C·115
Rockport	C·122
Annisquam	C·123
Essex	C·123
Ipswich	C·124
Newburyport	C·125

The Pine-Tree
John Greenleaf Whittier

Lift again the stately emblem on the Bay State's rusted shield
Give to Northern winds the Pine-Tree on our banner's tattered field.
Sons of men who sat in council with their Bibles round the board
Answering England's royal missive with a firm, "THUS SAITH THE LORD!"
Rise again for home and freedom!—set the battle in array!—
What the fathers did of old time we their sons must do today.

Tell us not of banks and tariffs,—cease your paltry pedler cries,—
Shall the good State sink her honor that your gambling stocks may rise?
Would ye barter man for cotton?—that your gains may sum up higher,
Must we kiss the feet of Moloch, pass our children through the fire?
Is the dollar only real?—God and truth and right a dream?
Weighed against your lying ledgers must our manhood kick the beam?

O my God!—for that free spirit, which of old in Boston town
Smote the Province House with terror, struck the crest of Andros down!—
For another strong-voiced Adams in the city's streets to cry,
"Up for God and Massachusetts!—Set your feet on Mammon's lie!
Perish banks and perish traffic,—spin your cotton's latest pound,—
But in Heaven's name keep your honor,—keep the heart o' the Bay State sound!"

> Where's the MAN for Massachusetts! —Where's the
>   voice to speak her free?—
> Where's the hand to light up bonfires from her
>   mountains to the sea?
> Beats her Pilgrim pulse no longer! —Sits she dumb in
>   her despair?—
> Has she none to break the silence?—Has she none to
>   do and dare?
> O my God! for one right worthy to lift up her rusted
>   shield,
> And to plant again the Pine-Tree in her banner's
>   tattered field!

Whittier's words capture the sense of oppression felt by colonial settlers throughout the Revolutionary War period. Again and again they struggled for freedom —"What the fathers did of old time we their sons must do today."

The Pilgrims came to America in 1620 to seek freedom from religious persecution — the freedom to believe in and practice their theocratic ideals. They were determined to institutionalize this freedom, as they did in their very first charter, the Mayflower Compact. That agreement encouraged all citizens to abide by the will of the majority, a principle that led to the eventual success of the Revolution, but not without cost. For in some settlements religious zeal recreated the intolerance of England, forcing those of different beliefs to again seek out the freedom they thought they had found.

The success of the Plymouth colony — in contrast to the dismal failures at Jamestown and nearby Weymouth — depended on knowledge that the Pilgrims did not bring with them from Europe. It was the Indians who taught them how to fish for cod and mackerel, how to rotate their crops, how to build canoes, how to make clothing from leather, and how to mold pots from local clay. The Pilgrims survived because they had the Indians, and the Indian lifestyle, to guide them.

If their religious ideals led the early settlers to seek their freedom, their commercial success allowed them to achieve it. As the shipping industry prospered, the colonists quite naturally resisted the British control imposed by the Acts of Trade and Navigation (beginning in 1650), the Stamp Act (1765), and the Tea Act (1773). Battles at Lexington, Concord, and Bunker Hill precipitated the Revolution and the eventual defeat of the British overlords. The freedom sought by the Pilgrims in 1620 was finally achieved a century and a half later.

The South Shore

The South Shore stretches from Plymouth, at the edge of the Cape, along the coast to Quincy, right outside Boston.

Plymouth

Plymouth County Development Council
Box 1620
Pembroke
826-3136

Plymouth Town Information Booth
South Park Avenue
Plymouth
746-4799

Mayflower II
Water Street
Plymouth
746-1622

Plymouth Rock
Water Street
Plymouth

The itinerary begins in Plymouth, where the spirit of religious freedom led to the settlement of a new country.

Contact the **Plymouth County Development Council** before you go, or stop in at the **Plymouth Town Information Booth** (it's open mid-April through November), for maps and information.

Start your tour of the area where the Pilgrims did, at the harbor. The **Mayflower II**, a replica of the Pilgrim's *Mayflower*, was built in England in 1955, and sailed two years later for Plymouth under the command of Alan Villiers. The bark is only 106 feet long, 25 feet wide — a very small area for a hundred people and their baggage on a two-and-a-half-month trip. And the ship was even more cramped than it seems now: The replica has a foot more headroom than the original.

Cranberries — probably named for the cranes who enjoyed them in the bogs — are a regional industry. The Pilgrims began using the tart berries for food because the Indians told them that the berries tasted good and had the power to heal wounds. Soon the berries were being carried aboard ships to supplement salt pork diets and prevent scurvy. An industry was born!

For a close-up look at that industry, stop in at **Cranberry World** on Water Street (747-1000). Here you'll find working bogs, antique harvesting tools, a scale model of a cranberry farm, and daily cooking demonstrations — all free!

Plymouth Rock is right down the street from *Mayflower II*. The symbolic birthplace of this vast nation is actually quite small. It sits under a granite portico, protected from weather and souvenir hunters by a fence. On it is engraved the date—December 21, 1620—when seventeen men waded ashore on the desolate coast.

There are other sights to see right in town: **Pilgrim Hall** is filled with things the Pilgrims used—furniture, paintings, pewter, textiles, even Peregrine White's cradle. There's also an extensive library of rare manuscripts and books. **Jenney Grist Mill** is a replica of a mill the Pilgrims built in 1636. Corn, wheat, and rye are still ground by waterpower, and old crafts demonstrations take place daily.

Thanksgiving is a special time to be in Plymouth. Many of the townspeople dress in period clothes, a small group representing those who survived the first winter in America. And there's Thanksgiving dinner in Memorial Hall. Tickets can be purchased at the door by the first two thousand people to arrive. Call 746-3377 for information.

Plimoth Plantation is about 3 miles from the center, on Route 3A. Nowhere else can you sense the hardship of life in those early years so clearly, or appreciate the courage of those who survived it.

Pilgrim Village has been recreated according to the descriptions of Governor William Bradford and Edward Winslow, archaeological research, and other records. In 1627 fifty families lived here, with the cattle, poultry, pigs, goats, sheep, and horses necessary for farming. Costumed guides create a living folk-museum, performing everyday tasks as they were done in the seventeenth century. Inside some are cooking in large open fireplaces, sewing, or making barrels; outside others are thatching roofs, chopping wood, or firing their muskets in a twice-daily militia drill. And there's more: an orientation program, movies, and exhibits.

Commonwealth Winery is in an old hemp factory on Court Street, the remnant of a once

Pilgrim Hall
75 Court Street
Plymouth
746-1620

Jenney Grist Mill
8 Spring Lane
Plymouth
746-4604

Plimoth Plantation
85 Samoset Street
Plymouth
746-1622

Duxbury

Old Burying Ground
Chestnut Street
Duxbury

Alden House
Alden Road
Duxbury
934-2745, 934-6647

Miles Standish Monument
Crescent Street
Duxbury

Scituate

Duxbury Beach
Route 139
Duxbury

prosperous industry. You can tour the working winery, learn how wines are made, and taste a selection of current production. For information call 746-4138.

From Plymouth take Route 3A north to Duxbury. In the village visit the **Old Burying Ground**, where you'll find the graves of Captain Myles Standish, John and Priscilla Alden, and their son, Colonel John Alden. Longfellow, a descendant of John Alden, often walked through this cemetery. And he wrote about John and Priscilla in *The Courtship of Miles Standish*. Nearby is **Alden House**, with gunstock beams and clamshell ceilings. A couple of miles away, the **Miles Standish Monument** offers a lovely view of the bay and Plymouth.

Most of the beaches along the South Shore are reserved for residents of the towns. However **Duxbury Beach** is open to the public. **Powder Point Bridge**, the longest wooden bridge in the country, is the gateway to this beautiful 9-mile stretch of sand.

Continue north along Route 3A to Scituate. The harbor is the most protected deep-water harbor on the South Shore, and yachts of all sizes and commercial fishing boats create a constantly changing scene here.

The story of Scituate's "Army of Two" was told in the *Boston Evening Transcript* in 1879 by Farnham Smith, who heard it from two ladies who were young girls during the War of 1812. It seems Rebecca and Abby saw boats being lowered from two British ships in the harbor, and knew that they were on their way to ravage flour-laden American ships. So the two girls stood behind a barn and played a fife and drum with such vigor that the British thought a group of settlers was about to attack them. As the British retreated in haste to their ships, the girls gave them a parting tune: "Yankee Doodle." Wonderful!

THE SOUTH SHORE

The "Doorstep to America" where the first Pilgrim settlers came ashore on December 21, 1620.

PLYMOUTH

The Mayflower II, *a full-scale reproduction of the type of ship that brought the Pilgrims to America.*

PLYMOUTH

The Plimoth Plantation reproduces the first crude homes and early lifestyle of the Plymouth settlers.

PLYMOUTH

C·81

On March 16, 1956, the 7,000-ton *Etrusco* ran aground on Cedar Point outside Scituate during a northeaster. Everyone said she would be there until she rusted away, but a retired admiral who'd been involved in the salvage work at Pearl Harbor worked out a scheme using dynamite and bulldozers to free her. She floated off in high water, and was towed to Boston for repairs and a new life at sea.

Try **Barker Tavern** (545–6533), a marvelous restaurant on Barker Road. The building was constructed in 1634, and has wide floorboards and low wooden beams. Paintings of ships line the walls.

Cohasset

A few miles north on Hatherly Road you come to the edge of Cohasset, which was settled in the seventeenth century. Perched high on one side of the town common is **Saint Stephen's Episcopal Church**; the fifty-one bell carillon rings every Sunday. The **First Parish Church**, built in 1745, the town hall, and lovely old homes line the other sides of the common.

Cohasset Historical
  Society
Lothrop House
14 Summer Street
Cohasset
383–6930

The **Cohasset Historical Society** maintains three museums: **Historic House** (tools and furnishings) and **Maritime Museum** (ship models, models of Minots Light, relics of shipwrecks, and area artifacts dating back to 1700) on Elm Street; and the **Independence Gown Museum** (more than six hundred gowns dating from 1750 to 1950) around the corner on South Main. The **Lothrop House**, where the historical society is headquartered, is being renovated and will eventually open as a museum.

If you're in the mood for seafood, try **Hugo's Lighthouse** (383–1700) on Border Street in Cohasset Harbor.

Follow Atlantic Avenue to Jerusalem Road, out of town. **Moore's Rocks Reservation**, an untouched stretch of granite ledge on the ocean side of the road, offers a view of the surf pounding on massive rocks below. Look toward the east, where **Minots Ledge Lighthouse**, a 114-foot tower built in 1860, sits in the Atlantic.

Jerusalem Road leads right into Hingham. Your first stop: the **Old Ship Church** on Main Street. Go inside and look up from the box pews. The ceiling is built of oak beams in the shape of an upside-down ship's hull. The church was built in 1681 by ship's carpenters, and is the only seventeenth-century church still standing in Massachusetts. Since 1825 it's been owned and used by the American Unitarian Association.

Old Ordinary is the home of the Hingham Historical Society. Enjoy furnishings, a tool collection, the taproom, and the garden. The historical society and the chamber of commerce both offer more information about the town.

For a great view of the harbor islands and Boston, head for **World's End Reservation**. The 200-acre preserve on an ancient drumlin has wide gravel trails, perfect for hiking.

Don't leave town without walking through the center. Stop at **Talbots** (749-4340) for beautiful women's clothing; **Roebuck Caterers** (749-7713) for pastry, meat, fish, and cheese; and **Brigham's** (749-9842) for ice cream.

From Hingham it's just a few miles north on Route 3A to Quincy, where your first stop should be the chamber of commerce or city hall, for maps and information.

Two presidents were born in Quincy—John Adams and John Quincy Adams—and the **Adams National Historic Site** centers on their lives. Begin your tour on Franklin Street, at the two seventeenth-century saltboxes where the presidents were born. John Adams was born at Number 133 in 1735; his son, at Number 141 in 1767. There's a hiding place in the chimney (in case of attack by Indians) at Number 141.

Hingham

Old Ship Church
90 Main Street
Hingham
749-1679

Old Ordinary
21 Lincoln Avenue
Hingham
749-0013

Hingham Chamber of Commerce
739 Thaxter Park
Hingham
749-7415

World's End Reservation
Martin's Lane
Hingham
698-2066

Quincy

Quincy-South Shore Chamber of Commerce
36 Miller Stile Road
Quincy
479-1111

HISTORIC BOSTON AND THE BAY COLONIES

**Adams National
Historic Site**
135 Adams Street
Quincy
773-1177

About a mile away, on Adams Street, is the home for four generations of the Adams family. Furnishing shows the development of styles from 1788 to 1927. Look for the John Singleton Copley painting of John Adams, the Trumbull engraving, the three-hundred-year-old grandfather clock, the Louis XV safe, and the high-cushion chairs, specially designed for the hoopskirts of the day.

End your tour of the national historic site in Quincy Square, at the church where the presidents and their families worshipped and are buried.

Hancock Cemetery
Hancock Street
Quincy

While you're here, stop across the street at the **Hancock Cemetery**, where sixty-nine veterans of the Revolutionary War are buried. You'll enjoy reading the amusing and unusual poetry on the grave markers. Then head out Hancock Street to the **Dorothy Quincy Homestead**, the home of Dorothy Quincy, who later married John Hancock. The house was built in the seventeenth century, enlarged in the eighteenth. There's a secret chamber here too, where American patriots hid during the Revolution.

**Dorothy Quincy
Homestead**
1010 Hancock Street
Quincy
472-5117

The **Patriot's Trail** takes you through twenty-seven towns, most of them along the South Shore, stopping at cultural, historical, and recreational sites. For information and a map contact the Norfolk County Tourist Council, 357 West Squantum Street, North Quincy, 328-1776.

Boston

Boston is a complex city. We could try to categorize it for you by its history, literature, education, culture, architecture, even geography. Instead we offer a composite itinerary, a cross-section of possibilities drawn from our many discoveries in this fascinating city.

For information before you go and while you're here, contact the **Boston Convention & Tourist Bureau** or the **National Historical Park**

Visitor Center. The **Boston Common Information Booth** is open for on-site visits only. You can pick up a copy of "Boston Byweek"—a monthly calendar of current activities—at any of these visitors' centers or at most hotels.

There's entertainment for everyone in Boston, much more than you'll have time to enjoy. Try the Boston Symphony Orchestra or the Boston Pops, the Opera Company of Boston, or the Boston Ballet. Pick up tickets for a Broadway-bound show at the Colonial, Shubert, or Wilbur theaters. Or catch a professional production at the Boston Shakespeare Company, the Charles Playhouse, or the Next Move. Need more? Schools, museums, and churches around the area offer a nonstop schedule of concerts, theater, and lectures.

For even more ideas and information, pick up a copy of the *Boston Globe*'s Thursday edition, and look through Calendar, a weekly listing of entertainment in the Hub.

Whenever we travel in Europe, we always head first for the tallest church, winding up worn stone steps to the top for a view of the city. With map in hand, we identify landmarks to fix our visual perspective before choosing our route for the day. In Boston you can enjoy an overview of the city and harbor from several spots. The **Sky Walk** in the fifty-two-story-high Prudential Tower offers a restaurant and shops along with the scenery. There's also a narrated description of local history. The **John Hancock Observatory** provides a panoramic view, exhibits of Boston past and present, a topographical model, and *Cityflight*, a seven-minute film tour of the city from a helicopter. A great introduction to the city: *Where's Boston?* is a montage of the voices, pictures, music, and sounds of the city today. The music track combines eighteenth-century hymns with the twentieth-century theme. You'll find the show near Faneuil Hall, at 60 State Street. Phone 367-6090 for information.

Boston Convention &
  Tourist Bureau
Prudential Plaza
Boston
267-6446

National Historical
  Park Visitor Center
15 State Street
Boston
242-5642

Boston Common
  Information Booth
Tremont Street
Boston

Prudential Tower
800 Boylston Street
Boston
267-1757, 236-3318

John Hancock
  Observatory
John Hancock Tower
Clarendon Street
Boston
247-1977

The Freedom Trail

Unless you're already familiar with historic Boston, start your tour with the Freedom Trail. You can pick up a map at any visitors' center, and then walk along the red-signed path.

Hardy souls cover the whole trail—from downtown Boston across the river to Charlestown. But with children, try a shorter loop. You could visit the North End and stop at the four sites there: Paul Revere House, Paul Revere Mall, Old North Church, and Copp's Hill Burying Ground. Another short tour begins at the State House, and stops at Park Street Church, Granary Burying Ground, King's Chapel, the Benjamin Franklin Statue, the Old Corner Bookstore, and the Old South Meeting House. In a third tour Faneuil Hall, Quincy Market, and the Old State House are grouped together.

There isn't a single sequence of sites along the trail. We like to explore it slowly, stopping when the spirit moves us. Usually we begin at **Faneuil Hall**, the "Cradle of Liberty." The building, topped with a grasshopper weathervane, was given to the city in 1742. Through the years it's been the site of hundreds of open meetings. On the top (third) floor you'll find the Ancient and Honorable Artillery Company and exhibits.

Quincy Market, a low granite building in Greek Revival style, is a shopper's paradise. Set a time limit, or you may spend the day in the tantalizing maze of specialty shops here and in the north and south markets next door.

From the Marketplace, walk up State Street to the **Old State House**. The Declaration of Independence was read from a balcony here on July 18, 1776. The building now houses a museum filled with ship models, revolutionary relics, and other memorabilia. Outside, at the intersection below the Old State House, the **Boston Massacre** site is marked by a ring of cobblestones. Here, on March 5, 1770, nine British soldiers were confronted by a crowd of angry Bostonians, throwing

Faneuil Hall
Dock Square
Boston
223-6098

Old State House
206 Washington Street
Boston
242-5655

rocks. The Redcoats fired into the crowd, killing five men.

Up Washington Street is the **Old South Meeting House**, where plans were laid in 1773 for the Boston Tea Party. In the museum are a model of the city in 1775, and copies of historic documents. Benjamin Franklin's birthplace is marked by a plaque just around the corner, on Milk Street. The **Old Corner Bookstore**, across Washington Street, was once a gathering place for Longfellow, Lowell, Whittier, Hawthorne, Thoreau, Stowe, Howe, and Holmes. Today, amongst the first editions and period furnishings, you'll find a bookstore filled with New England titles.

Old South Meeting House
310 Washington Street
Boston
482-6439

Old Corner Bookstore
Washington and
 School Streets
Boston
929-2602

Up School Street, four bronze panels at the base of the **Benjamin Franklin Statue** depict him signing the Declaration of Independence and a peace treaty with France, working as a printer, and experimenting with lightning and electricity. Look carefully: One side of Franklin's face is smiling; the other, sober.

Benjamin Franklin
 Statue
School Street
Boston

Early settlers believed that free public education was a citizen's right. And the people in Massachusetts were largely responsible for the early development of education in this country. The first public school in the country was built in Boston in 1635. You can read about it on the plaque outside Old City Hall, on School Street, right near the Franklin statue. And Harvard was founded in nearby Cambridge one year later.

At the corner of Tremont and School sits **King's Chapel**, the oldest stone church in Boston. In its steeple hangs a bell made by Paul Revere. The graves of Governor Winthrop and William Dawes are in the **Burying Ground** outside. In *The Scarlet Letter* Nathaniel Hawthorne, who often walked here, wrote about the small gravestone of Elizabeth Paine, which is on the southern edge of the cemetery. In 1683 she was tried for the murder of her child and acquitted, but some people say they can see the letter A on her gravestone. In *The*

King's Chapel and
 Burying Ground
58 Tremont Street
Boston
523-1749

HISTORIC BOSTON AND THE BAY COLONIES

Granary Burying Ground
Tremont Street
Boston

Park Street Church
Tremont and Park Streets
Boston
523-3383

State House
Beacon Street
Boston
727-3676

Scarlet Letter Hester, who's forced to wear a red letter A embroidered on her dress, imagines an angel writing an A on the stone.

In the **Granary Burying Ground** across the street are the graves of John Hancock, Robert Treat Paine, Samuel Adams, Paul Revere, Benjamin Franklin's parents, the victims of the Boston Massacre, and Mary Goose (the creator of Mother Goose).

You may hear the bells of the **Park Street Church**, around the corner, before you see the building. They chime every day at noon. The sails for the USS *Constitution* were made here, and brimstone for gunpowder was stored in the cellar during the War of 1812. Over the years **Boston Common** has been used for hanging criminals, grazing cows, and training militia. Today the criminals, cows, and militia are gone, but soapbox orators and sidewalk musicians are here in force. Come in the summer to wade in Frog Pond, hear a band concert, or feed the pigeons; in winter, to skate. People watching, we're happy to report, is available year-round.

The **Boston Public Garden**, across Charles Street, is a lovely spot. You can feed the ducks, ride the swan boats, or find a bench and just watch the world go by.

Walk up Park Street to the gold-domed **State House**. Meetings of the legislature are open to the public. In the **Archives Museum** are modern documents and proclamations, as well as famous written records from our colonial past.

From the State House cross over Beacon Hill, through Government Center, under the expressway, to the North End. This area has been the first home for different groups of immigrants. Now an Italian-American neighborhood, its narrow streets are lined with grocery stores, vegetable stands, and cafes serving espresso and cappuccino. There are four Freedom Trail stops in the area.

The first, **Paul Revere House**, was purchased by Revere in 1770 when it was already a hundred years old. There are four rooms (and he lived here with his sixteen children!) filled with seventeenth- and eighteenth-century furnishings. From here head up Hanover Street, and stop at **Paul Revere Mall**. Look for the equestrian statue of Revere. **Old North Church**, on the back side of the mall, was the site of the historic lantern signal—"one if by land, two if by sea"—that set off the midnight ride of Paul Revere. The church was built in 1723. The bells in the steeple, rung by Revere when he was a fifteen-year-old member of the Bell Ringers' Guild, are still rung every Sunday morning. Cross Salem Street to Hull Street, to Snowhill, where you'll find **Copp's Hill Burying Ground**. Some of the stones still display bullet marks made by the Redcoats, who used them for target practice.

Paul Revere House
19 North Square
Boston
523-1676

Paul Revere Mall
Hanover Street
Boston

Old North Church
193 Salem Street
Boston
523-6676

Copp's Hill Burying Ground
Snowhill and Charter Streets
Boston

Paul Revere's Ride
Henry Wadsworth Longfellow

Listen, my children, and you shall hear
    Of the midnight ride of Paul Revere,
On the eighteenth of April, in '75;
    Hardly a man is now alive
Who remembers that famous day and year
    He said to his friend, "If the British march
By land or sea from the town tonight,
    Hang a lantern aloft in the belfry arch
Of the North Church tower as a signal light—
    One, if by land, and two, if by sea;
And I on the opposite shore will be,
    Ready to ride and spread the alarm
Through every Middlesex village and farm,
    For the country folk to be up and to arm."
Then he said, "Good night!" and with muffled oar
    Silently rowed to the Charlestown shore...
Meanwhile, his friend, through alley and street,
    Wanders and watches with eager ears,
Till in the silence around him he hears
    The muster of men at the barrack door,

The sound of arms, and the tramp of feet,
    And the measured tread of the grenadiers,
Marching down to their boats on the shore.
    Then he climbed the tower of the Old North Church
By the wooden stairs, with stealthy tread,
    To the belfry chamber overhead,...
By the trembling ladder, steep and tall,
    To the highest window in the wall,
Where he paused to listen and look down
    A moment on the roofs of the town,
And the moonlight flowing over all...
    A moment only he feels the spell
Of the place and the hour, and the secret dread
    Of the lonely belfry and the dead;
For suddenly all his thoughts are bent
    On a shadowy something far away,
Where the river widens to meet the bay—
    A line of black that bends and floats
On the rising tide, like a bridge of boats,
    Meanwhile, impatient to mount and ride,
Booted and spurred, with a heavy stride
    On the opposite shore walked Paul Revere.
Now he patted his horse's side,
    Now gazed at the landscape far and near,
Then, impetuous, stamped the earth,
    And turned and tightened his saddle girth;
But mostly he watched with eager search
    The belfry tower of the Old North Church,
As it rose above the graves on the hill,
    Lonely and spectral and somber and still.
And lo! as he looks, on the belfry's height
    A glimmer, and then a gleam of light!
He springs to the saddle, the bridle he turns,
    But lingers and gazes, till full on his sight
A second lamp in the belfry burns!...

There are several Freedom Trail sites across the river in Charlestown. You can walk across Charlestown Bridge, or pick up your car and follow the signs to Charlestown City Square and Constitution Road off I-93.

The **USS Constitution** is at the Charlestown Navy Yard. The forty-four-gun frigate was launched in 1797, and was never defeated in its twenty-four battles. The flavor of sea life is everywhere: from the camboose (galley stove), the scuttlebutt, and the grog tub; to the bilge pumps and the anchor capstan; to the captain's cabin, officers' quarters, and crew's hammocks. Look up and you'll see on each mast a fighting top—a platform where marines stood to fire muskets at the decks of enemy ships. And all around are guides in 1812 naval uniforms ready to answer questions and share the ship's history.

> USS Constitution
> Charlestown Navy Yard
> Charlestown
> 242-5670

The USS *Constitution* took part in a number of memorable battles, including two with the British frigate *Guerrière* in 1812. In the first, Captain Isaac Hull, caught in a calm amongst a squadron of British ships, used his kedge anchors to escape. A boat went ahead, perhaps a half mile, and dropped the kedges; the men hauled on the long hawsers, drawing the ship up to the point where the anchors lay. Then the whole process was repeated. In two days the *Constitution* had outdistanced the enemy, and when the wind came sailed for Boston.

In the second adventure with the *Guerrière* patience was the byword. The men held their fire until the ships were abreast, close aboard. Then Captain Hull ordered, "Now, boys, pour it on them!" and the *Guerrière*'s mizzenmast and rigging crashed down. She was helpless. It was during this battle that one of the British sailors pointed to the undamaged *Constitution*, and shouted, "Huzza! Her sides are made of iron!" "Old Ironsides" was born.

In 1830, her battles long over, the *Constitution* was scheduled to be destroyed. Oliver Wendell Holmes wrote a poem about the ship that moved the public to save her.

The **USS Constitution Museum**, across the drydock, has a number of exhibits and hands-on displays, including knot tying and swinging in a sailor's hammock. Nearby you can see the **USS**

> USS Constitution Museum
> Charlestown Navy Yard
> Charlestown
> 426-1812

USS Cassin Young
Charlestown Navy
  Yard
Charlestown
242-5604

Cassin Young. This ship, launched in September 1943, saw action in the Philippines and Japan, and sank four Japanese carriers in the battle at Cape Engano. She represents all of the many ships built at the navy yard that served the country during World War II. Across the water from the USS *Constitution*, in the Bunker Hill Pavilion, is **The Whites of Their Eyes**—a sound-and-light show that recreates the Battle of Bunker Hill. Call 241-7575 for information.

Old Ironsides
Oliver Wendell Holmes

Ay, tear her tattered ensign down!
  Long has it waved on high,
And many an eye has danced to see
  That banner in the sky;
Beneath it rung the battle shout,
  And burst the cannon's roar;—
The meteor of the ocean air
  Shall sweep the clouds no more.

Her deck, once red with heroes' blood,
  Where knelt the vanquished foe,
When winds were hurrying o'er the flood,
  And waves were white below,
No more shall feel the victor's tread,
  Or know the conquered knee;—
The harpies of the shore shall pluck
  The eagle of the sea!

Oh, better that her shattered hulk
  Should sink beneath the wave;
Her thunders shook the mighty deep,
  And there should be her grave;
Nail to the mast her holy flag,
  Set every threadbare sail,
And give her to the god of storms,
  The lightning and the gale!

The **Bunker Hill Monument** is just a few blocks north of the navy yard in a section of Charlestown that is gradually being restored. (Ask for directions at the yard.) The monument commemorates the battle of June 17, 1775. The British lost 1,054 men that day; the Americans, 450.

From Charlestown, take I-93 south to the Dock Square–Callahan Tunnel exit; then follow the signs to the **New England Aquarium**. Here you'll find the world's largest circular glass tank. A highlight: watching divers in the tank feed the sharks and giant sea turtles. When you've finished exploring the multilevel exhibit galleries (and the more than seven thousand fish they display), head next door to the *Discovery* to watch otters, seals, sea lions, and dolphins performing in a large pool.

From the aquarium drive south on Atlantic Avenue to Purchase Street, where you'll bear right (Atlantic Avenue becomes one way the wrong way); turn left on Congress Street and follow the signs to the **Boston Tea Party Ship and Museum**. Here you can explore the brig *Beaver II*, a full-sized replica of one of the three original Tea Party ships. Audiovisual programs tell about the original Tea Party and the replica's voyage from Denmark. (The *Beaver II* was built in Denmark, and sailed to Boston in 1973.) There's also a model of eighteenth-century Boston, which traces the route of the Tea Party participants.

The next wharf off Congress Street, Museum Wharf, houses the **Children's Museum**. Children can climb through City Slice, a three-story section of a house and street; dress up in Grandmother's Attic; explore the Giant's Desk Top, where everything is twelve times normal size; learn about another culture in the Japanese House; and stop at the Resource Center to ask questions. It's a marvelous, noisy, try-your-hand-at-everything place.

Bunker Hill
 Monument
Breed's Hill
Charlestown
242-5641

Off the Trail

New England
 Aquarium
Central Wharf
Boston
742-8870

Boston Tea Party Ship
 and Museum
Congress Street
 Bridge
Boston
338-1773

Children's Museum
Museum Wharf
300 Congress Street
Boston
426-6500

Museum of Science
Science Park
Boston
723-2500

The **Museum of Science** is on the Charles River Dam Bridge between Leverett Circle and Lechmere Square. The museum is filled with exhibits about space, technology, and biology. Among them are many push-a-button-and-do-it-yourself exhibits, including one that reveals your skeleton and a generator that you operate to produce electric lighting. Visit **Hayden Planetarium** for a forty-five-minute program about the stars. Then head for the cafeteria or sandwich shop for a snack.

Museum of Fine Arts
465 Huntington Avenue
Boston
267-9300

Boston's **Museum of Fine Arts** is one of the most comprehensive museums in the Western Hemisphere. Enjoy the vast collections, and the library, research laboratory, restaurant, children's programs, gallery talks, and special lectures and films. The museum is on Huntington Avenue, which you can pick up at Copley Square.

Gardner Museum
280 the Fenway
Boston
566-1401

Around the corner is the **Gardner Museum**, Isabella Stewart Gardner's home until she died in 1924. The building is of Italian design, and is filled with Mrs. Gardner's eclectic collection of paintings, tapestries, stained glass, and furniture. The enclosed central courtyard, filled with flowers year-round, is used for chamber music concerts.

Boston's shopping ranges from the specialty shops lining Newbury Street and the Marketplace, to the ambiance and bargains of Filene's Basement. The area beyond downtown is filled with discount outlets and factory stores. Our favorites: **Calverts** (444-8000) in Needham for clothes to suit the whole family; **China Fair** (566-2220) in Brookline for pots and pans and dishes and more; **Bed and Bath** (443-8958) in Sudbury for linens and towels; and **The Shed** (237-1818) in Wellesley for shoes and sneakers.

John F. Kennedy Library
Columbia Point
Dorchester
929-4567

From downtown, take I-93 south to exit 17, and follow the signs to the **John F. Kennedy Library**. After an excellent introductory film, walk through exhibits depicting Kennedy's childhood, war experiences, Senate term, and days as presi-

BOSTON

BOSTON

The restoration of the historic Quincy Market, Faneuil Hall Market Place, attracts millions of people annually with its cosmopolitan melange of boutiques, restaurants, gift shops, and exhibits.

CAMBRIDGE

The USS Constitution, "Old Ironsides," floats quietly at her dock at the entrance to the Boston Navy Yard.

BOSTON

Visitors can trace the Kennedy family story in exhibits and film at the John Fitzgerald Kennedy Memorial Library.

dent. There's a small exhibit, too, about Robert Kennedy. The library itself—which most visitors don't go into—contains films and documents from the Kennedy administration, and other materials (including a fine collection on Ernest Hemingway).

Franklin Park Zoo
Franklin Park
Dorchester
442-2005

A few miles away is the **Franklin Park Zoo**, now being reconstructed and enlarged. Bird's World, a walk-in aviary, is open, and so is the range area, where you can see llamas, deer, antelope, camels, and other animals. To come: a children's zoo filled with baby animals.

Boston Harbor Islands

The Boston Harbor Islands, low and sandy, stand in marked contrast to the city's skyscrapers. The more than thirty islands offer eighteenth-century forts and ruins to explore, and picnicking, fishing, boating, swimming, camping, and hiking. Pick up a copy of the *AMC Guide to Country Walks Near Boston*, which describes several walks on the islands.

Ferry schedules are available from **Bay State-Spray & Provincetown Steamship Company** (723-7800), **Boston Harbor Cruises** (227-4321), and **Massachusetts Bay Line** (542-8000). All stop at Georges Island, where you board a free water taxi to the other islands.

Department of
  Environmental
  Affairs
100 Cambridge Street
Boston
727-3180

Eighteen of the islands now make up the Boston Harbor Island State Park. For complete information, contact the **Department of Environmental Affairs**.

The problem isn't finding good restaurants in Boston; it's choosing one. Our favorites: For first-rate seafood try **Legal Seafoods** (426-4444) at the Boston Park Plaza Hotel. We can vouch for the smoked Irish salmon, mixed sashimi, fried oysters, and fried clams; and everything else going by us looked delicious too! **Durgin Park** (227-2038) has been open in the Marketplace for over 135 years. Come for New England boiled dinners, Boston baked beans, and Indian pudding. On nearby Union Street, the **Union Oyster House** (227-2750) features shore dinners, lobster, and an oyster bar. **Maison Robert** (227-3370) on School Street serves both lunch and dinner on the patio behind the Franklin statue. Inside, floor-to-ceiling windows enhance the upstairs dining room.

Across the Charles from Boston sits Cambridge, a city rich in historical and cultural traditions. The city boasts two of the nation's finest universities—Harvard, the first college founded in America, and MIT, a leading research center in science and technology.

Harvard University opened in 1636. It was originally funded by John Harvard, who donated his library, farm, and money to begin the school. Today the campus sprawls from the river through Harvard Square, and beyond.

Start your explorations in the square, at the **Harvard Information Center**. This is the place for area maps and activity schedules. Then walk through **Harvard Yard**, past **Widener Library** and a fine collection of eighteenth-century buildings, to the **Harvard University Museum**. Actually the building houses four different museums: the **Botanical Museum** (look for the glass flowers), the **Mineralogical Museum**, the **Museum of Comparative Zoology**, and the **Peabody Museum**.

Around the corner are two other museums: The **Busch-Reisinger Museum** houses a fine collection of sculpture, paintings, drawings, and prints. The **Fogg Art Museum** has one of the richest university collections in the world. Here you'll see paintings, sculpture, prints, and silver.

The **Massachusetts Institute of Technology** was chartered in 1861, and moved to its present location on Massachusetts Avenue in 1916. Eero Saarinen designed the cylindrical **MIT Chapel**; the aluminum bell tower atop it was sculpted by Theodore Roszak. The lighting inside is reflected from the surrounding moat through high arches.

Cambridge

Harvard Information
  Center
1353 Massachusetts
  Avenue
Cambridge
495-1573

Harvard University
  Museum
24 Oxford Street
Cambridge
495-1910

Busch-Reisinger
  Museum
29 Kirkland Street
Cambridge
495-2338

Fogg Art Museum
32 Quincy Street
Cambridge
495-2387

MIT Chapel
Massachusetts Avenue
Cambridge
253-7975

Frances Russell Hart
Nautical Museum
77 Massachusetts
Avenue
Cambridge
253-5942

Charles Hayden
Memorial Library
116 Memorial Drive
Cambridge
253-4680

Cambridge Historical
Commission
57 Inman Street
Cambridge
498-9040

Longfellow National
Historic Site
105 Brattle Street
Cambridge
876-4491

Across the street, in the **Frances Russell Hart Nautical Museum**, are ship and engine models that trace the development of marine engineering. Around the corner, in the **Charles Hayden Memorial Library**, is the **Hayden Gallery** and its exhibits of contemporary art.

There is life beyond the universities. Contact the **Cambridge Historical Commission** for the "Old Cambridge Walking Guide," a brochure that describes thirty sites in the area. Among them is the **Longfellow National Historic Site**, once lived in by George and Martha Washington. Henry Wadsworth Longfellow later lived here for forty-five years, and was married to Fanny Appleton in the house. Most of his furnishings and belongings are still here. In the library are several paintings of Minnehaha Falls (Yes, there is a Minnehaha Falls. It's in Minneapolis), the setting of *The Song of Hiawatha*.

On your way out Brattle Street, at Number 56, you pass the **Blacksmith House** (354-3036), where Longfellow's village blacksmith lived. Stop in for Viennese and Parisian pastries.

Longfellow isn't the only literary figure to make Cambridge home. At one time or another Oliver Wendell Holmes, Margaret Fuller, James Russell Lowell, Robert Frost, E. E. Cummings, and Thomas Wolfe all lived here too.

There are a number of interesting side trips in the greater Boston area. We mention two that you might miss because they are out of the way: Sharon and Lowell.

Sharon

Kendall Whaling
Museum
27 Everett Street
Sharon
784-5642

From Boston take I-93 south to I-95 south to Route 27 east into Sharon. Turn onto Moose Hill Parkway and follow the signs to the **Kendall Whaling Museum**. This unique museum has a fine collection of whaling objects from all different times and places. You'll see paintings from the Greenland Whale Fishery; Delft tiles; British, German, and French scrimshaw; Japanese scrolls;

and paintings, prints, scrimshaw, and ship models from American whaling. Also here: a whaleboat from the last New Bedford whaler, the *John R. Manta*; whaling tools; figureheads; harpoons and lances; and logbooks and journals. On the grounds an unexpected pleasure—a doll museum housing one of the finest collections in the country.

From Boston take I-93 north to I-495 south; then follow the signs to Lowell, a center of the state's industrial development. From 1821, when the potential power of the Merrimack River was first realized, through the beginnings of the Industrial Revolution, men and women left their New England farms to work in the city's mills. After World War I, labor troubles and later the depression led slowly to the eventual shutdown of those mills. But today Lowell is coming back to life.

The **Lowell National Historical Park**, established in 1978, commemorates the significance of the Industrial Revolution in shaping our modern industrial society. Exhibits portray the lives of ordinary working people—from the factory girls working fourteen-hour days, six days a week, to today's unionized workers—during 150 years of economic and social change. And there are canal trips and river walks, and mills, boardinghouses, and museums to visit.

Lowell's ethnic neighborhoods add to the era's history the story of immigrant workers. Jack Kerouac grew up in Lowell, and wrote about those workers and the city in several of his novels. Look for *The Town and the City*, *Vanity of Duloz*, *Maggie Cassidy*, *Visions of Gerard*, *Dr. Saw*, and *Book of Dreams*.

Lowell

Lowell National
  Historical Park
Market Mills
Market Street
Lowell
459-1000

The Trail of the Minutemen

In the spring of 1775 Massachusetts was "a bonfire waiting for a match." The Continental Congress had authorized an army of 18,000 men, but only 4,000 had been collected. England decided to take advantage: General Thomas Gage was ordered to subdue the provincials while they were still "a rude rabble." But, the "rude rabble" pieced together the British plans on April 15, 1775, when General Gage relieved his best troops of their routine duties. Paul Revere rode to Lexington to warn John Hancock and Samuel Adams, then went to Boston to arrange a special signal from the steeple of Old North Church. Meanwhile Adams and Hancock began moving supplies and arms to new hiding places. Three nights later, as seven hundred Redcoats boarded boats on the Charles River, two lanterns glowed in the Old North's steeple, and Revere and William Dawes rode off to warn the Minutemen.

The Minutemen, led by Captain John Parker, gathered on the green in Lexington. As the British marched onto the green someone fired a shot — no one knows from where — and in just a few minutes eight Minutemen had been killed, shot in the back. The Redcoats marched on to Concord and took the town, then moved on to North Bridge. There "the shot heard round the world" set them on their heels. They panicked and ran.

As the defeated troops marched back to Boston along Battle Road, local patriots fired at them from behind trees, Indian style. A thousand reinforcements arrived, allowing the Redcoats time to rest and treat their wounded, but still the provincials harassed them. The British, angry at this method of fighting, began killing any civilian unlucky enough to be in the way, even innocent men sitting in a tavern. Forty-nine Americans died that day, forty-one were wounded, and five were reported missing; the British lost seventy-three dead, close to two hundred wounded, and twenty-six missing. This was the beginning of the American Revolution.

Lexington

Lexington Chamber
of Commerce
1875 Massachusetts
Avenue
Lexington
862-1450

Lexington Historical
Society
Meriam Street
Lexington
861-0928

From Boston take Route 2 west to Waltham Street; then follow the signs into Lexington Center. Stop at the chamber of commerce for maps and information, and to see a diorama of the battle, which should help you get the historical pattern into focus.

Then walk out onto **Battle Green**, where it began early in the morning of April 19, 1775. In summer you'll find young guides eager to share the story. The **Minutemen Statue** of Captain John Parker was designed by Henry Hudson Kitson.

The **Lexington Historical Society** operates a visitors' center just off Massachusetts Avenue. Here you'll find another diorama of the clash on the green, pamphlets about local shops, and information about bike and walking trails to Concord. And guides are on hand to help you chart your course.

The society maintains three historic houses: **Buckman Tavern**, on the green, was where the Minutemen gathered before the early-morning skirmish. It's been restored with eighteenth-century furniture, mugs for making "hot flip," signs limiting travelers to four in a bed, and a display of colonial clothing. A few minutes away is the **Hancock-Clarke House**, where Paul Revere rode to warn John Hancock and Samuel Adams that the British were coming. **Munroe Tavern**, back out Massachusetts Avenue toward Arlington, was used by Earl Percy as his headquarters and as a refuge for wounded British soldiers.

Nearby, off Route 2A, is the **Museum of Our National Heritage**. There are four galleries here, each with a display about the growth and development of the United States.

Minute Man National Historical Park sprawls across three towns: Lexington, Lincoln, and Concord. There are several visitors' centers in the park, each with informed staff, maps, and pamphlets. The first center you come to as you drive along Battle Road (Route 2A) is the **Battle Road Visitor Center** in Lexington (862-7753). Follow signs to the parking lot; then walk along the winding path through the woods to the striking modern cedar building nestled in the pines. There are exhibits, a movie, an electric map, and a bookstore.

Park headquarters are in the **North Bridge Visitor Center** (page 102) in Concord.

Buckman Tavern
1 Bedford Street
Lexington
861-0928

Hancock-Clarke
  House
36 Hancock Street
Lexington
862-5598

Munroe Tavern
1332 Massachusetts
  Avenue
Lexington
862-1703

Museum of Our
  National Heritage
33 Marrett Road
Lexington
861-6559

From Lexington Center follow Battle Road (Route 2A) into Concord. On your right, before you come into the center of town, are several historical houses.

Concord

Grapevine Cottage
491 Lexington Road
Concord

The Wayside
Lexington Road
Concord
369-6975

Orchard House
399 Lexington Road
Concord
369-4118

Museum of the
  Concord
  Antiquarian Society
200 Lexington Road
Concord
369-9606

Sleepy Hollow
  Cemetery
Bedford Street
Concord
369-7526

Old North Bridge
Monument Street
Concord

North Bridge Visitor
  Center
171 Liberty Street
Concord
369-6993

Grapevine Cottage is one of the oldest houses in town. In the yard is the original Concord grapevine, still bearing fruit in late summer. **The Wayside** was the home of Nathaniel Hawthorne, the Alcotts, and Margaret Sidney, who wrote the Five Little Peppers series. And beyond Alcott Road, you come to **Orchard House**, where Louisa May Alcott wrote *Little Women*. Look for her "mood pillow." When she set it on end, pointed up, she was in a good mood; but when she laid it flat, watch out!

Beyond Orchard House, on the left, is the **Museum of the Concord Antiquarian Society**. Here are fifteen rooms with furniture dating from the seventeenth to the mid-nineteenth century. Also here: one of the two lanterns that hung in Old North Church, Emerson's study recreated with its original furnishings, a copper kettle used by Louisa May Alcott during the Civil War, and a diorama of the fight at North Bridge.

Continue on Route 2A to the rotary, and take a right onto Route 62 (Bedford Street). In **Sleepy Hollow Cemetery**, on the left, look for **Author's Ridge**, where Hawthorne, Emerson, Thoreau, and the Alcotts are buried. Gravestone rubbing is allowed.

Turn back on Bedford Street and follow it straight out onto Monument Street. Park on the right, then cross the street to **Old North Bridge**, where the "shot heard round the world" was fired. Standing nearby is Daniel Chester French's famous statue of the Minuteman.

Most people see Old North Bridge from land; but you can also see it from water. The **South Bridge Boat House**, on Route 62 a mile west of Concord Center, rents canoes and runs guided boat tours to historic sites along the Concord River. Phone 369-9438 for information.

From the bridge it's a short walk up to the Buttrick mansion, where you'll find the **North Bridge Visitor Center**. There are exhibits, a room where children can try on colonial clothing, and a fully stocked bookstore. Outside you may see a colonial regiment recreating a battle.

On your way out, stop at the **Old Manse**, just to the right of the bridge. Reverend William Emerson, Ralph Waldo Emerson's grandfather, and Nathaniel Hawthorne both lived here at different times.

Old Manse
 Monument Street
Concord
369-3909

Concord Hymn
Ralph Waldo Emerson

By the rude bridge that arched the flood,
    Their flag to April's breeze unfurled,
Here once the embattled farmers stood
    And fired the shot heard round the world.

The foe long since in silence slept;
    Alike the conqueror silent sleeps;
And Time the ruined bridge has swept
    Down the dark stream which seaward creeps.

On this green bank, by this soft stream,
    We set to-day a votive stone;
That memory may their deed redeem
    When, like our sires, our sons are gone.

Spirit that made those heroes dare
    To die, and leave their children free,
Bid Time and Nature gently spare
    The shaft we raise to them and thee.

Follow Monument Street back into Concord Center. You can stop at the chamber of commerce in Monument Square or the information booth on Haywood Street (open summers only) for more information about the area. Then finish up at the **Thoreau Lyceum**, where you'll find exhibits about Concord's history and Thoreau memorabilia. There's even a replica of his cabin at Walden Pond.

The site of that original cabin is a couple of miles away, at **Walden Pond State Reservation**. Thoreau, having taken Emerson's essay "Nature"

Concord Chamber of
 Commerce
½ **Main Street**
Concord
369-3120

Thoreau Lyceum
156 Belknap Street
Concord
369-5912

Walden Pond State Reservation
Route 126
Concord
369-3254

to heart, believed that every person should have an original relationship with the natural world. When Emerson offered him the use of the land around the pond for his own "original relationship," Thoreau jumped at the chance. The cabin he built in 1845 cost $28.12½ (12½ cents!), and measured 10 by 15 feet. Thoreau lived here for two years, writing in his journal:

> It will be a success if I shall have left myself behind. But my friends ask me what will I do when I get there. Will it not be employment enough to watch the progress of the seasons?... I have, as it were, my own sun and moon and stars, and a little world all to myself.

Thoreau on the changing seasons at Walden: "At the approach of spring the red-squirrels got under my house, two at a time, directly under my feet as I sat reading or writing, and kept up the queerest chuckling and chirruping and vocal pirouetting and gurgling sounds that ever were heard.... When the warmer days come, they who dwell near the river hear the ice crack at night with a startling whoop as loud as artillery.... When the frogs dream, and the grass waves, and the buttercups toss their heads, and the heat disposes to bathe in the ponds and streams, then is summer begun.... October is the month of painted leaves, of ripe leaves, when all the earth, not merely flowers, but fruits and leaves are ripe. With respect to its colors and its seasons, it is the sunset month of the year."

The pond itself is interesting: Its water level does not rise and fall rapidly with wet and dry spells as it does in other ponds nearby; also it remains pure and clear while the quality of the water changes in other ponds. The reasons are geological: The other ponds in the area are made up of nonporous clay; Walden was formed from a glacial remnant that remained stationary as sand and gravel built up around it. When the ice melted, a glacial kettle hole resulted. Rainwater quickly fills up clay-bottomed ponds, while the sand and gravel sides around Walden absorb much of the moisture. And this debris forms a natural underground reservoir that supplies the pond with water in times of drought. The sand and gravel play a part in the water quality too, acting as a filter.

The woods around the pond are filled with hickory, red and black oak, red maple, birch, white pine, hemlock, black chokeberry, sumac, and blueberry. In this varied woodland Thoreau would have seen loons, deer, grey squirrels, chipmunks, rabbits, skunks, raccoons, red fox, kingfishers, blackbirds, bluejays, chickadees, and thrush, ducks, and Canada geese.

Today the pond is busy year-round. Come for swimming, hiking, canoeing, fishing, picnicking, ski touring, and snowshoeing.

From the pond continue south on Route 126 about 7 miles to Route 20 in Wayland; follow Route 20 west about 6 miles to Wayside Inn Road, on the right.

Longfellow's Wayside Inn was called How's Black Horse Tavern when it was licensed in 1661. Travel was slow, uncomfortable, and difficult in those days, and the inn offered a welcome respite for travelers from Boston to Worcester or Hartford. The original building had two rooms, one above the other; in 1716 another section of two rooms was added to the left of the entrance, and the name was changed to the Red Horse Tavern. More rooms and the west wing were added later. In 1897 the name was changed to the Wayside Inn by owner Edward Rivers Lemon.

Longfellow visited the inn with a group of professors who encouraged him to write *Tales of a Wayside Inn*. He used his own memories as well as those of his friends to create a poet, a musician, a student, a theologian, a Spanish Jew, and a Sicilian; Lyman Howe (over the years the spelling changed) was the landlord-narrator.

Sudbury

Longfellow's Wayside Inn
Wayside Inn Road
Sudbury
443-8846

A turning point in the evolution of the old hostelry came in 1923, when Henry Ford began collecting articles that originally belonged to the inn as well as old stage coaches, fire engines, and other historic memorabilia. In 1926 he brought the **Redstone School**, the setting for "Mary Had a Little Lamb," from Sterling to Sudbury. (Mary was Mary Elizabeth Sawyer; John Roulston wrote the poem.) He built the **Martha-Mary Chapel** in honor of his and his wife's mothers. In 1929 the **Gristmill** was added. The mill operates today as it would have long ago: You can see the water wheel, the gears on the first floor of the three-story structure, and the grinding stones. There's even a miller filling bags with flour.

Tales of a Wayside Inn
Henry Wadsworth Longfellow

One Autumn night, in Sudbury town,
   Across the meadows bare and brown,
The windows of the Wayside Inn
   Gleamed red with fire-light through the leaves
Of woodbine, hanging from the eaves
   Their crimson curtains rent and thin.

As ancient is this hostelry
   As any in the land may be,
Built in the old Colonial day,
   When men lived in a grander way,
With ampler hospitality;
   A kind of old Hobgoblin Hall,
Now somewhat fallen to decay,
   With weather-stains upon the wall,
And stairways worn, and crazy doors,
   And creaking and uneven floors,
And chimneys huge, and tiled and tall....

A fire in 1955 destroyed a great deal of the inn, but it's been restored, with interior and furnishings as they were. Come for traditional colonial fare, and a tour of the inn and the lovely grounds.

To get back to Boston, follow Route 20 to I-95 (Route 128) south, to I-90 (the Massachusetts Turnpike) east.

The North Shore

The North Shore winds along the coast from Marblehead, a lovely sailing center, through Salem and Cape Ann, to Newburyport, a town steeped in seafaring tradition.

Marblehead

From Boston take the Callahan Tunnel to Route 1A north, to Route 129 east. (For one last look at Boston's skyline, take Route 1A into Lynn and follow Nahant Road to the ocean.) Continue on Route 129 through Swampscott, past the lovely homes on Atlantic Avenue, into Marblehead.

Old Marblehead—it was called Marble Harbor then—was settled in 1629 by fishermen from Cornwall and the Channel Islands; it remained a part of nearby Salem until 1649. In the late 1600s the town was the scene of some verbal and physical sparring. The issue? Whether or not to celebrate Christmas. Dr. Pigot, who had recently arrived as vicar of the Episcopal church, planned to hold a Christmas service; the Puritans, not to be outdone, scheduled a lecture at the same time. Dr. John Barnard, parson of the Puritan church, argued against the celebration. He maintained that Christ was born in October and that Christmas was merely a pagan custom. Dr. Pigot replied in a paper entitled "A Vindication of the Practice of the Ancient Christian as well as the Church of England, and other Reformed Churches in the Observation of Christmas-Day; in answer to the uncharitable reflections of Thomas de Laune, Mr. Whiston and Mr. John Barnard of Marblehead." Universalists and Catholics, as well as Episcopalians, fought for the observance of Christmas. Gradually, the Puritans weakened, and in 1681 the law against Christmas was repealed. That year "December Relaxation" brought a polar bear to Boston Common; the following year, a pair of camels, a sea lion, and a leopard were on display in Dock Square. Salem's celebrations centered around a "sapient dog" who could read, write, and fire a gun!

The best way to see **Marblehead** is on foot. Antique shops, boutiques, and historical houses fill the narrow winding streets. Visit **Abbot Hall** to see the *Spirit of '76*. The painting by Archibald Willard was given to the town by General John Devereux, whose son was the model for the drummer boy. You'll also see the deed to the town, written in 1684, that transferred the land from the Nanepashemet Indians to the settlers for $80. And there's an information booth here too.

The Marblehead Historical Society owns and maintains the **Jeremiah Lee Mansion**, near the intersection of Washington and Hooper streets. This home is a fine example of Georgian architecture, with beautiful furniture from all over the world. Colonel Lee entertained Washington and Lafayette here.

You can enjoy wonderful harbor views from **Crocker Park** and **State Street Landing**, both on Front Street. The harbor of this sailing center is so packed with fine boats, you can practically walk across it! Farther up Front Street is **Fort Sewall**. It was built in the seventeenth century and "modernized" in 1742; only half-buried buildings remain today. During the War of 1812 guns from the fort saved the USS *Constitution*. The view from here is great too. Bring a picnic lunch and enjoy.

Heading out of town on Atlantic Avenue, take a left onto Ocean Avenue, and continue out the causeway to **Marblehead Neck**. There's a marked bicycle path (you can drive it too) around the peninsula, past beautiful homes. Watch for the signs to the Massachusetts Audubon Society's **Marblehead**

Abbot Hall
Washington and Lee Streets
Marblehead

Jeremiah Lee Mansion
161 Washington Street
Marblehead
631-1069

Neck Sanctuary. Farther out, at the very end of the neck, are **Marblehead Light** and **Chandler Hovey Park** – the best vantage point for watching the sailing competition during Marblehead's **Race Week**, the last week in July.

Marblehead Neck Sanctuary
Risley Road
Marblehead

Salem

From Marblehead take Route 114 into Salem – the city of witchcraft, of a long marine tradition, and of Hawthorne.

In 1623 Roger Conant and a group of fishermen crossed the Atlantic and settled on Cape Ann. They found the soil there so rocky and the harbors so open and unprotected, that they sailed southwest to a cove they called Naumkeag, later Salem. In 1628 the Dorchester Company was chartered and organized here, with Captain John Endecott as leader, and the settlers began building homes along Washington Street. Two years later Governor Winthrop arrived on the *Arbella* with the charter of the Massachusetts Bay Company.

A taste treat! Several years ago we received a package of sailboat-shaped almond buttercrunch candies called "sweet sloops." They were delicious, and our first introduction to **Harbor Sweets**. Ben Strohecker, the owner, is a candy craftsman. He designs special candy for the Boston Symphony Orchestra, the Museum of Fine Arts, the USS Constitution Museum, the Peabody Museum in Salem, the Metropolitan Opera Company, and Saks Fifth Avenue. Write or phone for a catalog (Box 150, Marblehead, 745-7648), or stop in at the shop on Leavitt Street in Salem.

Although the city is steeped in the lore of witchcraft – much to the dismay of many of its residents – the actual witch hysteria lasted just a little bit over a year. Between February 1692 and May 1693 some four hundred people were accused of the crime of witchcraft; and nineteen of them were put to death on Gallows Hill. The executions stopped when the wife of Governor Phipps was accused. He immediately released all suspected witches from jail and stopped the hangings.

Salem's witches were accused of voodoolike powers. It was believed that they made clay or wax images of their victims, and in destroying those images (in fire or water, or with a knife) would kill their victims. People also believed witches could fly, using a magic ointment on themselves and their broomsticks.

Although the hysteria was uncontrolled, the procedure for trying the witches was a specific one. It began with an accusation, a warrant for the suspected witch's arrest, and an examination by at least two magistrates. Then came indictment and trial. If found guilty—and only if he or she did not confess—the witch was hung the same day.

Why did people "cry out" against witches? Some enjoyed the feeling of importance; others sought revenge for real or imagined slights; still others wanted to divert suspicion away from themselves.

Salem's marine tradition goes back to the seventeenth century, and began with fishing. Soon sailing vessels were carrying dry cod, whalebone, whale and fish oil, and furs from Salem to the rest of the world, and returning with spices and luxury items.

There are many stories about the men who sailed out from Salem on long voyages and then died at sea; it's been said that their spirits always returned home. In a tale reminiscent of Coleridge's "Rime of the Ancient Mariner," a sailor aboard the *Neptune* reported seeing a ship four times her size bearing down upon her. He threw the wheel over hard to avoid a collision. The other vessel veered slightly, and came along the starboard side without a sound. There was no rush of water, no crunch of wood splitting, no straining of lines and canvas—only a glowing silence. And there wasn't a seaman in sight. As the ship faded away in the distance the sailor said, "It's the Ghost Ship. A proper Salem man has died somewhere and the ship is bringing his spirit home to Salem, home for Christmas."

The Mermaid

'Twas Friday morn when we set sail,
    And we were not far from the land,
When the captain spied a lovely mermaid,
    With a comb and a glass in her hand.

Oh! the ocean waves may roll,
    And the stormy winds may blow,
While we poor sailors go skipping to the tops,
    And the landlubbers lie down below, below, below,
And the landlubbers lie down below.

Then out spake the captain of our gallant ship,
    And a well-spoken man was he:
"I have married me a wife in Salem town,
    And to-night she a widder will be."

Then out spake the cook of our gallant ship,
    And a fat old cookie was he:
"I care much more for my potties and my kets
    Than I do for the depths of the sea."

Then out spake the boy of our gallant ship,
    And a well-spoken laddie was he:
"I've a father and a mother in Boston city,
    But to-night they childless will be."

"Oh! the moon shines bright and the stars give light;
    Oh! my mammy'll be looking for me;
She may look, she may weep, she may look to the deep,
    She may look to the bottom of the sea."

Then three times around went our gallant ship,
    And three times around went she;
Then three times around went our gallant ship,
    And she sank to the depths of the sea.

Through the eighteenth century the shipyards in Salem were busy producing ships of up to two hundred tons. During the Revolutionary War, when both Boston and New York were occupied by the British, the town's citizens converted existing ships into armed privateers. They also built larger vessels designed to capture prizes from the British. After the war this enterprising spirit was transferred to world trade. Salem's ships traveled to the East Indies, China, Russia, and Japan in a burst of trade that lasted some fifty years. Hurt by the embargo of 1807 and the War of 1812, the final blow came with the newer, larger clipper ships. Salem's harbor was too shallow to handle them.

The chamber of commerce operates two visitors' centers: in the Old Town Hall and at Pickering Wharf. Pick up a copy of the "Best of Salem and the North Shore," published weekly, which lists information about all kinds of entertainment, restaurants, and tourist attractions.

Start your tour at the brick mall on Essex Street. In the **Peabody Museum** are many of the articles brought back to Salem from exotic ports by captains and their crews, as well as paintings, figureheads, models, navigational instruments, and a professional library.

The nearby **Essex Institute** is a museum, art gallery, library, and publishing house. Lectures, conferences, and workshops—all about and for the heritage of Essex County—are held in the remarkable main building. On the grounds are several houses that have been restored and opened to the public: the **John Ward House** (1684), the **Crowninshield-Bentley House** (1727), the **Gardner-Pingree House** (1804–1805), and the **Andrew-Safford House** (1818–1819). The **Peirce-Nichols House** (1782) and **Assembly House** (1782), on Federal Street, are also owned by the institute.

The **Salem Witch Museum** is around the corner from the institute. Here life-size dioramas tell the story of the witchcraft hysteria with sound and light. More witches? Backtrack down Essex Street to the **Witch House**, the site of some of

Peabody Museum
East India Square
Salem
745-1876

Essex Institute
132 Essex Street
Salem
744-3390

Salem Chamber of Commerce
32 Derby Square
Salem
744-0004

Salem Witch Museum
19½ Washington Square North
Salem
744-1692

Witch House
310½ Essex Street
Salem
744-0180

THE NORTH SHORE

Lowell National Historical Park trolley "The Whistler" in front of the Boott Mill.

LOWELL

The Old North Bridge where the Minutemen fired the "shot heard around the world."

CONCORD

The House Of The Seven Gables, immortalized in the novel by Nathaniel Hawthorne.

SALEM

House of the Seven Gables
54 Turner Street
Salem
744-0991

Salem Maritime National Historic Site
Derby Street
Salem
744-4323

the trials. Once the home of Judge Jonathan Corwin, the house has been restored and furnished with antiques.

From the witch museum cross Salem Common and turn off Essex Street at Turner. The **House of the Seven Gables** was built in 1668 by Captain John Turner, whose family later sold it to the Ingersoll family. In the 1840s Nathaniel Hawthorne visited his cousin Susan Ingersoll, and saw the structure in the attic that supports the gables. He was just finishing his novel of the same name, and used the house for various scenes: the parlor where Colonel Pyncheon sat dying in the oak chair; the shop where Hepzibah sold scents and candy; the secret staircase that led to Clifford's room.

To preserve its rich heritage in world trade, contemporary Salem has added the **Salem Maritime National Historic Site** to its waterfront. Stop at the visitors' center in the **Custom House**, where Hawthorne was a surveyor from 1846 to 1849. (His description of the building forms the first chapter of *The Scarlet Letter*.) Then walk through **Bonded Warehouse** and **Derby House**.

Right next to the national historic site is **Pickering Wharf**, a reconstructed village filled with shops and restaurants, and a theater where you can travel to exotic ports aboard the *India Star*.

Try **Connolly and Wellington** (744-2456) on Derby Street for spices, coffees, and teas. Buy some to take home, or sit at a table and enjoy your choice here, savoring the heavenly smells. **300 Derby Street** (745-9608) is a fine restaurant in a century-old ship's chandlery.

There are more fine shops and restaurants at the **Essex Street Mall** near the Peabody Museum. The **Lyceum** (745-7665) on Church Street offers delectable French cuisine, for lunch, dinner, or Sunday brunch. A real find for inexpensive and delicious food is **Cafe L'Espresso** (744-1741) on Essex Street. Come for espresso or cappuccino or tea (fourteen kinds), fresh salads, homemade soups, sandwiches, and heavenly desserts. Food comes with newspapers, magazines, and games (checkers, cribbage, backgammon), and classical music in the background.

A few minutes out of Salem Center, off Route 1A, you'll find **Pioneer Village**. Here the Salem of 1630 has been recreated with thatched-roof houses and wigwams.

Pioneer Village
Forest River Park
Salem
744-0180

Cape Ann, a 55-square-mile peninsula jutting out into the Atlantic, is 30 miles from Boston. The region includes Gloucester and Rockport on the cape proper, and Manchester and Essex at the approach. Along its 25-mile coastline are six scenic harbors, twenty-four coves, and more than twenty sandy beaches—a natural beauty that's drawn artists and writers to the area.

Cape Ann

Small but good beaches are all around Cape Ann. In Gloucester try **Good Harbor Beach**, off Thatcher Road (Route 127A). The drop-off is gradual, but the surf can be heavy. Continue along Route 127A to South Street and Penzance Road, to **Cape Hedge Beach**. At low tide you'll find sand; at high tide, stones. Farther on, along Penzance Road, is **Pebbly Beach**, a half mile long. (Parking at both Cape Hedge Beach and Pebbly Beach is by sticker only; you'll have to park along the road and walk in.) Rockport Center boasts **Front Beach** and **Back Beach**, each 150 yards long, clean, and sandy, and a favorite of skindivers.

From Salem take Route 1A to Route 127, the coast road to Gloucester. You'll pass sections of elegant homes, particularly in Manchester. Turn off Route 127, at the sign for Magnolia, onto Hesperus Avenue, and watch for **Rafe's Chasm**. Leave your car and walk through the small shrubs to the 200-foot-long, 60-foot-deep chasm. The granite rocks pounded by the Atlantic make a spectacular setting for lunch.

Gloucester

**Hammond Castle
Museum
80 Hesperus Avenue
Gloucester
283-2080**

Continue on Hesperus Avenue, and follow the signs to **Hammond Castle Museum**. John Hays Hammond, Jr., an inventor and collector of medieval art, designed the castle for his collections. The Great Hall is 100 feet long, 58 feet high, and 25 feet wide. Concerts are held here year-round on the 8,000-pipe organ. The inner courtyard, filled with tropical plants, has its own weather system that can produce a tropical downpour and then turn back to sunlight. And there's a rooftop cafe where you can enjoy pastries baked in the castle.

Follow Hesperus Avenue out to Route 127 (Western Avenue). As you enter Gloucester, facing the harbor, stands the **Fisherman's Statue**, a bronze memorial to the ten thousand men lost at sea over the centuries. Every August there's a service in honor of those men, the Gloucestermen who "go down to the sea in ships."

Psalm 107

They that go down to the sea in ships.
They that do business in great waters.
These see the works of the Lord
And His wonders in the deep.

Longfellow captured the danger of seafaring on this reef-strewn coast in "The Wreck of the Hesperus."

The Wreck of the Hesperus
Henry Wadsworth Longfellow

It was the schooner Hesperus,
That sailed the wintry sea;
And the skipper had taken his little daughter,
To bear him company.

Blue were her eyes as the fairy-flax,
Her cheeks like the dawn of day,
And her bosom white as the hawthorn buds,
That ope in the month of May.

The skipper he stood beside the helm,
    His pipe was in his mouth,
And he watched how the veering flaw did blow
    The smoke now West, now South.

Then up and spake an old Sailor,
    Had sailed the Spanish Main,
"I pray thee, put into yonder port,
    For I fear a hurricane.

"Last night the moon had a golden ring,
    And tonight no moon we see!"
The skipper, he blew a whiff from his pipe,
    And a scornful laugh laughed he.

Colder and louder blew the wind,
    A gale from the Northeast,
The snow fell hissing in the brine,
    And the billows frothed like yeast.

Down came the storm, and smote amain
    The vessel in its strength;
She shuddered and paused, like a frighted steed,
    Then leaped her cable's length.

"Come hither! come hither! my little daughter,
    And do not tremble so;
For I can weather the roughest gale
    That ever wind did blow."

He wrapped her warm in his seaman's coat
    Against the stinging blast;
He cut a rope from a broken spar,
    And bound her to the mast.

"O father! I hear the church-bells ring,
    O say, what may it be?"
"'Tis a fog-bell on the rock-bound coast!"
    And he steered for the open sea.

"O father! I hear the sound of guns,
    O say, what may it be?"
"Some ship in distress, that cannot live
    In such an angry sea!"

"O father! I see a gleaming light,
    O say, what may it be?"
But the father answered never a word,
    A frozen corpse was he.

Lashed to the helm, all stiff and stark,
    With his face turned to the skies,
The lantern gleamed through the gleaming snow,
    On his fixed and glassy eyes.

Then the maiden clasped her hands and prayed
    That saved she might be;
And she thought of Christ who stilled the wave,
    On the Lake of Galilee.

And fast through the midnight dark and drear,
    Through the whistling sleet and snow,
Like the sheeted ghost, the vessel swept
    Tow'rds the reef of Norman's Woe.

And ever the fitful gusts between
    A sound came from the land;
It was the sound of the trampling surf
    On the rocks and the hard sea-sand.

The breakers were right beneath her bows,
    She drifted a dreary wreck,
And a whooping billow swept the crew
    Like icicles from her deck.

She struck where the white and fleecy waves
    Looked soft as carded wool,
But the cruel rocks, they gored her side
    Like the horns of an angry bull.

Her rattling shrouds, all sheathed in ice,
    With the masts went by the board;
Like a vessel of glass, she stove and sank,
    Ho! ho! the breakers roared!

At daybreak, on the bleak sea-beach,
    A fisherman stood aghast,
To see the form of a maiden fair,
    Lashed close to a drifting mast.

> The salt sea was frozen on her breast,
>   The salt tears in her eyes;
> And he saw her hair, like the brown sea-weed,
>   On the billows fall and rise.
>
> Such was the wreck of the Hesperus,
>   In the midnight and the snow!
> Christ save us all from a death like this,
>   On the reef of Norman's Woe!

Some say Longellow wrote the poem after reading a newspaper account of a wreck on Norman's Woe Reef; others say the poet took bits and pieces of many shipwreck legends, and used them here. We know there was a real-life parallel some fifty-seven years after Longfellow's poem was published. In February 1898 the *Asia* foundered on Nantucket Shoals with Captain George Dakin, his wife, and their eleven-year-old daughter, Lena, on board. Knowing that Captain Dakin would obey the tradition of the sea and be the last to leave the ship, his chief mate offered to look after Lena. And he did. He lashed himself and the child to the ship. They were found later, not drowned, but frozen to death, still tied together.

Longfellow was not the only writer to set a work in Gloucester. Rudyard Kipling wrote with feeling about the unpretentious heroism of the town's fishermen in *Captains Courageous*. That heroism shows strongly too in Winslow Homer's many paintings of the sea and Gloucester's fishing fleet.

Another sea legend involves pirates, not shipwrecks, and has a happier ending. In 1720 pirates boarded a ship off the Massachusetts coast. Their leader, Captain Pedro, intended to kill everyone on board until he heard a baby cry. He went below and found a mother and newborn baby girl. He promised not to harm the ship or passengers if the mother would name her baby after his own mother, Mary. She agreed, and Pedro released the captives. Then he handed the mother a bolt of beautiful silk for "Ocean-born Mary's" wedding gown. The ship landed in Boston, Mary's father died, and the mother and child moved to Henniker, New Hampshire. Mary grew up to be a tall, beautiful woman with red hair and green eyes. She married and had four sons.

Eventually Captain Pedro moved to Henniker, built a lovely colonial home, and asked Mary to live with him. One night the captain returned with a large chest, which he buried in the yard, some say with the body of his pirate helper. When he died a year later Mary buried him, as he had requested, under an 8-foot slab in front of the kitchen hearth. After Mary died the legend tells of strange things happening in the house and orchard, where the chest was buried: It seems Mary's ghost still walks down the stairs inside the house, and into her coach-and-four for drives; and out in the yard the pirate's helper moans as he guards the treasure.

Gloucester's legends also tell of sea monsters. One huge sea serpent was sighted in August 1817. A witness wrote that the serpent had a head as large as a 4-gallon keg and a body as large as a barrel, and was 40 feet long. A watcher on shore fired at the creature, who sank straight down into the sea like a "caterpillar," then reappeared 100 yards away. And one believer later killed a 3-foot snake, thinking it was a baby sea serpent.

Gloucester has its very own ghost town! **Dogtown Commons** sits in the center of the peninsula, accessible from Washington Street or Route 128. (Be sure to bring a map of the area along with you.) The community was settled in the 1600s, and thrived until the Revolutionary War. With all the men off fighting, the women were left alone with only dogs for protection. Strange derelicts and toothless old crones moved in—and the people who had lived there began moving out.

Today all that remains are ruins of foundations and cellars, and a hearthstone here and there among the blueberry bushes. And the population? Otters, foxes, raccoons, rabbits, pheasants, and all kinds of birds.

The fishing industry has existed longer in Gloucester—since 1623—than anywhere in the United States. (There's a Gloucesterman's saying that if the mackerel are running even a wedding can be postponed.) Gloucester's ships brought in fish, square-riggers came heavily laden with salt, and racks of drying salted fish were everywhere. Today modern plants process more fish here than in any other city in the country. Spend some time on the piers watching the ships unload in the harbor. For more information stop at the booth on Route 127 near the Fisherman's Statue or contact the chamber of commerce.

The **Gloucester Fishermen's Museum** is a unique "atticy" kind of museum. You can follow a series of numbered hands-on exhibits—tasting, reading, using, and handling artifacts and marine animals. A sign reading "Help us shape this mast" invites you to use old shipwright's tools to shape the wood. You can also try to drill a hole in a block with a hand drill. It's not easy, and it took eleven thousand holes to build a 100-foot schooner. (Electric drills weren't invented until the 1920s.) The museum is the place to sign up for a four-hour whale-watching cruise on Stellwagen Banks. If you can, go on an overcast day, when the sea is a little rough and the whales surface often.

Hungry? Try **Captain's Courageous** (283-0007), in the harbor area, for great seafood.

Follow signs around Gloucester Harbor to **Rocky Neck**, where there's a small art colony with galleries, a book shop, a restaurant, and several working boatyards—all untouched by tourism.

Cape Ann Chamber
 of Commerce
128 Main Street
Gloucester
283-1601

Gloucester
 Fishermen's
 Museum
Rogers and Porter
 Streets
Gloucester
283-1940

A boat trip? Come aboard the *Dixie Bell* or the *Daunty*, which leave from Rocky Neck, East Gloucester, and the Gloucester House Restaurant downtown. Call 283-5110 for information.

A fishing trip? **Yankee Fleet** operates half- or full-day excursions. Call 283-0313 for information.

> **Beauport**
> **Eastern Point**
> **Boulevard**
> **Gloucester**
> **283-0800**

On the other side of Rocky Neck is **Beauport**. The house was built by Henry Davis Sleeper, a Boston architect and interior designer. He wanted each of the twenty-five rooms in the mansion to reflect a different period, and they do. Each was designed around a particular object or collection of objects, in different styles, colors, and shapes.

From Beauport follow the road to the end of Eastern Point (ocean views, **Eastern Point Light**, and **Dog Bar Breakwater**). Then double back to Farmington Avenue and Atlantic Avenue, and follow the coast into Rockport.

Rockport

Rockport, once a fishing village and stone quarry, is now a year-round artists' colony, a town full of shops and galleries. The imposing sea wall of granite blocks makes the harbor one of the loveliest anywhere.

On **Bearskin Neck** stands **Motif Number 1**, the red house that's been painted by hundreds of artists, an appropriate symbol of Cape Ann. The original shack was destroyed in a blizzard in 1978, but funds were raised to rebuild it. Many of the other buildings on the neck are now used by artists and craftsmen for shops and studios. The area can be very crowded during the summer.

> **Rockport Art**
> **Association**
> **12 Main Street**
> **Rockport**
> **546-6604**

The **Rockport Art Association** is in an old tavern built in 1770. Here you'll find paintings, drawings, and sculptures by more than two hundred artists. The association also offers information about local art galleries and artists' homes that are open to the public.

Main Street turns into Granite Street as you continue along to the quarry. Today the workers are gone. In their place: a bird sanctuary and beautiful lake for diving. Also on Granite Street: the **Old Farm Inn** (546-3237), a 1799 farmhouse that's now a restaurant.

In 1710 Joshua Norwood began using pieces of granite for mooring stones. He would drill a hole in the center of a stone, and push an oak tree, roots and all, through the hole. The roots and slab sat at the bottom of the sea, and the boat was moored to the top of the tree! How's that for Yankee ingenuity?

On the hill above town, off Route 127, is the **Paper House**. This unique house, made entirely of newspaper, was built by the Stenman family in 1922. Even the furnishings are made of paper.

Paper House
Pigeon Hill Street
Rockport

Continue north on Granite Street to Gott Avenue on the right, and **Halibut Point Reservation**. Follow a path through the woods to the rocky point, the outermost tip of Cape Ann. The view is superb. If you come when the fog is in, expect an eerie mist full of the sound of the sea crashing below.

Halibut Point
  Reservation
Gott Avenue
Rockport
698-2066

Annisquam

Continue along Route 127 to Annisquam, where you can drive out to **Annisquam Lighthouse** on Wigwam Point. The stark white building with its black top is a welcome beacon to yachtsmen entering Ipswich Bay and the Annisquam Canal, which cuts through the peninsula to Gloucester. This is an area of long tidal inlets that empty out at low tide.

Essex

Follow Route 127 to Route 128 south, to Route 133 toward Essex. Stop at **Farnhams** (768-6643), or drive on to **Woodman's** (768-6451) for clams, lobster, and the world's best fried onions. During the summer Woodman's features a clambake: steamed clams, lobster, corn, watermelon, and a drink, all at a special price.

In 1668 the town set aside an acre of land on the river for shipbuilding, an industry that

Essex Shipbuilding Museum
28 Main Street
Essex
768-7451

flourished and is still providing maintenance and repair. Cross the Essex River Bridge and look to the right for the **Arthur D. Story Shipyard**, which has produced over four hundred ships through the years. Farther along Main Street is the **Essex Shipbuilding Museum**.

Ipswich

From Essex turn off Route 133 at North Gate Road to beautiful **Crane's Beach**, one of the best beaches on the Atlantic seaboard. From the parking lot you can follow **Pine Hollow Trail** through the dunes, or walk up to **Castle Hill**. The Georgian-style estate, the second at the site, is a center for performing arts.

From the beach follow Argilla Road to Route 1A, to Ipswich. The town has an historical, industrial, and culinary claim to fame. Here was the first denunciation of taxation without representation; here was the birthplace of the lace-making and hosiery industries in this country; and here is the home of the famous Ipswich clam.

John Whipple House
53 South Main Street
Ipswich
356-2811

Thomas Franklin
 Waters Memorial
40 South Main Street
Ipswich
356-2644

Visit the **John Whipple House**, built in 1640, which contains a collection of seventeenth- and eighteenth-century furnishings and a lovely seventeenth-century garden. The **Thomas Franklin Waters Memorial** (John Heard House), just across the street, is a large Federal house built in 1795. It's filled with treasures from the Orient and a collection of carriages.

The Ipswich River is a favorite of canoeists. Begin at the bridge on Route 97 in Topsfield, and paddle for 7 miles through a marsh sprinkled with gnarled oaks and maples, and grapevines. Around you: the **Ipswich River Wildlife Sanctuary**, a 2,400-acre preserve maintained by the Massachusetts Audubon Society. What's here? Fifteen hundred species of trees and shrubs, over two hundred species of birds, and deer, muskrat, red fox, and otter; miles of hiking trails through woods and marsh, ponds and wild flower gardens;

and camping (with advance reservations) on Perkins Island.

Follow Route 1A to Newburyport, at the mouth of the Merrimack River. Stop at the chamber of commerce for information.

Shipowners and captains built a series of Federal-style homes along **High Street**, many of them three stories tall and very elegant. The **Cushing Museum**, once the home of Caleb Cushing, now houses the Historical Society of Old Newbury. Here you'll see collections of paintings, furniture, needlework, clocks, silver, china, and carriages, and a library.

Farther up High Street you come to **Piel Craftsmen** (462-7012), where ship models are still made by hand. The expert craftsmen, consultants to several national museums, are happy to answer questions about their work. By the river, on Merrimack Street, the **1690 House** (465-8430) displays Towle silver and pewter. (Don't be fooled by the name. The house was built in 1738.) Nearby **Market Square** has been restored, and is filled with shops specializing in antiques and handcrafted products.

Down the street **Custom House** exhibits tell the story of Newburyport's shipping heritage. Also here: treasures from foreign lands, local artisans' crafts, and a professional library.

Follow Water Street to the causeway to **Plum Island**, a 9-mile strip of sand that acts as a breakwater. Cross the bridge and turn right to the **Parker River National Wildlife Refuge**. Here, along the 7-mile stretch of beach and dunes, is an activity for everyone—swimming, picnicking, hiking, clamming (with a permit), even picking cranberries.

The **Plum Island Lighthouse** is now at the northern tip of the island; it was moved because the ocean eroded the shoreline. This light is crucial to seamen, protecting them from the treacherous reefs that have claimed hundreds of ships over the years.

Newburyport

Newburyport
Chamber of
Commerce
29 State Street
Newburyport
462-6680

Cushing Museum
98 High Street
Newburyport
462-2681

Custom House
25 Water Street
Newburyport
462-8681

Parker River National
Wildlife Refuge
Plum Island
Newburyport
465-5753

The Wreck
Walter De la Mare

Storm and unconscionable winds once cast
    On grinding shingle, masking gap-toothed rock,
This ancient hulk. Rent hull, and broken mast,
    She sprawls sand-mounded, of sea birds the mock.
Her sailors, drowned, forgotten, rot in mould,
    Or hang in stagnant quiet of the deep;
The brave, the afraid into one silence sold;
    Their end a memory fainter than of sleep.
She held good merchandise. She paced in pride
    The uncharted paths men trace in ocean's foam.
Now laps the ripple in her broken side,
    And zephyr in tamarisk softly whispers, Home.
The dreamer scans her in the sea-blue air,
    And sipping of contrast, finds the day more fair.

You can return to Boston on I-95 (pick up Route 113 in Newburyport to I-95), or continue up the coast along Route 1A, into New Hampshire and the next itinerary.

The itinerary you've just completed covers very little distance—a mere 150 miles from Plymouth to Newburyport—but this small section of coastline is filled with history. Nowhere else in the country can you sense so tangibly what it was like to live in the seventeenth and eighteenth centuries. Colonial America reappears here, beneath the overlays of more recent eras, as the fundamental shape of our civilization.

ITINERARY D

ACADIA NATIONAL PARK

ITINERARY D

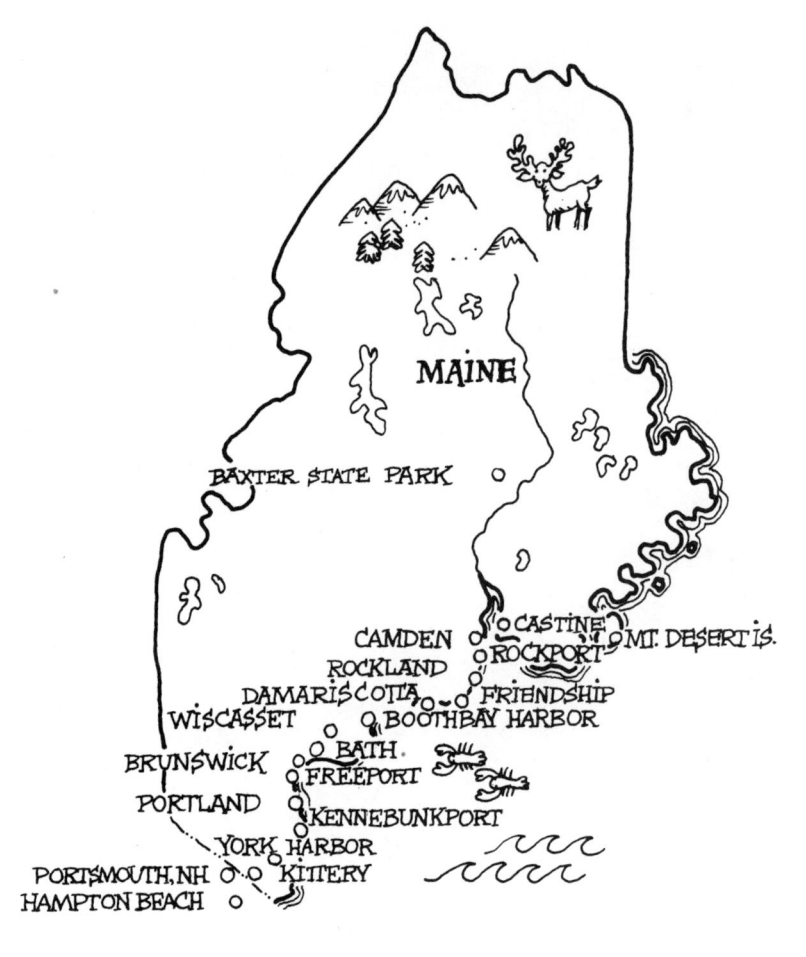

(Suggested Time: 7 days; 228 miles/365 kilometers)

Down East

Hampton Beach	D·131	Bath	D·145
Portsmouth	D·131	Popham Beach	D·146
Isles of Shoals	D·132	Wiscasset	D·147
Kittery	D·135	Boothbay Harbor	D·147
York	D·136	Damariscotta	D·148
York Harbor	D·138	Pemaquid Point	D·148
Cape Neddick	D·138	Friendship	D·148
Ogunquit	D·138	Tenants Harbor	D·149
Wells	D·139	Monhegan Island	D·149
Kennebunk	D·139	Rockland	D·149
Kennebunkport	D·139	Vinalhaven	D·149
Portland	D·140	Rockport	D·150
Freeport	D·141	Camden	D·150
Brunswick	D·141	Castine	D·151
The Harpswells	D·141	Deer Isle	D·152
Orrs Island	D·145	Isle au Haut	D·153
Bailey Island	D·145	Mount Desert Island	D·153

Away Down East

There's a famous fabled country never seen by
    mortal eyes,
Where the punkins are a-grow-in', and the sun is
    said to rise,
Which man doth not inhabit, neither reptile, bird,
    nor beast.
But one thing we're assured of, it's AWAY DOWN EAST!

It is called a land of notions, of applesauce
    and green,
A paradise of punkin pies, a land of pork and
    beans.
But where it is who knoweth? Neither mortal, man,
    nor beast.
But one thing we're assured of, it's AWAY DOWN EAST!

Once a man in Indiana took his bundle in his hand,
And he went to New York City for to find this
    famous land.
But how he stares on learning this curious
    fact at least:
He'd nowhere near begun to get AWAY DOWN EAST!

So he traveled on to Bangor, whereby he soiled
    his drabs,
And the first that greets his vision is a pyra-
    mid of slabs.
Oh, sure this must be Egypt, 'tis a pyramid, at
    least.
And he thought that with a vengeance, he had
    found DOWN EAST.

Visitors to New England often wonder why locals say they're going Down East when they travel from Boston to New Hampshire or Maine. After all, you're really heading "Up East." Puzzled? Then look at a map. With all those peninsulas cutting up the Maine coast, the best way to reach that coast, at least until recently, was by sea. And if you sail from Boston up to Maine, you sail downwind in the prevailing southwesterly.

New Hampshire

The first permanent settlement in New Hampshire was established in 1623 on Odiorne Point in Rye. Dover, Portsmouth, Exeter, and Hampton were settled soon after, and the five were the only towns in the area for years. Their isolation did not create good feelings among the settlements: Bitter arguments arose over land deeds and religion. And infighting was not their only problem. At one point Massachusetts tried to take over the New Hampshire villages—a dispute that was settled by the crown in 1629.

Apart from the brief coastal plain, so much of New Hampshire is mountainous that small agricultural communities tended to remain isolated and self-sufficient throughout the eighteenth and early nineteenth century. But during the second half of the nineteenth century industry swept into the state. Rivers provided power for mills, and cities like Manchester and Concord grew. Some of these mill towns still flourish; others have turned to different kinds of industries to survive. As in neighboring Vermont, much of New Hampshire's development in recent years has been built on tourism.

Hampton Beach

From Newburyport follow Route 1A along the coast to Hampton Beach. Here you can stop for a swim in the ocean, a stroll along the boardwalk, or a ride at the amusement park. More activity? There's often a talent show or a fishing derby going on in this busy resort town.

Portsmouth

Continue up Route 1A into Portsmouth, New Hampshire's only seaport. The city is also a service center for the naval base across the river in Kittery.

Little Harbor Road is on the right just after you enter town. Here you'll find the **Wentworth-Coolidge Mansion**, an excellent example of early

Wentworth-Coolidge Mansion
Little Harbor Road
Portsmouth
436-6607

DOWN EAST

Strawbery Banke
Hancock Street
Portsmouth
436-8010

Moffatt-Ladd House
154 Market Street
Portsmouth
436-8221

Portsmouth Chamber of Commerce
Market Street Extension
Portsmouth
436-1118

John Paul Jones House
43 Middle Street
Portsmouth
436-8420

Isles of Shoals

American architecture. The house was the official residence of New Hampshire's first royal governor, Benning Wentworth, from 1741 to 1746.

Strawbery Banke, a 10-acre area along the Piscatagua, was settled in 1630. In the late 1950s the town began a major restoration project here, a project that's still under way. Pick up a map at the entrance and head to the orientation building for a film. Then watch potters and silversmiths and carpenters (Strawbery Banke dories are made here) at work. And there are several restored homes to visit.

Across the street, on the banks of the river, is **Prescott Park**. Come in summer for beautiful flower gardens, free outdoor concerts, and art and craft exhibits.

The **Moffatt-Ladd House** was built in 1763 as a wedding gift for Samuel Moffatt from his father, an English sea captain named John Moffatt. John's son-in-law, William Whipple, a signer of the Declaration of Independence, later lived here. There are three floors of eighteenth-century furnishings, a cellar with a secret passageway to the wharves, and beautiful gardens.

While you're on Market Street, stop at the chamber of commerce for more information about the city. Then turn onto Deer Street, and take a left on Maplewood Avenue to Route 1, and the **John Paul Jones House**. The boardinghouse where Captain Jones stayed while the *Ranger* (1776–1777) and the *America* (1781–1782) were being built now houses the Portsmouth Historical Society and its collections of furniture and china.

Hungry? There are lots of good restaurants in town. Our favorites: **Pier II Restaurant** (436-0669) at Prescott Park, **Puddle Dock Pub** (431-4731) on State Street, and **Strawberry Court** (431-7722) on Atkinson.

For your first taste of Down East, board the **Viking Queen** and cruise to the Isles of Shoals.

The islands, which lie 8 miles out of Portsmouth Harbor, were discovered in 1614 by Captain John Smith. They developed as a prosperous fishing center until the Revolution, when most of the residents moved to the mainland.

Star Island still maintains a little stone chapel that's over 150 years old, and a graveyard that's supposedly hiding pirate treasure. Or is the treasure on **Appledore**? Rumor has it that Captain Kidd killed one of his men here so that he would haunt the spot where the treasure lies. And Old Bab's been seen, with white face and a ghostly light emanating from his body, wearing a red ring around his neck.

Viking Queen
Market Street Dock
Portsmouth
431-5500

Captain Kidd

Oh! my name was Robert Kidd, as I sailed, as I sailed,
Oh! my name was Robert Kidd, as I sailed,
My name was Robert Kidd, God's laws I did forbid,
And most wickedly I did, as I sailed, as I sailed,
And most wickedly I did, as I sailed.

Oh! my parents taught me well, as I sailed, as I sailed,
Oh! my parents taught me well, as I sailed,
My parents taught me well, to shun the gates of hell,
But against them I rebelled, as I sailed, as I sailed,
But against them I rebelled, as I sailed.

I murdered William Moore, as I sailed, as I sailed,
I murdered William Moore, as I sailed.
I murdered William Moore and left him in his gore,
Not many leagues from shore, as I sailed, as I sailed,
Not many leagues from shore, as I sailed.

And being cruel still, as I sailed, as I sailed,
And being cruel still, as I sailed,
And being cruel still, my gunner I did kill,
And his precious blood did spill, as I sailed, as I sailed,
And his precious blood did spill, as I sailed....

Take warning now by me, for I must die,
Take warning now by me, for I must die,
Take warning now by me, and shun bad company,
Lest you come to hell with me, for I must die, I must die.
Lest you come to hell with me, for I must die.

Old Bab may not be real, but the treasure was. In the early 1800s Captain Haley found silver bars on **Smuttynose Island** while he was digging a well. Haley, who owned a mill and a ropewalk, kept a lighted lamp in the window for ships at sea. In 1813 the *Sagunto* foundered off the island. Three survivors crawled toward his light in vain. They were buried on the island. (Look for the millstones near the mill.)

And Smuttynose saw more tragedy. In 1873 Louis Wagner rowed out to search for treasure, and killed two of the three women living on the nearly deserted island. The survivor, Maren Hontvet, escaped to tell the horrible story. The well where Wagner tried to wash the blood from his hands is still here.

⇜ Maine ⇝

Maine: waves crashing on rocky shores, crisp mornings licked by wisps of fog, huge jumbled rock formations. The bedrock of the state was formed during the Precambrian era, which produced weathered formations from sandstone and limestone; other sections with rich beds of fossils date from the Paleozoic era. During the Ice Age the weight of the icecap caused the land to sink below sea level. Water flooded into long valleys, creating fjords and coves, and leaving clay as much as 75 miles away from the modern shoreline. Some clay deposits, exposed by running streams and excavations, are now 500 feet above sea level. As the glacier dissolved, mountains that were near the shore became islands, and those that were farther inland became headlands jutting into the sea, creating a drowned coastline that's one of the most fascinating anywhere in the world.

The first inhabitants of Maine were roving hunters, Indian descendants of Asian immigrants who crossed the land bridge when the Bering Strait was dry. Their graves, found in more than fifty tribal cemeteries, contain red ochre (powdered hematite), which gave them the name Red Paint People. Heavy stone tools were found in the same graves. Later Indians called themselves Wabanackis, which means "easterners" or "dawnlanders"; their language was that of the Algonquian tribes. Today there are two tribes left: the Passamaquoddies and the Penobscots.

The first Europeans to arrive in Maine were probably the Vikings, who had occupied islands and coastal towns in the North Sea from the late eighth to the late twelfth century, then pushed west to colonize first Iceland and Greenland, then Newfoundland and Nova Scotia. Leif Erikson sailed to Newfoundland in 1003, and continued past Maine to Cape Cod. Several years later his brother Thorvald landed in Maine, probably at Somes Sound, a fjord cutting into Mount Desert Island, where he was killed by Indians.

In 1496 John Cabot and his sons Lewis, Sebastian, and Sancius received permission from King Henry VII of England to look for and occupy new lands. Between 1497 and 1499 they made a number of voyages along the Maine coast—voyages that formed the basis of England's claim to Maine and other parts of North America. In 1524 Giovanni da Verrazano, an Italian explorer serving under the French flag, also reached Maine, but he did nothing to establish a settlement. And a year later, Esteban Gomez, a Spanish explorer, left too when he did not find the gold he was looking for. Not until the seventeenth century did the European explorers realize the treasure that was here in fish, fur, and timber.

In 1614 Captain John Smith arrived in Maine and named the coastline from Nova Scotia to Cape Cod, New England. The origin of the state's name isn't clear: Some believe the name was a tribute to Queen Henrietta Marie, because she ruled the French provinces of Meyne or Maine; others believe the name was derived from "mainland." But to sailors none of it mattered. Maine was always Down East. Why? Because the prevailing winds blew from the southwest, and you could only get here from other parts of New England by running downwind.

Kittery

Kittery, incorporated in 1647, is the state's oldest town, and has long depended on shipbuilding for its major industry. The *Ranger*, which sailed to France under the command of John Paul Jones to announce Burgoyne's surrender, was built here. And today the Portsmouth Navy Yard and a number of smaller boatyards are carrying on the tradition.

Lady Pepperell House
Route 103
Kittery

Fort McClary
  Memorial Park
Route 103
Kittery

Kittery Point is the oldest part of town. There are several interesting homes to visit here, including **Lady Pepperell House**, a striking white Georgian mansion built in 1760. The house is listed in the National Register of Historic Places, and is beautifully furnished and maintained. There is an interesting old graveyard beyond the house, overlooking the harbor. Look for Browning's epitaph for the husband of poet Celia Thaxter. Names on other old stones are still well known in the area.

Farther up the road you come to **Fort McClary Memorial Park**. The fort—all that remains is the hexagonal blockhouse—dates back to 1809. Sit back and enjoy the view of the outer harbor: hundreds of sailboats bobbing on moorings, fishing boats going in and out, and a maze of lobster pots everywhere.

There are several good beaches along the southern coast of Maine. **Fort Foster** in Kittery Point is actually two beaches: one 200 feet long, one 400 feet long. Both are clean and sandy, and sprinkled with rocks. **Sea Point Beach**, off Route 103 on Cutts Island Road, is also sandy with some rocks. **Ogunquit Beach** (page 138) is spectacular. And in Wells there are three beaches: **Moody**, **Drake's Island**, and **Wells** (where you can surf).

York

York, north of Kittery on Route 1A, is part of a national historic district. Many of the seventeenth- and eighteenth-century homes in the village are open. Turn off Route 1 at Lindsay Road, and park your car in the lot. Then walk through the **Old Burying Ground**. Mary Nason's grave is covered with a giant stone slab. Legend says she was a witch, and the slab was put there to keep her soul in the grave. The truth is almost as good: It seems her heartbroken husband, a wealthy man, placed the stone there to keep the village pigs from grazing on her grave.

At the other end of the graveyard you come to the **Emerson-Wilcox House**, where you can buy a combination ticket for all the sites in the village. The house was built in 1740 on church land, then leased for 999 years. It was once a tailor shop, tavern, and general store, and then a post office. Today its rooms are furnished in a series of different period styles. One of them boasts a local treasure: the Mary Bulman bed hangings, the only complete set of eighteenth-century American crewelwork hangings in the country.

Across the street you'll find the **Old Gaol Museum**. It was a king's prison from 1719 through the Revolution, and continued to be used as a jail until 1860. You can walk through the jailer's quarters, the cells, and the dungeon—a special treat for children.

From the Old Gaol cross York Street (Route 1) to the **First Parish Congregational Church**, on the green. Reverend Samuel Moody laid the cornerstone in 1747. Reverend Joseph Moody, his son, was the subject of one of Hawthorne's short stories, "The Minister's Black Veil." Moody accidentally killed a friend while they were out hunting. He felt so guilty, he wore a handkerchief over his face for the rest of his life.

Head back across York Street to the other end of Lindsay Road, near the parking lot. Here you'll find the **Old Schoolhouse**, which was built in 1745, and **Jefferds' Tavern**. The tavern was built in 1750 in Wells, where it was a neighborhood pub and a stagecoach stop. It was moved here in the 1940s, and restored. Come inside and look for the mural of the village.

From here you can drive or walk (it's about a mile) down Lindsay Road to the river. The **John Hancock Warehouse** (Hancock was one of the owners) houses an exhibit about life and industry on the York River. The eighteenth-century commercial building—the only surviving one in the area—

Emerson-Wilcox House
Lindsay Street
York
363-3872

Old Gaol Museum
Lindsay Road
York
363-3872

First Parish
Congregational
Church
York Street
York
363-3647

Jefferds' Tavern
Lindsay Road
York
363-4703

is set up as a period warehouse. Outside you can enjoy a picnic lunch by the water.

The Elizabeth Perkins House sits beside the river at Sewall's Bridge. Perkins, who died in the 1950s, and her mother were largely responsible for the preservation work in the village. The eighteenth-century colonial house, once the Perkins's summer home, is filled with their marvelous collection of furnishings from all over the world.

Elizabeth Perkins
House
South Side Road
York
363-4723

York Harbor

York Harbor's waterfront is bustling. Don't miss **Cliff Walk**, which begins along the boardwalk at the ocean end of Harbor Beach Road, and ends on a rocky beach near Cow Beach Point. Along the way: wonderful views of the coastline (look for Nubble Light to the north) and lovely homes, and the sounds of waves crashing over the rocks.

Cape Neddick

Follow Route 1A to Nubble Road, to the tip of Cape Neddick. Next to **Nubble Light** is the six-bedroom Victorian lightkeeper's house. Captain Bartholomew Gosnold landed here in 1602, and named the point Savage Rock because of an encounter he had with the Indians on shore. The lighthouse was built in 1879 after the rock had claimed several wrecks.

From the point you can see **Boon Island Lighthouse**, 6½ miles southeast of the cape. Celia Thaxter describes the lonely life of the lightkeeper and his family in *The Watch of Boon Island*.

Ogunquit

Continue on Route 1A up the coast to Ogunquit. The 2½-mile-long beach here is one of the finest in New England—but the water is cold! **Marginal Way**, a path along the ocean, begins at the parking lot at the end of Cherry Lane, and ends at Shore Road in **Perkins Cove**. The cove is filled with artists and craftsmen, lobstermen and fishing boats, and lots of good restaurants. Look for the double-leaf draw-footbridge, the only one in Maine, which is raised for every boat that sounds a horn.

Wells is about 5 miles north of Ogunquit, on Route 1. The **Wells Auto Museum** is fun for the whole family. You'll find collections of cars, bicycles, motorcycles, even license plates, and nickelodeons. And you can take a ride in an antique car.

The **Rachael Carson National Wildlife Refuge**, off Route 9, not far from the junction with Route 1, is a lovely spot to commune with nature.

Continue up the coast along Route 1 to Kennebunk. Main Street boasts an interesting church and the **Brick Store Museum**, where you'll find a collection of early American pewter, maritime exhibits, old wedding gowns, and antique fire engines. Ask for a map of the other historic homes in town (most aren't open to the public). There's a legend about one of them – the **Wedding Cake House**. The sea captain who built the house created the elaborate trimming for his disappointed bride. You see they had married so quickly, there wasn't time to bake a wedding cake.

In Kennebunkport you'll find the oldest commercial building in the area. It began as Perkins' West India Goods, then became a boardinghouse, a post office, a harness shop, a fish market, an artist's studio, and finally a book shop. It's in **Dock Square**, a good spot for watching the Kennebunkport world go by.

The **Kennebunkport Historical Society** has exotic treasures brought back by sea captains, exhibits about local shipwrecks, and other memorabilia. Many of the towns along the New England coast had their own ropewalks – long platforms with a spindled wheel at either end. The ropemakers would walk between the wheels, spinning flax as they went. Thomas Goodwin built a

Wells

Wells Auto Museum
Route 1
Wells
646-9064

Kennebunk

Brick Store Museum
117 Main Street
Kennebunk
985-4802

Wedding Cake House
Landing Road
Kennebunk

Kennebunkport

Kennebunkport
 Historical Society
North Street
Kennebunkport
967-2751

ropewalk on Ocean Avenue, Kennebunkport, in 1806. (It's now a yacht club.) The platform here was 600 feet long. Because each wheel had six spindles, six men would have worked spinning flax here.

Stop at the **Seashore Trolley Museum** for a ride on an old-fashioned trolley. Also here: a slide show, exhibits from horsecars to streamliners, and craftsmen at work restoring the collection.

Seashore Trolley Museum
Log Cabin Road
Kennebunkport
967-2712

Don't leave town without stopping for lunch or supper at one of the many restaurants. Our favorites: the **Old Grist Mill** (967-4781), built in 1749, on Mill Lane; the **Breakwater** (967-3118) on Ocean Avenue; the **White Barn Inn** (967-2321) on Beach Street; and **Arundel Wharf** (967-3444) on the waterfront.

Portland

From Kennebunkport take Route 9A to I-95, to Portland. Stop at the chamber of commerce for information about the **Portland History Trail** and a free bus tour of the historic area.

Then head for the waterfront and the **Old Port Exchange**. The area, devastated by the Great Fire of 1866, was rebuilt in the 1960s. It's filled with shops, restaurants, pubs, and recreational facilities. Along the wharves you'll see fish-processing plants and warehouses. And the harbor is busy with ferries and boats heading out to Nova Scotia and Casco Bay. You can wander around endlessly, watching the waterfront activity and savoring that Maine smell.

Portland Chamber of Commerce
142 Free Street
Portland
772-2811

Every morning at eleven a red double-decker bus sets off from the Old Port Exchange for a three-hour tour of Portland's historic area. It's fun and it's free! Call or stop at the chamber of commerce for more information.

There are two good restaurants nearby: the **Hollow Reed** (773-2531) on Fore Street, and **F. Parker Reidy**'s (773-4731) on Exchange Street. Or bring a picnic and enjoy the fine view over the bay on **Eastern Promenade**, a good spot for watching Fourth of July fireworks. (Across the harbor, **Falmouth Foreside** offers a fine anchorage for visiting yachts.)

On Congress Street you'll find the **Wadsworth-Longfellow House**, built in 1785 by General Peleg Wadsworth. The house is furnished with pieces used by the family during the hundred years they lived here. At one time only fields separated the house from the sea; today buildings and highways block the view.

Wadsworth-
  Longfellow House
481 Congress Street
Portland
772-1807

From Portland follow I-95 north to Freeport, and a shopping spree at **L. L. Bean** (865-4761). Here is everything you could possibly want for camping, fishing, skiing, snowshoeing, and hunting. Even if you're not an outdoorsman, you'll love poking around this fabulous place.

Freeport

Continue on I-95 to Brunswick, the home of **Bowdoin College**. On campus stop to see paintings by Stuart, Copley, Homer, and Eakins in the **Museum of Art**. Nearby, exhibits in the **Peary-MacMillan Arctic Museum** outline the history of polar expeditions and display belongings of the two arctic explorers.

Brunswick

Museum of Art
Walker Art Building
Brunswick
725-8731

Travel along the central Maine coast, from Portland to Bar Harbor, has always been easier by sea than by land. For a glimpse of unspoiled Maine, you must be willing to drive up and down the necks. Here you'll find old saltwater farms, their land split between two or three necks (the dory was as important a tool as the plow), and small coves with lobstermen's houses and piers.

To see some of this country, drive down Route 123 from Brunswick along Harpswell Neck, a narrow finger into the sea, 1½ miles across at its widest point. In the tiny village of Harpswell Center the 1757 **First Meetinghouse** is a fine example of early church architecture.

The Harpswells

Peary-MacMillan
  Arctic Museum
Hubbard Hall
Brunswick
725-8731

The area abounds with legends. You may see a headless horseman riding through South Harpswell. Come at midnight when the moon is bright. Or you might catch the Ghost Ship of Harpswell, fully rigged and under sail. That ship is part of a tragic legend about two young friends, George Leverett and Charles Jose, who fell in love with Sarah Soule. Jose left town; Leverett stayed and built a ship he named *Sarah*. He sailed into Portland to pick up cargo, and there saw a black ship armed with a cannon. It was the *Don Pedro*, and it was sailed by his rival, Jose. The *Don Pedro* attacked, and all on board the *Sarah* were killed except Leverett; he was tied to the mast of his ship, and she was pushed out to sea. Now legend says the *Sarah*'s dead crew set sail and turned the ship toward home. The ghostly crew took Leverett ashore and left him with his logbook on the beach, where he was rescued. The *Sarah* was sighted from **Harpswell House** in 1880. She gleamed in the sun, headed straight for the harbor, and then disappeared, as though she'd come home for the last time.

Harpswell House
9 Gilman Avenue
South Harpswell
725-7694

The Dead Ship of Harpswell
John Greenleaf Whittier

What flecks the outer gray beyond
    The sundown's golden trail?
The white flash of a sea-bird's wing,
    Or gleam of slanting sail?
Let young eyes watch from Neck and Point,
    And sea-worn elders pray,–
The ghost of what was once a ship
    Is sailing up the bay!

From gray sea-fog, from icy drift,
    From peril and from pain,
The home-bound fisher greets thy lights,
    O hundred-harbored Maine!
But many a keel shall seaward turn,
    And many a sail outstand,

MAINE

HARPSWELL

One of the many small harbors that fishermen and lobstermen call home.

KENNEBUNK

The Wedding Cake House is renowned for its unique architecture and embellishing woodwork.

PEMAQUID POINT

Typical of Maine's many lighthouses which protect the seafarer from the rocky shore.

When, tall and white, the Dead Ship looms
    Against the dusk of land.

She rounds the headland's bristling pines;
    She threads the isle-set bay;
No spur of breeze can speed her on,
    Nor ebb of tide delay.
Old men still walk the Isle of Orr
    Who tell her date and name,
Old shipwrights sit in Freeport yards
    Who hewed her oaken frame.

What weary doom of baffled quest,
    Thou sad sea-ghost, is thine?
What makes thee in the haunts of home
    A wonder and a sign?
No foot is on thy silent deck,
    Upon thy helm no hand;
No ripple hath the soundless wind
    That smites thee from the land!

For never comes the ship to port,
    Howe'er the breeze may be;
Just when she nears the waiting shore
    She drifts again to sea.
No tack of sail, nor turn of helm,
    Nor sheer of veering side;
Stern-fore she drives to sea and night,
    Against the wind and tide.

In vain o'er Harpswell Neck the star
    Of evening guides her in;
In vain for her the lamps are lit
    Within thy tower, Seguin!
In vain the harbor-boat shall hail,
    In vain the pilot call;
No hand shall reef her spectral sail,
    Or let her anchor fall.

Shake, brown old wives, with dreary joy,
    Your gray-head hints of ill;
And, over sick-beds whispering low,
    Your prophecies fulfill.
Some home amid yon birchen trees
    Shall drape its door with woe;

> And slowly where the Dead Ship sails,
>   The burial boat shall row!
>
> From Wolf Neck and from Flying Point,
>   From island and from main,
> From sheltered cove and tided creek,
>   Shall glide the funeral train.
> The dead-boat with the bearers four,
>   The mourners at her stern,–
> And one shall go the silent way
>   Who shall no more return!
>
> And men shall sigh, and women weep,
>   Whose dear ones pale and pine,
> And sadly over sunset seas
>   Await the ghostly sign.
> They know not that its sails are filled
>   By pity's tender breath,
> Nor see the Angel at the helm
>   Who steers the Ship of Death!

Orrs & Bailey Islands

Off Route 123 there's a road to the right that takes you to Route 24. Head south, through the area where a murdered pirate supposedly stands guard over buried treasure (some say they've seen his light and heard him moaning). Between Orrs Island and Bailey Island, separated by Will Straits, is an uncemented granite-block bridge that's laid out like a honeycomb so that the tides and rushing spring thaws can flow through freely. There's a statue of a Maine lobsterman at **Land's End** on the tip of Bailey Island. After a storm, when the surf is high, or any time, take the cliff walk for superb views of Casco Bay and Halfway Rock Light.

Bath

Head back up Route 24 to Route 1 or I-95 into Bath, Maine's cradle of shipbuilding. Some five thousand vessels have been launched here, including half of all the wooden sailing vessels built in the United States between 1862 and 1902.

Allow yourself time to visit the **Maine Maritime Museum** at its four sites: Sewall House, the

Maine Maritime Museum
Sewall House
963 Washington Street
Bath
443–6311

Winter Street Center
880 Washington Street
Bath
443-4185

Percy and Small Shipyard
263 Washington Street
Bath
443-6381

Apprenticeshop
375 Front Street
Bath
443-5638

Winter Street Center, the Percy and Small Shipyard, and the Apprenticeshop. **Sewall House**, museum headquarters, is a twenty-eight-room Georgian mansion. Here are collections of ship models and paintings, and exhibits on lobstering, fishing, and sailing. The **Winter Street Center** was once a church; now it houses ship models, half models, photographs, and historical exhibits. The **Percy and Small Shipyard** is the country's only surviving yard where large wooden sailing ships were once built. The *Seguin*, the oldest wooden steam tug still registered, is being restored here. In the **Apprenticeshop** the museum conducts programs for students who want to learn how to build classic Maine coast skiffs, dories, and sloops.

A recent *New York Times* article tells the story of a descendant of a Bath shipyard owner who is still trying to recover a Civil War debt from the government. In 1862 the yard built a 300-foot gunboat for the navy; it was commissioned and served for some time. Legitimate cost overruns pushed the final bill over what Congress had appropriated. Although both the navy and the U.S. Board of Claims recommended that the total bill be paid, Congress took no action. And the family has been pursuing the claim for over a hundred years. How much was the bill? In 1862 it came to $11,708.79.

Popham Beach

From Bath take Route 209 south to Popham Beach. Visit the site of Popham Colony, where a hundred English colonists arrived in 1607. Discouraged by the harsh winter and sickness, they stayed just a year, most of them returning to England on the *Virginia,* a ship they built themselves (the very first built in America).

At the **Fort Popham Memorial** you'll see the partial construction of a fort that was begun in 1861 and never finished. Displays here interpret the history of the area—the story of Popham Colony, Benedict Arnold's march through Maine, and the fort's construction.

The memorial is in **Popham Beach State Park**, a new facility extending along 4½ miles of fine sand. There are tidal pools, dunes, and rocky outcroppings, and warm water (for Maine). Come early. Parking is limited.

Continue up Route 1 to Wiscasset, one of the prettiest villages in Maine. **Castle Tucker**, where you'll find a freestanding elliptical staircase, has a beautiful view overlooking Wiscasset Harbor. It's furnished with original Victorian pieces. The **Musical Wonder House** has an unusual collection of music boxes, player pianos, gramophones, pipe organs, and period antiques. Many of the furnishings in the **Nickels-Sortwell House** are original. Its barn houses the **Lincoln County Fire Museum**, where you can see antique firefighting equipment and other vehicles. Stop at the **Maine Art Gallery** on Warren Street (882–7511). The gallery features work by local artists and hosts a special show during the summer.

Our favorite site: the resting place of the *Luther Little* and the *Hesperus* (not the one that was sunk on Norman's Woe), two four-masted schooners that lie in the harbor tide flats, picturesque reminders of the days of sail.

Popham Beach State Park
Route 209
Popham Beach
389–1335

Wiscasset

Castle Tucker
Lee and High Streets
Wiscasset
882–7364

Musical Wonder House
18 High Street
Wiscasset
882–7163

Nickels-Sortwell House
Main and Federal Streets
Wiscasset

The Dismantled Ship
Walt Whitman

In some unused lagoon, some nameless bay,
    On sluggish, lonesome waters, anchor'd near the shore,
An old, dismasted, gray and batter'd ship, disabled, done,
    After free voyages to all the seas of earth,
        haul'd up at last and hawser'd tight,
Lies rusting, mouldering.

Boothbay Harbor is on Route 27 south of Wiscasset. It's one of the finest and busiest of Maine's natural harbors, with commercial fishing boats, excursion boats, windjammers, and deep-sea fishing charters going in and out. In mid-July

Boothbay Harbor

Boothbay Harbor
  Chamber of
  Commerce
Route 27
Boothbay Harbor
633-4232, 633-2353

the harbor is the site of the three-day **Windjammer Festival**, but you can see these marvelous sailing ships here all summer long.

There are two fine museums in town: At the **Boothbay Railway Museum** you'll find antique cars and fire equipment, railroad society memorabilia, and a collection of antique dolls. When you're through exploring, take a ride on a narrow-gauge railroad. Then head for the **Grand Banks Schooner Museum**, actually a 142-foot fishing vessel that's been restored.

For more information about the town, stop at the chamber of commerce or the **Boothbay Region Historical Society** on Townsend Avenue.

Damariscotta

Chapman-Hall House
Main Street
Damariscotta

Continue on Route 1 to Damariscotta. Stop at the visitors' center on Main Street; then cross the street to the **Chapman-Hall House**. The house, built in 1754, is furnished with period pieces. Also here: a collection of eighteenth-century tools (crafts, farming, and shipbuilding) and an herb garden.

Pemaquid Point

Pemaquid Point
  Lighthouse
Lighthouse Road
Pemaquid Point

Colonial Pemaquid
  Restoration State
  Park
Route 130
Pemaquid Point
677-2423

Are you longing for the coast proper? Head south on Route 129 to Route 130, to Pemaquid Point. **Pemaquid Point Lighthouse**, which towers over the pounding surf, is a glorious spot to spend time. Enjoy the magnificent view, then visit the **Fisherman's Museum** in the lightkeeper's house next door.

In 1965 archaeologists began uncovering foundations of early Indian settlements and seventeenth-century houses at **Colonial Pemaquid Restoration State Park**, near Pemaquid Beach. There's a museum displaying much of the material from the site, where several thousand artifacts have been found.

Friendship

Continue up Route 1 to Route 220 south, to Friendship, home of the famous Friendship sloop. Come in late July when **Friendship Sloop Days** honor these vessels. In August there's the **Friendship Sloop Race**; over Labor Day weekend, the **Chowder Race**, with a fleet of fifty beautiful antique boats. From Friendship meander through the countryside to Cushing, where Andrew Wyeth summers and paints, and Thomaston, a village of beautiful sea captains' homes. Then go south on Route 131 to Tenants Harbor, a lovely fishing village. Stop for a swim in the magnificent clear quarry. Then buy fresh lobsters for dinner. (There's a distributor down the road from the quarry.)

Just beyond Tenants Harbor, from Port Clyde, you can take the mailboat **Laura B** (372-8848) to Monhegan Island, which lies 9 miles out to sea. Leif Erikson may have landed here in the year 1000; we know John Cabot did in 1498. Later Monhegan was a haven for pirates.

You can't bring your car, but the island is only a couple of miles long and a mile wide, and the views along the rugged cliffs on the off-shore side are well worth the walk. While you're exploring, plan a stop at the **Monhegan Museum**, in the former lightkeeper's house. What's here? Indian artifacts, exhibits about the island's wildlife, and an art gallery.

Follow Route 131 back to Route 1 and Rockland, where you'll find a large collection of Andrew Wyeth paintings in the **William A. Farnsworth Library and Art Museum**. Also in the museum's collection: the works of other nineteenth- and twentieth-century artists, among them Winslow Homer.

The **State of Maine Ferry Service** runs a ferry between Rockland and Vinalhaven. On the island, one of the oldest summer colonies in New England, are several interesting houses. Also here: a marvelous area for cruising and an active fishing

Boothbay Railway Museum
Route 27
Boothbay Harbor
633-4727

Grand Banks Schooner Museum
100 Commercial Street
Boothbay Harbor
633-4727

Tenants Harbor

Monhegan Island

Rockland

William A. Farnsworth Library and Art Museum
19 Elm Street
Rockland
596-6457

Vinal Haven

State of Maine Ferry
  Service
517 Main Street
Rockland
594-5543

Rockport

Camden

Camden Information
  Booth
Public Landing
Camden
236-4404

Camden Hills State
  Park
Route 1
Camden
236-3109

industry. Stop for a swim in one of the spring-filled granite quarries, explore a small cove, or just sit back and enjoy the view. Across a small strip of water to the north, you can see North Haven Island; to the southwest, sits Hurricane Island, where the first Outward Bound School was located.

Heading up the west shore of Penobscot Bay you come to Rockport, home of André the Seal. André used to swim 160 miles to Boston, to spend the winter at the aquarium there; and then back to Maine again in the spring. (These days he's wintering in Mystic.) His keeper, Harry Goodridge, has taught him a number of tricks, which he performs afternoons at four in his special floating pen near the head of the harbor.

Continue up Route 1 through Rockport to Camden, one of Maine's most interesting towns. The harbor is a fascinating place, busy with commercial and charter fishing boats, sloops, and a large fleet of windjammers (offering weekly cruises).

Stop at the **Camden Information Booth** off Main Street for a wealth of information about the area. Then enjoy the shops and restaurants, and the view of the waterfalls running through the center of town.

Camden is nestled against the **Camden Hills**, which rise majestically from the shore of the bay. Come for the view or the hiking—both are exceptional. The **Mount Battie South Trail** begins on Megunticook Street (north of the town square). The 1-mile path is steep, but the views from the ledges are worth the climb. Or take the easy way to the top (800 feet): the toll road from **Camden Hills State Park**.

Mount Megunticook Trail (3½ miles) begins at the warden's hut in the park's campgrounds. Enjoy beautiful views of the ocean as you wend your way up to the summit of Mount Megunticook

(1,385 feet); then come down on the **Tablelands Trail** to Mount Battie Road.

Bald Rock Mountain Trail starts 4 miles north of the park, on Route 1. (Look for a sign near telephone pole 106.) Follow yellow blazes along a logging trail to Bald Rock Summit (1,100 feet), where there are shelters if you want to spend the night. On a clear day you can see Northport and Lincolnville, Islesboro Island, Deer Isle, and even Pulpit Harbor on North Haven. The trail is 3 miles long.

Maiden Cliff, named for an eleven-year-old girl who fell to her death in May 1864, offers spectacular views of Megunticook Lake and the surrounding countryside. Follow Route 52 west from Camden to the Barrett Place parking lot, where the **Maiden Cliff Trail** begins. At the summit (1,204 feet) — it's marked by a wooden cross — pick up the **Scenic Trail** for your return trip. The total distance is 2½ miles.

Ragged Mountain Trail begins at the Camden Ski Bowl (take John Street from town) and continues up the lift line, right into the woods, and along the ridge to the summit (1,300 feet). You can see the ocean over Oyster River Pond, the Glen Cove area, and Maiden Cliff. Then come down any of the ski runs.

For fine dining in town, try **John Wanamaker** (236-8728) on the wharf, or the **Waterfront** (236-3747), in Harborside Square. There's great seafood, too, at the **Lobster Pound** (789-5550) on Route 1 in Lincolnville.

From Camden continue along Route 1 to Route 175 south, to Route 166A on the Nasket peninsula. Here you'll find Castine, a quiet town with a stormy history. In 1779 Commodore Saltonstall led Paul Revere and other patriots here in the Massachusetts Expedition. The expedition — a mission to dislodge the British from their base at Castine — failed miserably, and all the American

Castine

Fort George
Wadsworth Cove
Road
Castine

boats were lost. Because the abortive mission was such an embarrassment to several prominent patriots, it was never fully documented. And the British? They occupied the town again during the War of 1812.

You can learn more about the area's history at **Fort George**, where fortifications were constructed as early as 1626. The buildings have been razed and rebuilt many times since. Then stroll around the town, reading the historical markers and enjoying the fine examples of colonial architecture.

Maine Maritime Academy
Battle Avenue
Castine
326-4311

The **Maine Maritime Academy** offers tours of the *State of Maine*, a training ship. In August the academy also schedules walks (intelligent beachcombing) with staff members. These field trips on the natural history of the seashore last between two and three hours.

On your way down the Penobscot peninsula to Deer Isle, stop at North Brooksville on Route 175, where a bridge crosses over a rapids in the Bagaduce River. These rapids reverse with the tide. About 2 miles downriver is another reversing rapids, more vigorous than the first, where the current passes through a narrow rocky channel. You can launch a canoe or small boat near the bridge, and run the rapids either up or down the river, depending on the tide.

The stretch of river between the two rapids is a haven for seals. Come on a fine day at low tide, and you'll see them sunning on uncovered rocks.

Deer Isle

From Castine take Route 166 to Route 199, to Route 175 south. Continue on Route 175 to Route 15, crossing Eggemoggin Reach on a high suspension bridge. Deer Isle is a great area for exploring, for discovering something new and interesting around the next bend. What's here? Towns climbing into the hills, harbors active with lobstering, and scallop and sardine catches; historic homes; a musicians' retreat; an abandoned silver mine; a granite quarry; lilies floating on Ames Pond;

highly skilled craftsmen; and mounds of shells left by the Indians.

Friends tell us about a great place to buy fresh fish—right off the boat—for dinner. Driving along Route 15 from the village of Deer Isle toward Stonington, turn left on Oceanville Road (there's a filling station and a used car lot on the corner); then right on the dirt road marked "Northeast Boat Yard." The wharf is at the end of the road. The fishermen usually return with the day's catch between two and three in the afternoon. Come before the truckers start loading, and you'll find delicious fresh fish for anywhere from $.35 to $.80 a pound. A warning for the fainthearted: The fish are gutted but not cleaned.

Isle au Haut

From Stonington, at the tip of Deer Isle, you can take the mailboat to Isle au Haut, 6 miles out, a part of Acadia National Park. Named by Samuel de Champlain in 1604 for its high land, the island is relatively untouched, with just a few roads and trails around the perimeter. Bring your bike, or plan to hike.

Mount Desert Island

Meander up to Ellsworth through the Blue Hill region; then take Route 3 to Mount Desert Island.

This beautiful island was discovered by Champlain, who named it L'Isle des Monts Désert because the mountains looked so barren. In 1613 a group of Jesuits settled on Fernald's Point, but were driven out after only a month by the British. That skirmish was the first in a century and a half of fighting between French and British for control of the area.

Today, almost half of the island (along with parts of two nearby islands) makes up **Acadia National Park**. The terrain is varied—wooded valleys, lakes, mountains, and granite shore constantly lashed by the sea—and filled with beautiful trees and wild flowers, and birds and animals. Stop at the visitors' center in Hulls Cove for

Acadia National Park
Route 3
Hulls Cove
288-5262

maps, guidebooks, and information about trails (hiking and biking), self-guided nature walks, and special programs.

A tour of the park? **National Park Tours** (288-3327) in Bar Harbor offers a bus trip around the park. Or you can take a cruise from **Frenchman's Bay Boating Company** (288-5741) in Bar Harbor. Or you can rent a tape recorder and taped tour at the visitors' center, and drive yourself.

Bar Harbor is the largest and best known town on Mount Desert Island. At one time a fabulous summer resort, many of the elegant nineteenth-century "cottages" were destroyed in a disastrous fire in 1947. Plan to spend some time shopping; then head for one of the many good restaurants for lunch or dinner. Our favorites: **Abel's** (276-5837) on Route 198, the **Quarterdeck Restaurant** (288-5292) at Main and West, **Clipper Inn** (633-5152) and **Tugboat Inn** (633-4434) on Commercial Street, and **Rocktide Inn** (633-4455) on Atlantic Avenue.

Loop Road Trail begins at Bar Harbor, where several scenic overlooks offer magnificent views of Frenchman's Bay and Bar Harbor itself. **Sieur de Monts Spring**, farther out, has a nature center and a wild flower garden. Nearby, the **Abbe Museum** preserves the Indian history of the area. Not far from the museum, at the picnic area, the road becomes one way.

Abbe Museum of Stone Age Antiquities
Loop Road
Bar Harbor
288-3519

Hardy souls can stop for a swim at **Sand Beach**, off Ocean Drive, where the average temperature of the water in summer is a brisk 50 to 55 degrees. There is some surf although the beach is in a protected cove. A path from here leads to Otter Cliffs.

Don't miss **Thunder Hole**, where the waves crash in and out with a roar. And the view from **Otter Cliffs**—the highest headlands on the East Coast—is spectacular!

As you drive along the Atlantic shore, you can see **Cadillac Mountain** rising from the interior.

MAINE

The Boothbay Central RR steams along its tracks at the Railroad Museum.

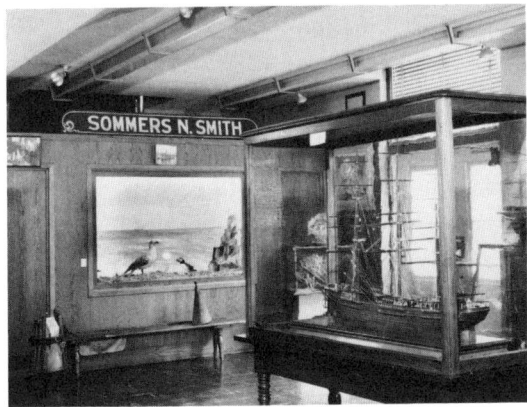

BOOTHBAY HARBOR

The Farnsworth Art Museum of marine art and artifacts.

ROCKLAND

Consisting of nearly 42,000 acres, the park is almost completely surrounded by the sea.

ACADIA NATIONAL PARK

You can reach the 1,530-foot mountain, the highest point on the Atlantic coast north of Rio de Janeiro, by heading north on Jordan Pond Road. From the summit you can see sparkling **Eagle Lake** to the northwest and **Somes Sound** to the west. The sound, the only natural fjord on the East Coast, creeps in so far that the island is almost cut in two. Swimmers: try **Sand Beach** (above) or **Seal Harbor Beach**, a community beach off Route 3, where the water temperature hovers around 57 degrees in summer. The surf is gentle; the drop-off, gradual. Less hardy souls can try swimming at the head of the sound in Somesville, where the water is actually warm.

For hikers Mount Desert is paradise. At the eastern end of the island you can walk the Champlain Mountains from south to north on the **Gorham Mountain Trail**. The 6-mile trail begins a mile north of Otter Cliffs at the Monument Cove parking area. The **South Ridge Trail** (7 miles) takes you to the summit of Cadillac Mountain. It begins at the campground on Otter Cove. Shorter trails to the top: the **West Face Trail** from Jordan Pond Road and the **North Ridge Trail** from the Bar Harbor side of Ocean Drive. Watch out for cars!

Pemetic Mountain Trail, an easy 2 miles, begins at the north end of Bubble Pond, off Jordan Pond Road, and goes along the ridge to the top of Pemetic Mountain (1,218 feet).

The Penobscot and Sargent mountains run along the west side of Jordan Pond. The **Jordan Cliffs Trail** begins at the **Jordan Pond House** (276–3316), a restaurant just north of Seal Harbor. The distance, if you circle back on the **Penobscot Mountain Trail**, is about 5 miles. Enjoy long views over Blue Hill Bay, the Atlantic, even Frenchman's Bay; then stop for lunch on your way out.

Norumbega Mountain Trail begins on Route 198 near Upper Hadlock Pond, and extends almost 3 miles. From the top (852 feet) you can see South-

West Harbor and Tremont. Be sure to bring along a pail or a basket if you're hiking in blueberry season.

Acadia Mountain Trail offers an easy walk through an area rich in history. An early French colony was formed here, on Saint Sauveur Mountain, but was later destroyed by the English. English patrols used to come to **Man o' War Brook** to fill their casks with fresh water, and to hunt and fish. The trail is 2½ miles long, and begins on Robinson Road, off Route 102, across from Echo Lake. Look for the sign to the summit (644 feet).

Hikers, climbers, and campers: You'll enjoy a drive inland to **Baxter State Park**, a lovely wilderness area of mountains and lakes. From Ellsworth follow Route 1A to Bangor; then take I-95 to the Millinocket exit, and follow the signs to the park. **Mount Katahdin**, at 5,267 feet, is one of the highest spots in the eastern United States. The Appalachian Trail, which begins in Georgia, ends here.

In 1930 Perceval P. Baxter bought the land and gave it "for the benefit of the people of Maine," to enjoy in its natural state. And enjoy it you will. You can swim, hike (be sure to check trail conditions with a park ranger), picnic, fish, canoe, and camp here. Write to Box 540, Millinocket (723-5140), or stop at the park office in town for maps, information, and a list of rules.

From Mount Desert Island, follow Route 3 into Ellsworth, to Route 1A, to I-95 in Bangor. Leave I-95 at Newport, and continue west on Route 2 across the state to Farmington and Bethel. Then cross the New Hampshire border to Gorham, the entrance to the Presidential Range of the White Mountains, the most impressive range of mountains in the Northeast, and the setting-off point for the next itinerary.

ITINERARY E

MOUNT WASHINGTON

ITINERARY E

(Suggested Time: 10–14 days; 694 miles/1,111 kilometers)

The White and Green Mountains

Mount Washington	E·162	Ripton	E·179
Jackson	E·163	Pittsford	E·179
North Conway	E·163	Proctor	E·179
Freedom	E·164	Rutland	E·180
Lincoln	E·164	Ludlow	E·181
Franconia	E·164	Weston	E·181
Kinsman Notch	E·165	Manchester	E·181
Hanover	E·166	East Dorset	E·182
Quechee	E·168	Dorset	E·182
Woodstock	E·168	East Rupert	E·182
Bridgewater	E·169	Sunderland	E·184
Bridgewater Corners	E·169	Townshend	E·184
Plymouth	E·169	Newfane	E·184
Sherburne	E·170	Brattleboro	E·185
Stowe	E·172	Jaffrey	E·185
Burlington	E·173	Peterborough	E·185
Grand Isle	E·176	Wilmington	E·186
Shelburne	E·178	Bennington	E·186
Middlebury	E·178	North Bennington	E·187

Although New England's mountains are not as rugged or spectacular as western ranges, these very old forested peaks are built to human scale. And, like old family friends, they have been around a while and have seen a lot of living.

New Hampshire

New Hampshire's White Mountains are rugged and irregular. Once much taller, these mountains have been ravaged by periods of folding, faulting, and terrific pressure from molten rock within them. What this has done is create a landscape cut by ravines and embellished with unusual contours.

Mount Washington

Mount Washington
Toll Road
Gorham
466-2222

Mount Washington
Cog Railway
Mount Washington
846-5404

Follow Route 2 from Maine into Gorham, where you take Route 16 south, through the **Presidential Range**. Mount Washington, at 6,288 feet, is the highest peak in the range, and in New England.

There are several ways to get to the top of Mount Washington. You can pick up the toll road at Glen House on Route 16. Or you can drive to the base station on the western side of the mountain, near Fabyan, and board the **Mount Washington Cog Railway**. The train's been operating since 1866. The trip takes an hour and a half each way, and is a lot of fun. Or you can stop at one of the local ski areas—Wildcat, Attitash, Mount Cranmore—and ride a lift to the top. Or you can pull on your hiking boots, and do it the hard way!

Tuckerman's Ravine at Pinkham Notch is the scene of a spring ritual for slightly crazy skiers and their only a bit more sane camp followers. The skiers carry skis and poles up the steep trail to the base of the ravine; the followers bring cameras, lunch, and the yen to watch. And what a show! A few skiers making it down the slope with style, the rest tumbling down the hill—all to the cheers and boos of the crowd.

At **Pinkham Notch** you'll see people doing just that—getting ready to climb one of the ravines on the east face of the mountain. Of course hiking is the best way to discover the beauty of the Presidential Range. The whole of the White Mountain National Forest is interlaced with well-marked hiking trails, lean-tos, and huts where you can get a bunk or a meal or both (reservations are a must in season). This network allows you to travel light even on an extended hiking trip. For information, guidebooks, and maps before you go, write to the chamber of commerce or the **Appalachian Mountain Club** (page xvii). The AMC also has a store in the camp at Pinkham Notch.

Whether you're hiking or driving or riding the rails to the top, dress warmly. Mount Washington records the highest wind velocities in the country, often well over a 100 miles an hour during the winter. And the weather on top is changeable. The average temperature at any time of the year is below 30 degrees, and there's snow every month of the year. Always carry sweaters and jackets.

Mount Washington
 Valley Chamber of
 Commerce
Main Street
North Conway
356-3171

Jackson

Continue down Route 16, through the covered bridge, into Jackson. There's good shopping here in the **Jackson Village Store** and the **Jack Frost Shop**, both in the center. And there's good food and lodging at several old inns in town. Stay for the night or just a meal at the **Christmas Farm Inn** (383-4313) on Route 16B, or the **Dana Place Inn** (383-6822) on Pinkham Notch Road.

North Conway

A few miles beyond Jackson pick up Route 302 south to North Conway, a busy place all year round.

The **Conway Scenic Railroad** leaves from the century-old restored train station in town for an hour trip on an 11-mile track. There's also a railroad museum and a roundhouse on the grounds.

For shoppers there's one long street of stores. You'll find **Eastern Mountain Sports** (356-5433), **Carroll Reed** (356-3122), **Yield House** (356-3141), a **Dansk Factory Outlet** (356-3493), and a **Bass Shoe Outlet** (447-5288). There's also a **Chuck Roast Outlet** (447-2052) in Conway where you can buy canvas and nylon bicycle bags, backpacks, and other camping equipment. Local crafts? Write to the **League of New Hampshire Craftsmen** for scheduled exhibitions in the area.

Just east of town, the **Mount Cranmore Skimobile** has been operating since 1938. Watch for hang gliders preparing for takeoff at the top.

Freedom

To the west of town you'll find **Echo Lake State Park**. (Follow the signs from the railroad station.) Come for a swim and a picnic, and two dramatic rock formations—**White Horse Ledge** and **Cathedral Ledge**. You can drive to the top (some 700 feet) for a beautiful view of the valley.

Freedom is about 20 miles southeast of North Conway, near the Maine border. (Take Route 302 to Route 153.) Come the second Saturday in August for the parade that marks the beginning of **Old Home Week**.

The **Luethi-Peterson International Camp** in town was established during the post–World War II period to promote understanding among people. Folk dancing is featured nightly, and visitors are welcome. Nearby: mountains, rivers, and lakes (Lake Ossipee and, farther south, Lake Winnipesaukee) to explore.

Lincoln

Loon Mountain
Kancamagus Highway
Lincoln
745-8111

From North Conway continue south on Route 302 to Route 16, to the turnoff for Route 112, the **Kancamagus Highway**. Along this 33-mile road is some of the most spectacular scenery in the White Mountains. Stop just outside Lincoln at **Loon Mountain** for a magnificent aerial ride—the longest in the state.

Franconia

From Lincoln pick up Route 3 north, which takes you right into **Franconia Notch State Park**, a lovely area surrounded by the White Mountains National Forest. Come to swim, to hike, to ski, to camp—to enjoy the natural beauty of the place.

Part of that natural beauty is the **Flume**. This narrow gorge has walls of granite rising 70 to 90 feet. The boardwalk along the 800-foot length of the gorge is lined with descriptions of its geological development, and leads to the 40-foot **Avalanche Falls**.

Beyond Whitehouse Bridge you come to the **Basin**, a granite glacial pothole 20 feet in diameter, which sits at the base of a waterfall.

A few miles north of the Flume, on the west side of Route 3, you'll find **Profile Lake**. Look up to see **Old Man of the Mountains** (he's sometimes called Great Stone Face) rising above the gorge. Plaques at the lake tell how the 40-foot-high profile was formed thousands of years ago.

Right beyond the park, at the junction of Routes 3 and 18, you'll find the **Cannon Mountain Aerial Tramway**. Ride up to the top, where gaps and notches give you a view right into the heart of the White Mountains.

Robert Frost spent summers and vacations from 1915 to 1920 in Franconia, a few miles north of the park. His home—**Robert Frost Place**—has been restored, and mementos and photographs depict the poet's life here. The house is now an arts center, where a summer program of concerts, readings, and lectures is conducted by a visiting poet in residence. To get here, take Route 116 (exit 38) off I-93 to Bickford Hill Road; turn right over the ridge, then left onto Ridge Road.

Franconia Notch State Park
Route 3
Franconia
823-5563

Cannon Mountain Aerial Tramway
Echo Lake Road
Franconia
823-5563

Continue on Route 112 about 6 miles west of North Woodstock, to Kinsman Notch and the **Lost River Reservation**. Lost River flows through a glacial gorge that is narrow, steep, and strangely shaped. Years ago boulders broke off and slid down into the gorge to form caverns. The **Giant Pothole** is a pear-shaped bowl, 28 feet across, worn smooth by swirling water. **Paradise Falls** was formed as the river flowed over two dikes and into a basin

Kinsman Notch

Lost River Reservation
Route 112
Kinsman Notch
745-8031

Hanover

at the bottom. Also here: a natural history museum, an ecology trail, and a garden.

Continue on Route 112 to Route 118, which you'll follow through Warren, Wentworth, and Dorchester, to Canaan. There you pick up Route 4 to I-89 into Lebanon; then go north on Route 120 to Hanover.

Dartmouth College was founded in Hanover in 1769 by Reverend Eleazar Wheelock. His mission: to spread Christian education among the Indians. You can join a tour of the campus at the college information booth on the east side of the green or at **Hopkins Center**, on the campus, during the summer. Don't miss **Dartmouth Row**, a series of four classroom buildings dating from 1784.

When you've finished enjoying the campus and, perhaps, a meal at the **Hanover Inn** (643-4300), take Route 12A south to I-89 west, into Vermont.

The Song of the Vermonters, 1779
John Greenleaf Whittier

Ho—all to the borders! Vermonters, come down,
    With your breeches of deerskin and jackets of brown;
With your red woollen caps, and your moccasins, come,
    To the gathering summons of trumpet and drum.

Does the "old Bay State" threaten?
    Does Congress complain?
Swarms Hampshire in arms on our borders again?
    Bark the war-dogs of Britain aloud on the lake—
Let 'em come; what they can they are welcome to take.

Yet we owe no allegiance, we bow to no throne,
    Our ruler is law, and the law is our own;
Our leaders themselves are our own fellow-men,
    Who can handle the sword, or the scythe, or the pen.

Hurrah for Vermont! For the land which we till
  Must have sons to defend her from valley and hill;
Leave the harvest to rot on the fields where it grows,
  And the reaping of wheat for the reaping of foes.

Come York or come Hampshire, come traitors or knaves,
  If ye rule o'er our land, ye shall rule o'er our graves;
Our vow is recorded — our banner unfurled,
  In the name of Vermont we defy all the world!

Vermont

The early history of man in Vermont begins with the Algonquians in 2000 B.C. Later the Algonquians, Iroquois, Mohicans, and Abnakis used Vermont as a trail from Massachusetts to New York. This Indian heritage is still very much present in the names around the state: Quechee, Bomoseen, Passumpsic, Winooski, Jamaica.

On July 4, 1609, Samuel de Champlain led the Algonquian Indians against the Iroquois. He killed two Iroquois chiefs and a number of warriors, incurring the wrath of the Iroquois for years to come. While here he named a mountain Le Lion Couchant (the crouching lion); it's known today as Camel's Hump. And he called the largest island in Lake Champlain Grand Isle. This French influence is also evident in other regional names: Montpelier, Vergennes, St. Johnsbury, Danville.

The first English settlement in the area was Fort Dummer, near Brattleboro, in 1724. The land was bought at auction by Sir William Dummer and Colonel William Brattle (Dummerston and Brattleboro were named for them). At that time Vermont was part of New York, which didn't keep New Hampshire from annexing land there. The matter was settled by King George II, who maintained that the land belonged to New York. In 1770 Ethan Allen and his Green Mountain Boys rallied to drive off the "Yorkers" who were following up on that claim. The same group responded to the call against the British during the Revolution. In 1777 Vermont declared itself an independent republic, which it remained for fourteen years before becoming a state.

The Green Mountains are probably the remains of the oldest mountain range in New England, dating back 440 million years. Erosion worked folds into the bedrock on a north-south axis, producing an even, rolling range with no jagged peaks or deep valleys. This *peneplain*, or flat plain,

E·167

THE WHITE AND THE GREEN MOUNTAINS

is interspersed with *monadnocks*, isolated mountains made up of very hard bedrock that did not erode as much as the land around it.

There are not many lakes in the Green Mountains, possibly because the movement of the glaciers was along the folds southward instead of across them. There was, however, one large glacial lake, Lake Vermont, which covered the Champlain lowland up to 700 feet above the present level of Lake Champlain.

Although the Green Mountains are fairly flat in the south, in the northern section they divide into three parallel ranges more rugged in appearance and filled with more separate peaks. Mount Killington, Mount Ellen, Camel's Hump, and Mount Mansfield are all over 4,000 feet. Some geologists believe that the mountains in the south were once much higher. They claim that the Taconic Mountains, which stretch between northern Connecticut and central Vermont on a north-south axis, were once the tops of the southern Green Mountains, which detached and moved a number of miles to the west. (This is called a *thrust fault* — an older rock formation settled over a younger one.)

Quechee

Continue on I-89 through White River Junction to Route 4, to Quechee. **Quechee Gorge**, Vermont's Little Grand Canyon, rises 165 feet over the Ottauquechee River. Stop for a good view of the gorge from the bridge on Route 4. Or hike along the **Quechee Gorge Trail**, which begins a third of a mile beyond the gorge near the state park entrance. Watch for the sign marked with blue blazes. The views along the trail are spectacular.

Stop at the **Sweater Store** (295-7920) about a mile west of the gorge for Fall River Knitting Mill sweaters. For fabrics, and kits for kilts, skirts, ponchos, capes, quilts, and pillows, backtrack to **Dewey's** (295-3545) on Route 4 near the junction of I-89 and I-91.

Woodstock

Woodstock Historical Society
26 Elm Street
Woodstock
457-1822

Continue along Route 4 to Woodstock, one of the prettiest towns in New England. Take time to walk around the green, past the charming antique homes. Nearby, the **Woodstock Historical Society** has nine restored rooms with collections of silver, glass, paintings, and period furniture, and a landscaped garden. On Central Street antique shops, galleries, bookstores, and boutiques now occupy restored eighteenth- and nineteenth-century buildings.

There is so much to discover in this town, a town that has valued and preserved its heritage while adapting it to modern living. Contact the chamber of commerce for more information about historic sites. It's the place, too, for information about nearby nature trails, **Faulkner** and **Mount Peg**.

John Freiden has written a wonderful book about bicycle trips in Vermont. And one of those trips begins and ends in Woodstock, with stops at South Pomfret, Hewetts Corners, and West Hartford. Bring the book and your bike, and enjoy.

From Woodstock follow Route 4 to Bridgewater, where you'll enjoy shopping in the **Bridgewater Mill Mall** (672-3332). The mall is in a beautifully restored nineteenth-century mill. What's here? A museum, craft shops, clothing stores, bookstores, fabric shops, and a food market.

Follow Route 4 into Bridgewater Corners; then turn left on Route 100A. The **Calvin Coolidge State Forest** outside town offers picnicking, hiking, and camping.

Continue on Route 100A to Plymouth, where, in 1872, Calvin Coolidge was born. You can visit the **Coolidge Birthplace**, then head to the **Coolidge Homestead**, where the president was sworn in. When President Harding died early in the morning of August 3, 1923, the news was carried from Bridgewater to the homestead by the telephone operator's husband—the Coolidges didn't have a phone! Well, they may not have had a phone, but they did have a notary public handy for the swearing in—Colonel John Coolidge, the vice president's father. Someone later asked the colonel how he knew he could administer the oath of office

Woodstock Chamber
of Commerce
4 Central Street
Woodstock
457-3555

Bridgewater

Calvin Coolidge State
Forest
Route 100A
Bridgewater Corners
672-3612

Bridgewater Corners

Plymouth

Coolidge Birthplace
and Homestead
Route 100A
Plymouth
672-3402

to his own son. His reply: "I didn't know that I couldn't."

The former president's son, John Coolidge, still lives in town. He runs **Plymouth Cheese** (672-3650), a cheese factory where everything is made by hand. Stop in to watch or buy.

Sherburne Center

Killington Ski Area
Killington Road
Sherburne Center
422-3333

About a mile west of Plymouth, pick up Route 100 north, which rejoins Route 4 at West Bridgewater. This stretch of road takes you into the **Killington Ski Area**. You can ride a gondola to the top of **Killington Peak**—a 4,241-foot ride, straight up—or drive a little farther up Route 4 to the 5-mile access road to the largest ski village in the East.

The skiing here is wonderful, but there's plenty to do even when the slopes are bare. Come in summer for riding or tennis or the **Adventure-Wilderness Trail Camp** (422-3333), a backpacking trip for adults and teenagers. The **Killington Playhouse** (422-3333), based at Ram's Head Lodge, schedules performances from June through Labor Day.

There are several shops along Route 4 near the junction of Route 100. Our favorites: the **Ski Shack** (775-2821) for outdoor clothing and equipment at discount prices; **Greenbrier** (775-1575) and **Gazebo** (775-4766) for gifts; and **Bill's Country Store** (773-9313) for all kinds of goodies.

And of course there's hiking. Try the trail over Deer Leap Mountain, which begins at Long Trail Lodge on Route 4, at the top of Sherburne Pass. You start out on a section of the mountain with fine views, and rejoin the Long Trail; then climb steeply to the south peak.

A word of caution: Don't head out on a trail with a guidebook as your only source of information. All hikers, regardless of their experience, need good topographic maps of the area they're exploring. **U.S. Geological Survey** maps are available at most bookstores and stationery shops.

VERMONT

MOUNT MONROE

On the Appalachian Trail, the view from Mount Monroe toward the Lakes of the Clouds Hut.

FRANCONIA NOTCH STATE PARK

The view from the aerial tram.

WEST ARLINGTON

The covered bridge on Batten Kill. Vermont has more covered bridges than all the other New England states combined.

Or you can write directly for them. The **National Survey** in Chester, Vermont, is another source of good maps.

The **Bucklin Trail** to Killington Peak begins at Brewers Corners on the west face of the mountain, and ascends through some old flat logging roads, then some steeper rocks. It crosses Brewers Brook several times, winds in and out of Calvin Coolidge State Forest, then joins the Long Trail until it bears right, up to the peak. On a clear day you can see the Green Mountains stretching north from nearby Pico Peak to distant Mount Mansfield; Glastenbury Mountain to the south; the Presidential Range to the east; and, the Taconic Mountains and the Adirondacks to the west. To reach the trail, follow Route 4 to Mendon, and turn left on Wheelerville Road. About 4 miles up you'll see a parking lot and the blue-blazed signs marking the path.

The **Long Trail** is a 263-mile footpath that stretches from Williamstown, Massachusetts, to the Canadian border near North Troy, Vermont. James Taylor, headmaster of Vermont Academy, came up with the idea for the trail in 1909. He organized a group of volunteers to clear a path linking the northern and southern peaks of the Green Mountains. His volunteers carried their equipment in pack baskets, clearing and building shelters as they went northward – a project that took twenty-two years.

Today the trail is maintained by the **Green Mountain Club** (page xvii), which awards end-to-end emblems to those who walk the trail completely. (Over twelve hundred have been presented.) There are sixty-five shelters along the way, each no more than a day's hike apart. The north end is marked by a marble monument, one side reading "United States"; the other, "Canada."

Stowe

From Sherburne Center continue north on Route 100, through Pittsfield (a typical Vermont town, with village green and bandstand) and Hancock (named for the patriot). You're going through beautiful mountain country, past major ski areas (Sugarbush, Mad River Glen), to Stowe.

In Stowe there is loads to do: You can discover the spectacular beauty of **Smugglers Notch**, ride the **Mount Mansfield Gondola**, try the **Alpine Slide**, or ski, ride, play tennis, hike, golf, bike, fish, or swim. For information contact the **Stowe Area Association**. The **Green Mountain Club** (page xvii) and the **University of Vermont Outing Club**, who maintain the area's trails, are your best sources for hiking information.

Mount Mansfield, at 4,393 feet the highest mountain in the state, towers over the countryside. There are several stories that explain the mountain's strikingly human look. One tells of a man named Mansfield who fell off the Camel's Hump when the camel knelt to drink, and now lies face up, a mountain profile. Another legend says the profile is the face of Mishawaka, the son of an Indian chief, who crawled up to the peak to prove his courage, and died there.

Did you love the *Sound of Music*? If you did, you have to stop at the **Trapp Family Lodge**. The building is new—the original was destroyed by fire in 1981—but the family's spirit is still here. Take a room, or just a meal, and hear about their dramatic flight from war-torn Europe. The inn, nestled in mountains not unlike those in the Trapps' native Austria, is off Route 108. Call 253-8511 for information.

Stowe boasts several fine restaurants: **Stowehof** (253-8500) on Edson Hill, the **Yodler** (253-7308) and **Topnotch at Stowe** (253-8585) on Mountain Road, and **Restaurant Swisspot** (253-4622) on Main Street. All are great, but the venison at the Topnotch is a special favorite.

From Stowe take Route 108 (it's closed during the winter) for a spectacular ride through mountain

Stowe Area
  Association
Box 1230
Stowe
253-7321

University of Vermont
  Outing Club
University of Vermont
Burlington
656-3439

Burlington

Lake Champlain
  Regional Chamber
  of Commerce
209 Battery Street
Burlington
863-3489

Richard Robbins
Box 195
Vergennes
759-2411

Lake Champlain
  Transportation
King Street Dock
Burlington
864-9804

North Beach
Institute Road
Burlington
862-0842

Ethan Allen Park
North Avenue
Burlington

passes, by nine ski areas, to Jeffersonville. Then follow Route 15 down through Cambridge, Essex Junction, and Winooski, to I-89 into Burlington. Burlington, the largest city in Vermont, is a college town with a busy industrial area. Contact the chamber of commerce or stop at one of the information booths — there are three: at Main Street and South Willard, at Burlington Square, and at University Mall — for area news.

Burlington sits on Lake Champlain. From the waterfront you can take a cruise on the **Richard Robbins**, a 58-foot schooner built in 1902. Or you can take an hour-long ferry ride from the King Street Dock to Port Kent, New York.

On the water, keep your eyes open. There are sea monsters in the lake! Way back in 1609, Champlain wrote about a creature he spotted that was 20 feet long and as thick as a barrel, with a head like a horse and a body like a serpent. In the 1870s "Champ" was sighted by hundreds of steamer passengers. And in 1977 a woman took a photograph of something that looks an awful lot like "Champ." So watch closely!

Battery Park, on the waterfront at Pearl Street, was the scene of defensive shooting at British warships during the War of 1812. Sit back and enjoy the fine view of the Adirondacks across the lake. For swimming, picnicking, and camping, drive out North Avenue, to Institute Road, to **North Beach**. Continue on North Avenue to **Ethan Allen Park**, part of the farm once owned by the fascinating leader of the Green Mountain Boys.

Legends about Ethan Allen mix fact and fabrication. Once when he was walking through the woods a huge bobcat sprang and landed on his back; Allen reached behind and wrenched the cat onto the ground, then strangled it. When he arrived where he was going he explained his delay by blaming the "Yorkers" for training and setting varmints against him. Another time he was said to have killed a bear by jamming his powderhorn down the animal's throat! Even a rattlesnake didn't get the better of Ethan Allen. One night after too much elbow-bending, Allen and a friend stopped for a nap. A rattler coiled on Allen's chest, struck him several times, then rolled off, staggered, burped, and fell asleep. The next morning Allen complained about the pesky "mosquito" that kept biting him during the night.

Allen's drinking caused him some trouble at home too. His wife, Fanny, finally worked out her own method for checking his sobriety. She pounded a nail high on the wall of their bedroom. In the morning, if she found his watch hanging on the nail, she knew he'd come home sober; if not, he was in for it. It didn't take Allen long to put one and one together. And after a while, no matter how much he was weaving about, he'd get that watch hooked on before he went to sleep.

When news leaked out of an impending real estate auction, Allen, his brother Ira, and the sheriff announced the sale would be delayed until one the next day. And it was—until one in the morning! Just after midnight the three men met. And at the stroke of one Ethan bid a dollar for the house, barn, and hundred acres; Ira bid two dollars; and the gavel fell.

Back in town, stop at the **Robert Hull Fleming Museum**. There's an Egyptian mummy, a Kang Hsi vase, and seventeenth-century Persian miniatures, and galleries and lots of exhibits.

If you're here between June and October, enjoy the **Mozart Festival**. Write ahead or call for a schedule of concerts. And every summer the **Champlain Shakespeare Festival** takes place at the **Royall Tyler Theater** on the University of Vermont campus.

Burlington offers gastronomic delights for everyone—in all tastes and price ranges. For an inexpensive meal stop at the **Fresh Ground Coffeehouse** (864-9663) on Church Street. On Wednesday nights the Burlington Folk Club meets

Robert Hull Fleming
   Museum
Colchester Avenue
Burlington
656-2090

Mozart Festival
Box 512
Burlington
862-7352

Champlain
   Shakespeare
   Festival
University of Vermont
Burlington
656-2094

there, and the songfest is open to all (bring your own instrument and voice). There are lots of choices on the blackboard menu: pocket sandwiches, quiches, Italian dishes, salads, coffees, and teas. The **Ice House** (862-9330) on Battery Street, right on the lake, is a pleasant place to spend some time. It features an oyster bar, creative salads, daily seafood specials, and a superb Sunday brunch. Like sandwiches? Try one at **Carbur's Restaurant** (862-4106) on Saint Paul Street. Vermont's largest sandwich menu offers over a hundred unbelievable concoctions, among them the Flashback, the Swinger Club, the Tricky Dick, the Oregon Plan, and the Pyramid Maul. If you can finish the Queen City Special, you've got quite an appetite! At **Ben & Jerry's Ice Cream** (862-9620) on Cherry Street, you get, not only terrific ice cream, but also your choice of homemade soups, crepes, salads, sandwiches, cappuccino, and espresso.

Goodies to go? Stop at the **Bagel Factory** (655-2660) for treats to take with you to the hinterland. On Saturdays, **Farmer's Market**, at the corner of Bank and Pine streets, has great fresh produce. And there's the **Cheese Outlet** (863-3968) on Pine Street for cheddars and delicious cheesecake.

Grand Isle

Department of Forests
and Parks
Montpelier
828-3375

From the city take I-89 north to Route 2; then follow the signs across the bridge to Grand Isle. This quiet island is a wonderful place to relax. Three parks—**Grand Isle State Park**, **Knight Point State Park**, and **North Hero State Park**—offer swimming, boating, and camping. Contact the **Department of Forests and Parks** for information about them.

Rent a boat and set off for **Valcour Island**, on the west side of the lake between Port Kent and Plattsburgh. The first major naval battle of the Revolutionary War was fought here on October 11, 1776.

In September of that year General Benedict Arnold assembled his naval forces between Valcour Island and the New York mainland. His fleet included the sloop *Enterprise*, the schooners *Royal Savage* and *Revenge*, and a number of smaller vessels. Captain Thomas Pringle led the British fleet—the schooners *Maria* and *Carleton*, and several dozen smaller ships. On the first day the British held the advantage, then tried to maintain a line south of the island to hold the Americans in place. But, in dense fog that night the Americans sailed north around the island, then south all the way to Crown Point (16 miles north of Ticonderoga). Eventually the British destroyed the American fleet, but General Arnold and his men escaped to Fort Ticonderoga. This battle upset British plans to capture the fort in 1776; instead they withdrew to Canada. In the meantime the Americans were able to strengthen their forces, and were victorious at Saratoga in 1777, the turning point in the war.

Today the island's 950 acres are uninhabited, preserved in their natural state. For birdwatchers there's a large rookery for great blue herons in the southeast corner; for hikers and campers there are 7 miles of trails and camping sites scattered around the island. For information, contact the New York State Environmental Conservation Department (518-474-2121).

Stop at **Allenholm Farm** (372-6611) in South Hero for apples (the island abounds with orchards), cheeses, jellies, and gifts. Driving along Route 2 you'll pass the **Hyde Log Cabin**, which is maintained by the historical society. It was built in 1783, the oldest log cabin in the country.

When you're through exploring, you can follow Route 2 through North Hero and Alburg Center to Route 78 to Swanton, to Route 36 along the east shore of the lake, back to Burlington. Or, if time's a problem, retrace your steps on Route 2 and I-89 into the city.

Shelburne

Shelburne Museum
Route 7
Shelburne
985-3346

From Burlington take Route 7 south to Shelburne. Here you'll find the **Shelburne Museum**, with a remarkably extensive and varied collection of Americana. The thirty-five buildings, spread out on 45 acres of land, house collections of quilts, textiles, tools, glass, ceramics, scrimshaw, furniture, dolls, carriages, and wagons. There are seven period homes, a general store, a blacksmith shop, a schoolhouse, a church, a livery stable, a smokehouse, the 220-foot sidewheeler SS *Ticonderoga*, a steam train, a railroad car, and galleries. Wear comfortable shoes (there is a shuttle bus for the foot-weary), and plan to spend the day.

Another one of John Freiden's bike tours begins in Shelburne. The route takes you through 18 miles of flat country against a backdrop of mountains. Start at the blinker on Route 7, heading south along Mount Philo Road. (Stop at **Harrington's** (985-2000), and the **Shelburne Country Store**, (985-3657), both near the intersection, for provisions.) Continue south on Mount Philo to Hinesburg Road, to Route 116, where you turn north toward Richmond. At the high school, turn left. When you come to a 90-degree angle in the road, go to the right; then turn left onto Irish Hill Road at the stop sign. This takes you back to Mount Philo Road (turn right), and back to Shelburne.

Middlebury

Vermont State Craft Center
Frog Hollow Lane
Middlebury
388-3177

Morgan Horse Farm
Weybridge Road
Middlebury
388-2011

Continue south on Route 7 to Middlebury, the home of **Middlebury College**. The lovely old Georgian and nineteenth-century buildings make this "college on the hill" just what a New England college should be.

One of our favorite stops is the **Vermont State Craft Center**, just off Main Street. Here you'll find crafts exhibitions, classes, and wonderful collections of wooden toys, stained glass, jewelry, pottery, pewter, and more—all for the buying.

To reach the **Morgan Horse Farm**, which is managed by the University of Vermont, head out Route 125 west to Route 23, and follow the signs. There's an audiovisual presentation about the Morgan horse and the farm, and a tour of the stables.

Continue south on Route 7. About 4 miles beyond Middlebury turn left on Route 125, to Ripton. Robert Frost lived here from 1939 until he died, in 1963. His home, the **Homer Noble Farm**, is 2 miles east of the town. You can visit the house and the cabin behind it, where Frost worked. Through the years, the poet became involved in the Breadloaf Writer's Conference at Middlebury College's summer campus, a few miles farther along Route 125. The **Robert Frost Interpretive Trail** begins at the farm and ends at the Breadloaf campus. You can read seven of his poems on plaques along the way.

Head back to Route 7, and follow it south into Pittsford. Here maple syrup aficionados will enjoy the **New England Maple Museum**. The museum houses a collection of antique sugaring equipment and a wall of panel displays that depict the development of the industry. There's also a ten-minute slide show about modern production methods. When you're through looking, step into the tasting area for a spoonful of fresh syrup.

At Pittsford Mills turn off Route 7 to Proctor, the center of another local industry—marble. Head for the **Marble Exhibit** on the grounds of the Vermont Marble Company, a couple of miles north of town. What's here? Samples of marble from all over the world, a view of the massive factory, a look at a sculptor at work, and movies that explain the quarrying process.

Between the Taconic Mountains and the Green Mountains, widening into Lake Champlain, lies the Champlain Valley. You can see marble in the rock all along the valley, where heat and pressure

Ripton

Homer Noble Farm
Route 125
Ripton

Pittsford

New England Maple
  Museum
Route 7
Pittsford
483-9414

Proctor

Marble Exhibit
Route 3
Proctor
459-3311

have combined with limestone. Vermont is one of the largest producers of marble in the nation. The best commercial marble in the state lies between Dorset and Brandon, and many of the quarries in the area—including the one in Proctor—are open for visits.

The town of Proctor was named for Colonel Redford Proctor, a descendant of Captain Leonard Proctor, who settled in Cavendish, Vermont, in 1780. Captain Proctor had a feud going with Salmon Dutton over Dutton's "turnpike," a toll road Proctor didn't see the need for. (In fact he built himself a "shunpike" through the same area—just to avoid paying Dutton's toll!) The family feud lasted seventy-five years, until Redford laid it to rest by marrying Emily Dutton in 1858.

Wilson Castle
West Proctor Road
Proctor
773-3284

From the town take West Proctor Road a mile south to **Wilson Castle**. The thirty-two-room nineteenth-century mansion sits on 115 acres. In the house are stained-glass windows, furnishings from Europe and the Orient, and an art gallery.

Rutland

From Proctor head down Route 3 to Route 4 east, into Rutland. The second largest city in Vermont was chartered in 1761 by Governor Benning Wentworth of New Hampshire. In the 1770s Rutland prospered as a frontier town, with both a gristmill and a sawmill. Later it, and the area, became famous for its superb marble. The New York Public Library, the John F. Kennedy Memorial, and the Supreme Court Building were all built from marble quarried here.

In town stop for lunch on Center Street at the **Back Home Cafe** (775-2104). The quiches, omelettes, salads, and homemade desserts are all delicious.

There are lots of factory outlet stores in the Rutland area. **Dunhams Footwear** (773-2796) and **Dexter Footwear** (775-4370) are on Route 4; **Hathaway Shirts** (775-7639), the **Way Station**

(773-6838), and the **Bass Shoe Outlet** (775-5822) on Route 7. Bring your checkbook, and enjoy!

From Rutland follow Route 7 to Route 103, into Ludlow. **Okemo Mountain**, on your way into town, offers skiing in winter and road rallies in summer. You can drive up to the top. In Ludlow, stop at the **Daken Mills Outlet** (228-7061) on Route 103 for sweaters, blouses, slacks, and ski clothes.

Ludlow

From Ludlow follow Route 100 west to Weston, a charming village slightly off the main line. The **Farrar-Mansur House**, built in 1797, is just off the common. Once a tavern, it's now a museum. Nearby the **Weston Playhouse** (824-5288) offers summer theater.

There are several shops in town. Our favorites: the **Vermont Country Store** (824-3184), the **Weston Village Store** (824-5477), and the **Weston Bowl Mill** (824-6219), where you'll find a large selection of wooden items and bins full of seconds. Plan a stop on Route 11, on your way out of town, at **The Barn** (824-3737) for London Fog coats.

Weston

From Weston head south on Route 100 to Londonderry, where you turn right on Route 11, to Manchester. Pick up Route 7 and follow it into Manchester Center.

The old town on the hill is an impressive collection of stately colonial homes. Mary Todd Lincoln and her son were visitors here, and Robert came back to stay until he died, in 1926. You can visit his home, **Hildene**, which was occupied by direct descendants of the family until 1975. The furnishings are original, and everywhere are memorabilia of the Lincoln family.

The Manchester area is filled with opportunities for outdoor activities: hiking, swimming, boating, and fishing. Fishermen everywhere know the town because the **Orvis Company** (362-3434)

Manchester

Hildene
Route 7
Manchester
362-1788

is here. You can visit the famous producer of fishing equipment at the plant on Route 7 between Manchester and Manchester Center.

Spring is really on the way when the canoes start appearing on the Batten Kill. The river flows south through the Vermont Valley, between the Green Mountains and Mount Equinox. From the town square in Manchester, follow Union Street east about three quarters of a mile to the Union Street Bridge—your boarding area. Oh, you may receive some glares from fishermen and leave a little paint on the rocks, but this river, with its very mild white water, is a joy to run. Where to stop? There's a campground north of Arlington, and another near Shushan, New York—both good spots to end your trip.

Don't leave town without stopping at the **Jelly Mill** (362-3494) on Route 7. There are three floors filled with gifts of every description. When you've shopped to your heart's content, treat your stomach to quiche, soup, salad, or a crepe upstairs in the **Buttery**. The **Reluctant Panther Inn** (362-2568), in Manchester Village, is another great place for a meal. One of our breakfast favorites here is the Panther Blossom—half orange juice, half cranberry juice—a great eye-opener.

East Dorset

Emerald Lake State Park
Route 7
East Dorset
362-1655

From Manchester take Route 7 north to East Dorset. There's a fine area for hiking near **Emerald Lake State Park**. Instead of going into the park, bear right at the sign for **Natural Bridge**. Leave your car in the parking lot. The climb is steep, leading up to a deep gorge spanned at the top by a 2-foot-wide natural bridge that's almost as thick.

Dorset and East Rupert

From Manchester take Route 30 north to Dorset. This charming village, with well-kept colonial houses, was the site of the first marble quarry in the country. The **Dorset Playhouse** (867-5777) is an established theater of professional caliber. Call for a schedule of performances. The

VERMONT

A Civil War soldier stands watch at the Windham County Courthouse.

NEWFANE

The old steamer Ticonderoga, *one of the many exhibits at the Shelburne Museum on the banks of Lake Champlain.*

SHELBURNE

First Congregational Church and cemetery where poet, Robert Frost, is buried.

BENNINGTON

E·183

Dorset Inn (867-5500) is just what you think of when you think of an inn in Vermont. Stay for the night, or just a meal.

Merck Forest
Route 315
East Rupert
394-7836

Continue on Route 20 into East Rupert; then take Route 15 for 2½ miles to the sign for **Merck Forest**. This 2,600-acre forest, a treasure for hikers, was given to the town by George W. Merck in 1950. There is a year-round program of reforestation and logging, and signs at seven stations along the main trail describe the wildlife in the area. Before you start, register at the information booth and pick up a pamphlet. After Station 3, you come to a barn, the center of the educational program. There are a number of trails to follow, including the steep trail to Mount Antone, and there are nine overnight shelters that can be used with a permit. The forest is open all year, and offers one of the finest cross-country ski terrains in Vermont.

Sunderland

Follow Route 7 south about 5 miles from Manchester, to Sunderland. Watch for the entrance to **Skyline Drive**, a steep narrow toll road to the top of **Mount Equinox**. The view from the 3,835-foot peak includes the spine of the Green Mountains, the backbone of Vermont and New York.

Townshend

From Manchester head southeast on Route 30 to Jamaica, where the white water canoe and kayak championships are held each spring, and on to Townshend. Here you'll find the longest covered bridge in Vermont — **Scott Bridge** — spanning West River. It was built in 1870, and extends 276 feet. In town the **Congregational Church** is the archetypical New England church. It was built in 1790, and it is beautiful. It's also a favorite of jigsaw puzzle manufacturers — so you may already be familiar with it.

Newfane

Newfane, 4 miles south of Townshend on Route 30, is one of the loveliest towns in the state.

The **Windham County Court House**, a Greek revival structure, was built in 1825.

Stop for a meal at the **Newfane Inn** (365-4427), right on Route 30. The inn's lovely (it was built in 1787), and so's the food. Then walk across the street to the **Newfane Country Store** (365-7916). Its four rooms are filled with kitchen accessories, foods (the bread is delicious), quilts, and all kinds of country gifts. If you're looking for older treasures, come on a Sunday between May and October for the **Newfane Flea Market**.

Follow Route 30 into Brattleboro. The site of the first settlement in Vermont, in 1724 at Fort Dummer, was once home to Rudyard Kipling. In 1892 the author married Caroline Starr Balestier of Brattleboro. On her family's estate they built **Naulahka**, a home that Kipling described as a ship with the propeller (furnace) and kitchen at the stern, his study and a piazza at the bow. It was here he wrote *The Jungle Book*, *The Seven Seas*, and *Captains Courageous*. During a family quarrel over land rights, Beatty Balestier, Kipling's brother-in-law, made threats on his life. Balestier was arrested, and Kipling and his family moved to England. Today you can see Naulahka from a distance, but it is not open to the public.

Hungry? Stop for a meal at the **Country Kitchen Restaurant** (257-0338) about 3 miles west of town on Route 9. Or try **Jolly Butcher's Tavern** (254-6043) nearby.

Brattleboro

Naulahka
19 Terrace Street
Brattleboro

Monadnock State Park in Jaffrey, New Hampshire, isn't far from Brattleboro. Take Route 9 east to Keene, to Route 124; then watch for signs to the park. Stop at the Ecocenter for information about hiking trails—there are dozens of them. (Although Monadnock is not a high mountain by New Hampshire standards, its top is above the tree line, which makes the climb worthwhile.) Or bring

Jaffrey and Peterborough

Monadnock State
  Park
Route 124
Jaffrey
532-8862

your bike to tour the area's rolling hills and quiet back roads.

From the park continue on Route 124 to Jaffrey; then take Route 202 to Peterborough. This lovely town is home to the **McDowell Colony**, a retreat for musicians, painters, and writers. (Thornton Wilder wrote *Our Town* here.)

In town stop at **Eastern Mountain Sports** (924-9212), one of our favorite places for outdoor equipment. Then have a bite at the **Folkway Restaurant** (924-7484) on Grove Street. We hear the food's terrific.

Wilmington

Molly Stark State Park
Route 9
Wilmington
464-5460

Head back to Brattleboro on Route 101, through Dublin, one of the loveliest towns in New Hampshire. Then pick up Route 9 again at Keene. For another interesting side trip drive west on Route 9 from Brattleboro to signs for **Molly Stark State Park**. Molly Stark was the wife of General John Stark, who was called out of retirement during the Revolution to lead a thousand men across Vermont, to protect munitions stored in Bennington. Stark wrote his wife:

> Dear Molly: In less than a week, the British forces will be ours. Send every man from the farm that will come and let the haying go.

She did as he asked and more; she sent two hundred townspeople along too. As he went into battle, General Stark said, "There are the Redcoats, and they are ours, or this night Molly Stark sleeps a widow." But she didn't. He won the battle and brought home a brass cannon, one of six taken from the British. (It's still on display in New Boston, New Hampshire, and is fired every Fourth of July.)

Bennington

Continue west on Route 9 to Bennington, the home of Ethan Allen's Green Mountain Boys — the Bennington Mob. On August 16, 1777, the Battle of Bennington was fought nearby (the actual battle site is near Walloomaac, New York). That battle marked a turning point in the war, weakening the British and forcing them to retreat.

The **Bennington Battle Monument**, a 300-foot-high obelisk built in 1891, commemorates General Stark's victory. Take an elevator to the top for a view of the countryside. Farther up Monument Avenue, you can walk around Old Bennington, and enjoy the lovely colonial homes, the green, and **Old First Church**.

About a mile beyond the center is the **Bennington Museum** and its collections of Bennington pottery, blown and pressed glass, paintings by Grandma Moses, costumes, and furnishings.

And don't leave without stopping at **Bennington Pottery** (447-7531) on County Street. You'll find a lovely gift shop, good buys on seconds, and, next door, a wonderful cafe for lunch.

Follow Route 67A out of Bennington to North Bennington, where you'll find the **Parke-McCullough House**. The Victorian mansion is furnished with period pieces. During the year, craft fairs, art exhibits, square dances, and other events are held here.

From Bennington head south on Route 7 into our last itinerary, which starts in Williamstown. As the Green Mountains fade into the Berkshires, you're entering the rich historic world of western Massachusetts and Connecticut.

Bennington Battle Monument
Monument Road
Bennington
447-0550

Bennington Museum
Route 9
Bennington
447-1571

North Bennington

Parke-McCullough House
West and Park Streets
North Bennington
442-2747

ITINERARY F

OLD STURBRIDGE VILLAGE

ITINERARY F

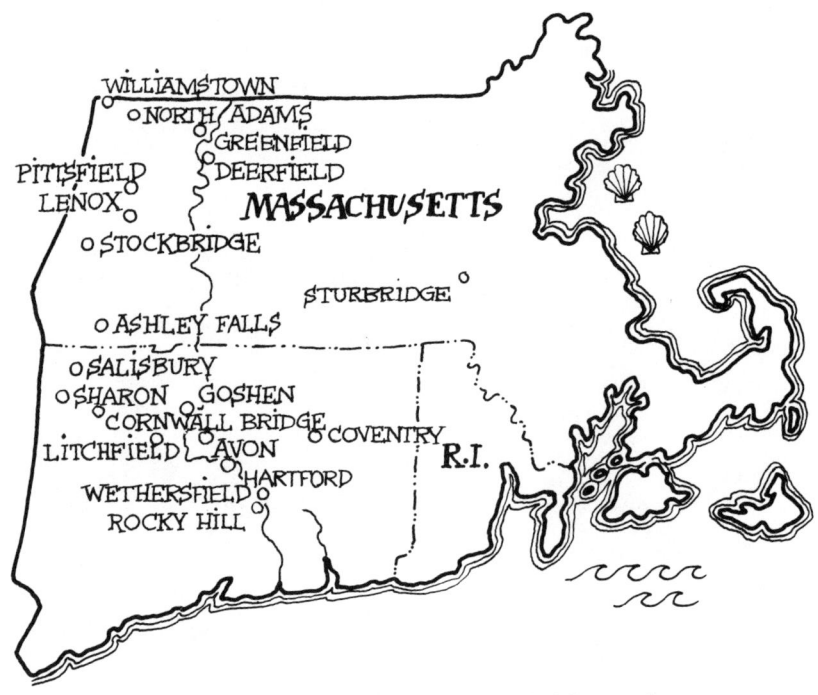

(Suggested Time: 7 days; 225 miles/360 kilometers)

The Western Circuit

Williamstown	F·193
North Adams	F·194
Deerfield	F·194
Pittsfield	F·195
Lenox	F·198
Stockbridge	F·198
Mount Washington	F·199
Ashley Falls	F·200
Salisbury	F·201
Sharon	F·201
Cornwall Bridge	F·202
West Cornwall	F·203
Cornwall	F·204
Goshen	F·204
Litchfield	F·204
Canton	F·206
Avon	F·207
Farmington	F·207
West Hartford	F·209
Hartford	F·209
Sturbridge	F·215
Coventry	F·217
Wethersfield	F·218
Rocky Hill	F·218

The Pesky Sarpent

On Springfield mountain there did dwell,
    A comely youth I knew full well.

      Ri tu di nu, ri tu di na,
      Ri tu di nu, ri tu di na.

One Monday morning he did go,
    Down in the meadow for to mow.

He scarce had mowed half the field,
    When a Pesky Sarpent bit his heel.

He took his scythe and with a blow,
    He laid the Pesky Sarpent low.

He took the Sarpent in his hand,
    And straitway went to Molly Bland

Oh Molly, Molly, here you see,
    The Pesky Sarpent what bit me.

Now Molly had a ruby lip,
    With which the pizen she did sip.

But Molly had a rotten tooth,
    Which the pizen struck and kill'd 'em both.

The neighbors found that they were dead,
    So laid them both upon one bed.

And all their friends both far and near,
    Did cry and howl they were so dear.

Now all you maids a warning take,
    From Molly Bland and Tommy Blake.

And mind when you're in love don't pass,
    Too near to patches of high grass.

Massachusetts

The Berkshires—from Williamstown to Ashley Falls—are full of special pleasures. There are three major mountains to climb or simply enjoy from a distance; there are lakes and streams to fish and swim in. The towns and villages abound with historic homes, antique shops, and fairs. And the whole region is touched with a rich heritage of literature, drama, art, and music.

Williamstown

Williamstown—the home of **Williams College**—is one of the most beautiful college towns in the country. On the campus: **Thompson Memorial Chapel**, a modern Gothic building; **Chapin Library**, with a fine collection of rare books; **Hopkins Observatory**; and the **Williams College Museum of Art**.

When you've finished exploring the college grounds, head for the **Sterling and Francine Clark Art Institute**. This wonderful museum is the setting for paintings by Botticelli, Lorrain, Rembrandt, Gainsborough, Homer, Sargent, Renoir, Monet, Degas, Gauguin, and Picasso. Also here: magnificent collections of silver, and sculpture by Rodin.

Stop for a meal in **The Williams Inn** (458-9371), on the green. Call ahead for reservations.

The **Mohawk Trail** begins at Route 2 in Williamstown. The trail was first used by the Indians, a path from the villages of central Massachusetts to the Finger Lakes of New York. Later it was used by colonial troops marching to New York during the French and Indian Wars. Still later, settlers followed the trail in their covered wagons and stagecoaches.

The trail winds through several forests: **Greylock Mountain State Reservation** (south of Route

Sterling and Francine
  Clark Art Institute
South Street
Williamstown
458-8109

2), and **Savoy Mountain State Forest** and **Mohawk Trail State Forest** (both along Route 2). There's good hiking and camping here, and the views are spectacular.

Greenfield sits at the end of the trail, in **Pioneer Valley** — an area of tobacco fields, apple orchards, and lovely villages. The Connecticut River formed this rich agricultural region, and was the main source of transportation for its early settlers.

North Adams

Hoosac Community
  Resources
  Corporation
121 Union Street
North Adams
664-6382

From Williamstown follow Route 2 east to North Adams. The town was able to turn the loss of its industry to advantage. It's now an art and craft center. The **Hoosac Community Resources Corporation** was formed in a nineteenth-century mill by weavers, leather workers, potters, and glassblowers. You can tour the building and buy their products.

North Adams is the site of the only natural **marble bridge** in North America. It's located 1½ miles northeast of the town on Route 8. It was formed by water erosion, and sits over a 60-foot-deep chasm that winds through 475 feet of rock. (That rock is over 550 million years old.) Hawthorne described the bridge in his *American Notebooks*.

Deerfield

Continue out Route 2 to Greenfield. Then take Route 5 and 10 to Deerfield. The town was settled in 1669 by Samuel Hinsdell, a squatter who began farming the fertile soil. He was soon joined by other settlers, and within six years the population reached 125. The Pocumtuck Indians, who had used the land to raise corn, tobacco, and pumpkins, were enraged. They attacked the settlement, and in the Bloody Brook Massacre of 1675 killed or drove away all the white settlers. The town stood empty for seven years; but slowly people began to return, and by 1686 Deerfield had held its first town meeting.

MASSACHUSETTS

In 1704, during Queen Anne's War, the Indians attacked again. They burned more than half the village, took a hundred people for slaves, and killed the fifty who resisted. Peace finally came in 1735.

You can learn more about the town's history in **Historic Deerfield**, where the Flynt family has restored many original homes and buildings. Henry N. Flynt first came to Deerfield in 1936 (he was bringing his son to the academy). He liked the town, and bought an inn; then he bought one home, then another, and another, restoring each in turn. Over the next twenty-five years, Flynt and his wife oversaw the restoration and furnishing of twelve buildings, acquiring more than eight thousand antique pieces in the process.

Stop first at **Hall Tavern**, the visitors' center, for tickets and information. Then enjoy the houses — among them a print shop, a tavern, a silver shop, and **Allen House**, the Flynt's own home — spread along the street.

Historic Deerfield
Routes 5 and 10
Deerfield
773-8689

From North Adams follow Route 8 south to Pittsfield, the capital of the Berkshires. Contact the **Berkshire Vacation Bureau**, or stop at the booth in Park Square for local and regional information.

Herman Melville lived in Pittsfield between 1850 and 1863. He wrote Moby Dick at **Arrowhead**, in a study that faced the whalelike Greylock range. In the house are all kinds of Melville memorabilia — his spectacles, his books, genealogical charts of the family, portraits, photographs, even his daughter's toys.

More Melville lore? Visit the library, the **Berkshire Athenaeum**, to see the **Herman Melville Memorial Room**. Here you'll find the secretary from his New York apartment (on which he wrote *Billy Budd*), manuscripts, first editions of his books, and pictures from his home.

The **Berkshire Museum**, on South Street, has ethnological, geological, and zoological displays,

Pittsfield

Berkshire Vacation
 Bureau
20 Elm Street
Pittsfield
443-9186

Arrowhead
780 Holmes Road
Pittsfield
442-1793

Berkshire Athenaeum
1 Wendall Avenue
Pittsfield
442-1559

Berkshire Museum
39 South Street
Pittsfield
443-3171

**Hancock Shaker
  Village
Route 20
Pittsfield
443-0188**

in addition to its collection of paintings and sculpture.

Follow Route 20 west about 5 miles to **Hancock Shaker Village**, a restored Shaker settlement dating from 1790. Highlights: The 1826 **Round Stone Barn**, the five-story **Brick Dwelling** (the kitchen dates from 1830), craft shops, and the herb garden. Come in early August for the **Shaker Kitchen Festival**. You'll see cooking demonstrations and take part in a Shaker meal.

Every summer the Berkshires come alive with music, theater, and dance. For performance schedules, contact the Berkshire Vacation Bureau (page 195), or stop at an information booth. You'll find one in Williamstown (at 22 Front Street), North Adams (at 1 Main Street, 69 Main Street, or 121 Union Street), Pittsfield (at Park Square), Lenox (on Walker Street), Lee (in the park on Main Street), Stockbridge (on Main Street), and Great Barrington (at 362 Main Street).

If there's something you're anxious to see, don't wait for tickets. You can order in advance for these performances:

- **Berkshire Center for the Performing Arts**, Berkshire School Campus, Route 41, Sheffield, MA 01257, 413-229-8084.
- **Berkshire Theatre Festival**, Main Street, Stockbridge, MA 01262, 413-298-5576 (summer), 413-298-5536 (winter).
- **Jacob's Pillow Dance Festival**, Box 287, Lee, MA 01238, 413-243-0745.
- **Shakespeare & Company at the Mount**, Plunket Street, Lenox, MA 01240, 413-637-3353.
- **Tanglewood**, West Street, Lenox, MA 01240, 413-637-1940 (summer); Boston Symphony Orchestra, Symphony Hall, Boston, MA 02115, 617-266-1492 (winter).
- **Williamstown Theatre Festival**, Box 517, Williamstown, MA 01267, 413-458-8146.

MASSACHUSETTS

The Old Corner House, an 18th-century landmark, displays delightful original paintings of Norman Rockwell and revolving exhibits from the Stockbridge Public Library's fine historical collection.

STOCKBRIDGE

A crowd gathers on a summer's evening for an outdoor concert at the Berkshire Music Center.

TANGLEWOOD

Youngsters enjoy a discovery at the Roaring Brook Nature Center.

CANTON

Lenox

From Pittsfield follow Routes 20 and 7 into Lenox, once "America's Lake District." In the nineteenth century, literary figures gathered here, among them Edith Wharton, Henry Wadsworth Longfellow, Nathaniel Hawthorne, Herman Melville, and Henry Adams. Around the turn of the century several large mansions were built as summer homes. You can catch glimpses of them, and a few small castles, half hidden by trees and set behind long green lawns. Most are still owned privately.

The homes are beautiful, and the shopping in town is marvelous. But the real treasure in Lenox is **Tanglewood** – the summer home of the Boston Symphony Orchestra. The concerts featuring the BSO, the Boston Pops, and other noted musicians draw more than a quarter of a million people each summer. Join them in the Music Shed or bring a picnic supper and find a spot on the lawn. Both the setting and the music are magnificent.

Stockbridge

Continue south on Route 7 to Stockbridge. You may recognize the wide main street lined with classic New England homes – a setting Norman Rockwell used often in his paintings.

Another Rockwell favorite was the **Red Lion Inn** (298-5545). This large white building on Main Street looks like a New England inn should. You can wander around inside (there's a nice gift shop), then have a meal in the **Widow Bingham's Tavern** or on the patio ablaze with impatiens in the summer.

Old Corner House
Main Street
Stockbridge
298-3822

Naumkeag
Prospect Street
Stockbridge
298-3239

The **Old Corner House**, next door to the library, contains a permanent collection of Rockwell's paintings. Here you'll see the originals of the magazine covers, posters, and prints we all know. The guide who takes you through is eager to share background information and to point out the humor inherent in the artist's work.

Turn off Main Street onto Pine Street, to Shamrock Street, to Prospect. **Naumkeag** was once the estate of Joseph Choate, an ambassador to England in the late nineteenth century. The twenty-six-room Norman mansion, built by Stanford White in 1885, is filled with beautiful antiques. In the gardens are fountains, a sculpted topiary, and a Chinese pagoda.

Chesterwood was the summer estate of Daniel Chester French, who sculpted the *Seated Lincoln* in the Lincoln Memorial and the *Minuteman* at Old North Bridge. You can visit the mansion, the studio, and the nineteenth-century barn (now a gallery); walk along a nature trail; and enjoy the gardens and the views of Monument Mountain. The sculptor once said: "I live here six months of the year—in Heaven. The other six months I live, well—in New York." To get to French's heaven take Route 102 west to Route 183. Turn left, and follow the signs.

A few miles up Route 102, in West Stockbridge, is the **Old Yankee Marketplace**, a restored New England village filled with shops.

Chesterwood
Route 183
Stockbridge
298-3579

From Stockbridge follow Route 7 south through Great Barrington, to Route 41. Continue on Route 41 through South Egremont to Mount Washington. This small town—a population of fifty—is on a hill near the summit of **Mount Everett**, one of the highest peaks in the state. The area is beautiful; the scenery, spectacular.

There are several good hiking trails nearby. You can follow the **Elbow Trail**, which begins off Route 41, near the Berkshire School, to **Guilder Pond**, the highest natural body of water in Massachusetts. Another, steeper trail takes you to **Bash Bish Falls**, a 50-foot waterfall in **Mount Washington State Forest**. Turn right south of Smiley's Pond at the Mount Everett–Bash Bish Falls sign, and follow the road west to the foot of the mountain. (There's a longer but easier path off Route 22 in New York, from a parking lot below the falls.) Legend tells of an Indian maiden,

Mount Washington

Mount Washington
  State Forest
East Street
Mount Washington
528-0330

saddened when her husband took another wife, who jumped from the cliff here into the water. It seems she heard her mother (a witch who lived underneath the falls) calling to her. Her husband jumped in to save her, and died. His body was found, but the maiden lives on with her mother behind the falls. You can still see her profile in the pool on moonlit nights.

Wherever you're hiking, be sure to bring a bucket or pail along. You're in blueberry country!

Ashley Falls

Bartholomew's Cobble
Weatogue Road
Ashley Falls
229-8600

Colonel John Ashley House
Cooper Hill Road
Ashley Falls
229-8600

From Route 41 follow the road into Sheffield; then take Route 7A into Ashley Falls. Watch for the signs along Weatogue Road for **Bartholomew's Cobble**. *Bartholomew* is a George Bartholomew who lived here in the late nineteenth century; *cobble* is a local term for a rock outcropping. This particular outcropping—a gigantic natural rock garden—was formed by glaciers. It's filled with over five hundred species of wild flowers, forty species of ferns, and a hundred species of trees and shrubs. Stop at the museum on the hill for a map before you set out. If you come in late June you'll find special programs and walks on **Annual Cobble Day**.

In town stop at the **Colonel John Ashley House**. The house, dating from 1735, is the oldest in the Berkshires. The Sheffield Declaration of Independence was drafted here in 1773.

∽ Connecticut ∾

Connecticut's topography divides the state into three areas: the western highland, with its small mountains and hills; the central lowland, a long wide valley centered on the Connecticut River; and the eastern highland, along waves of gently rolling wooded hills running north and south.

The formation began in Precambrian times, about 620 million years ago, with a major shifting of the earth's crust. Two more shifts, during the Paleozoic era, 230 to 500 million years ago, created a fault along the eastern side of the lowland that produced mountains. These mountains and those in the western part of the state developed a basalt crust (you can still see a basalt ridge at Talcott Mountain, west of Hartford).

A later shift of the earth's crust tilted the land, sloping it from northwest to southeast, producing cliffs on one side and a gradual slope on the other. Streams and rivers, their velocity increased by the tilt, began to erode the plain of the central lowland. Glaciers carried soil from northern New England, depositing it in Connecticut's valleys; boulders, too, scraped along, scouring rocks and leaving scratches you can still see today. Centuries later the smaller rocks were used to build the stone walls that line the roads and farms of the area; the larger ones stand where they've stood for hundreds and thousands of years, mute remnants of a bygone age.

Salisbury

From Ashley Falls continue south on Route 7, to Route 44 west to Salisbury. This resort town in the hills was settled by the Dutch from New York State. Later, during the Revolutionary War, the town's furnaces produced cannon, cannonballs, muskets, swords, sabers, shot, and grenades. In front of the town hall, a triphammer that once pounded hot iron is a reminder of that past.

North of town, off Route 41, in **Mount Riga State Park**, you can see the **Mount Riga Furnace**. This furnace was shut down when a breakdown in the bellows cooled material in the furnace into one solid mass, a "salamander." A salamander wasn't uncommon, and could sometimes be removed by firing into the furnace with a small cannon, but the Mount Riga Furnace didn't have enough money to start up again.

Most mountain towns have their legends about local recluses, and Salisbury is no different. Near Mount Riga live the "Raggies"—a group of people who keep apart from society, intermarry, and live in poverty.

Sharon

From Salisbury follow Route 44 to Route 41 south to Sharon. Along the way, sports car enthusiasts may want to detour on Route 112 to Lime Rock, where **Lime Rock Raceway** sits in a

Lime Rock Raceway
Lime Rock Park
Lime Rock
435-2572

Gay-Hoyt House
Main Street
Sharon
364-5688

Sharon Audubon
 Center
Route 4
Sharon
364-5826

Cornwall Bridge

beautiful 350-acre setting. Even if you're not a racing aficionado, you may still want to make the trip. This is one of Paul Newman's favorite tracks!

Sharon was settled in 1739 on the plateau of the Taconic Mountains. Along Main Street and Route 41 you'll pass elegant estates and mansions, some from Revolutionary War days.

The **Clock Tower** and **Congregational Church** face the green, the site in August of the **Clothesline Art Show**, and busy all summer and fall with flea markets and antique fairs. The **Gay-Hoyt House** nearby is made of brick. Its fireplaces are angled into the end walls, a regional architectural characteristic.

The **Sharon Playhouse** (364-5909) on Route 343 offers summer theater and an art gallery sponsored by the local art foundation.

As you head east on Route 4, stop at the **Sharon Audubon Center**, an interpretive museum in the former home of Mrs. Clement R. Ford. On the grounds: 11 miles of self-guided trails, an herb garden, and a museum shop. Come in late July for the **Sharon Audubon Festival**.

From Sharon continue east on Route 4 to Cornwall Bridge. This tiny village boasts its own ghost town. Take Dudleytown Road through Dark Entry, to **Dudleytown**. The town, built on a plateau above the Housatonic River, was founded in 1747, and was populated until 1900. Today all that remains are parts of collapsed stone walls, foundations, and wells.

Life in Dudleytown wasn't easy. The mountains surrounding the village kept the sunlight out, so the land couldn't be farmed. Instead villagers depended on charcoal for their livelihoods.

Some local residents refuse to believe the town failed on its own. They talk about the Dudleytown Curse, and point to odd happenings and bizarre deaths as proof of it. The story of the curse seems to start with the Dudley brothers, early residents of the town, who were descended from Edward and John Dudley, the dukes of Northumberland who plotted against the monarchy during the fifteenth and sixteenth centuries.

During the 1800s, when charcoal was the town's main industry, the residents may well have been affected by heavy concentrations of carbon monoxide in the air, which could have caused brain damage. Certainly some inhabitants were insane; others feebleminded. One story tells about a man who caught mussels in Spectacle Pond, let them sit until they were rancid, then made them into a stew. He gave the stew to a family he was feuding with; and when they died, he hung himself. Others tell about dogs and horses that refused to enter the village, almost as though they sensed something terrifying in the air.

From Cornwall Bridge take Route 7 north to the **Housatonic Meadows State Park** — 450 acres of parkland for fishing, hiking, and camping.

At the junction of Route 7 and 128 in West Cornwall stands a one-lane covered bridge that won a national award for restoration in 1973. Originally designed by Ithiel Town in 1827, it is the longest of the four over the Housatonic.

How about a trip along the Housatonic? Bring your canoe, kayak, or raft. Spot one car at Housatonic Meadows State Park; then drive north on Route 7 west on Route 112 (past the track) to Dugway Road, and put in by the power plant in Falls Village. Plan to get here about eleven thirty; the plant lets water out between nine and ten every morning, and within an hour the river is usually full. The first 3 miles are flat; then you hit 2 miles of rocks, ripples, and rapids. Just before the bridge in West Cornwall you'll hear hissing and see white rapids. You can pull over and choose one of three courses under the bridge; or if the river is very high and fast, you can portage around. After that, the going is easy right to the state park.

Housatonic Meadows State Park
Route 7
Cornwall Bridge
672-6139

West Cornwall

Cornwall

Need more information? Contact **Riverrunning Expeditions** (824-5579) on Main Street in Falls Village or **Clarke Outdoors** (672-6365) on Route 7 in West Cornwall.

Follow the back roads from West Cornwall into Cornwall, a lovely town spread along the Housatonic.

Cathedral Pines, a forest of two-hundred-year-old pines, is a couple of miles from town. Head out Route 4 and, about a half mile beyond the junction of Route 128, turn left on Bolton Hill Road, then right on Jewell Street. At the next fork turn left, and watch for the white blazes that mark the Appalachian Trail. The trees here reach as high as 150 feet, some with diameters of over 3 feet.

Goshen

Mohawk State Forest
Route 4
Goshen
491-3620, 491-3572 (tower)

Continue on Route 4 toward Goshen, a farming village where the first commercial hard cheese in America was made. Several miles outside town you'll find the entrance to **Mohawk State Forest**. You can drive in 2½ miles to a wooden observation tower for a panoramic view around the compass. Park your car and walk to the tower. Then follow blue-blazed **Mattatuck Trail** to the ruins of a great stone tower. You can climb to the top—1,683 feet, straight up—for views of the Riga Plateau (Mounts Everett, Race, and Bear), the Catskills, Canaan Mountain, and Mount Tom. Then you follow the trail for 3¼ miles, or Mattatuck Road to Toumey Road, back to your car.

Litchfield

From Goshen follow Route 4 to Route 63 south, into Litchfield, one of the most beautiful towns in the state. It was settled in 1720 by Deacon John Buel of Lebanon, who felt the location on the hill offered protection from the Indians. That location, along natural routes from New York, Albany, Hartford, and Boston, later made the town a busy center of commerce.

The village today has not been restored; it's a living museum, maintained over time by its residents. You can see this care in the elegant white clapboard homes that line the green along North and South streets. Most are privately owned but open their doors in mid-July, on **Open House Day**.

Start your exploration of the town on the green, where you can pick up a map of a walking tour at the information center. Then head for the **Congregational Church**, perhaps the most photographed church in New England, which sits majestically nearby.

The **Litchfield Historical Society**, at one corner of the green, houses a fine collection of early American paintings, furniture, and decorative arts. Farther down South Street, the **Tapping Reeve House and Law School** is the site of America's first law school. In the house you'll find hand-stenciled walls in the front hall, a lovely paneled dining room, and fine period furnishings, many of which belong to the Reeve family. The school, 100 feet from the house, is a one-room building where, in 1784, legal education in this country began. Among its graduates: Aaron Burr, John C. Calhoun, and several early members of Congress.

Other landmarks in the area: the birthplaces of Ethan Allen and Harriet Beecher Stowe, and **Sheldon's Tavern**, where George Washington (who else?) slept when he came to town.

There's great shopping in Litchfield. Stop at **Davidson's Dress Shop** (567-8664) on West Street for Pendleton, Jantzen, Skyr, and Leon Levin—all at moderate prices. The **Wilderness Shop** (567-5905) on Route 202 features outdoor clothes, and camping and hiking equipment. **White Flower Farm** (567-9415) on Route 63 offers 3½ acres of exotic gardens and greenhouses, and tea on the terrace on Open House Day.

More? We have three favorites in nearby towns. **Woodbury Pewterers** (263-2668) in Woodbury

Litchfield Historical
  Society
East and South
  Streets
Litchfield
567-5862

Tapping Reeve House
  and Law School
South Street
Litchfield
567-8919

Sheldon's Tavern
North Street
Litchfield

offers discounts of 20 to 50 percent on factory seconds. Come for pewter bowls, candlesticks, coffee pots, mugs, tankards, and teapots. In Riverton stop on Route 20 at the **Hitchcock Chair Factory** (379-4826), where you'll find reproductions of original Hitchcock furniture — some at reduced prices. Also in Riverton on Route 20 is the **Seth Thomas Clock Shoppe** (379-1077), where the clocks are marked 35 to 40 percent less than retail.

White Memorial Conservation Center
Route 202
Litchfield
567-0857

Mount Tom State Park
Route 202
Litchfield
567-8870

The **White Memorial Conservation Center**, 2 miles west of town on Route 202, is the largest nature center in the state. On its 4,000 acres: trails, recreation areas, a museum, a natural history library and bookstore, an operating sawmill, observation towers, swimming facilities, and campgrounds. **Mount Tom State Park** is farther out Route 202. Take the 1½-mile trail to the tower — it's an easy one — for a view of the countryside.

The **Haight Vineyards and Winery** is on Chestnut Hill Road, off Route 118, a couple of miles east of town. The first Rieslings and Chardonnays were produced here in 1979 from 15 acres of grapes. Come May through October for tours and wine tasting. Call 567-4045 for information.

Canton

Roaring Brook Nature Center
Gracey Road
Canton
693-0263

From Litchfield follow Route 202 east to Canton, to visit the **Roaring Brook Nature Center**. You'll find interpretive displays with year-round nature exhibits, a store, a resource room, and 115 acres of woodland trails.

One of the trails — the **Tunxis Trail** — winds for almost 8 miles through Satan's Kingdom, a very steep gorge. It begins 2½ miles west of the junction of Routes 202 and 179. From the parking lot follow the blue-blazed signs along Pine Hill Road and Tipping Rock Ledge (where a glacial rock did in fact tip over) to Queen Mary Ledge and Rome Spare Outlook. Look for the sign that reads "Charcoal Kiln." It marks the spot where wood was cut, piled into a circle, covered with earth, and burned (with very little air) – all to produce charcoal. When you come to the end of the trail at Rome Spare Outlook, retrace your steps to Tipping Rock Ledge; then continue down to Satan's Kingdom Road, which leads back to Pine Hill.

From Canton follow Route 202 into Avon. Hikers will enjoy a day along the **Metacomet Trail**. From Routes 44 and 10, follow Route 44 a little bit over 2 miles to the sign for Reservoir 6. Park in the lot, and walk to the far end, bearing left on the dirt road, where you'll see blue-blazed signs marking the trail. The path leads to **Heublein Tower**, an ornate observation tower built in 1914. The view from the top on a clear day reaches as far as Mount Monadnock to the north, Long Island Sound to the south. Follow the trail along the other side of the reservoir on your way back.

Hungry? Stop for a meal at the **Avon Old Farms Inn** (677-2818) at the intersection of Routes 44 and 10. The Sunday brunch here is delicious. Then visit the **Farmington Valley Arts Center** in an historic stone building, once an explosives plant. Here you'll find artists' studios, a gallery, and a bookstore – and wonderful exhibitions and programs.

Avon

Farmington Valley
Arts Center
Avon Park North
Avon
678-1867

From Avon follow Route 10 south to Farmington, the scene in mid-May of the annual **Children's Services Horse Show and Country Fair**.

The **Farmington Museum** is in the **Stanley-Whitman House**, which was built in 1660. The Elizabethan and Jacobean architecture of the original has been fully restored, and the building is filled with seventeenth-century furnishings. Also here: displays of old manuscripts, glass, china, silver, and pewter.

The **Hill-Stead Museum** is in the elegant mansion designed by Stanford White for millionaire Alfred Pope. You'll see paintings by Manet, Monet,

Farmington

Farmington Museum
37 High Street
Farmington
677-9222

Hill-Stead Museum
671 Farmington
Avenue
Farmington
677-9064

Degas, Cassatt, and Whistler, among others, and a collection of Ming dynasty porcelains.

Love canoeing? Then you'll love the 9½-mile trip from Farmington to Weatogue on the lower Farmington River. This stretch is smooth, and there are no portages. Spot one car in Weatogue, at the end of the bridge along Route 185. (There's a large lot at the east end of the bridge a few yards down Nod Road.) Then head back to Route 4 in Farmington to start off. The trip takes you past tall maples, sycamores, and oaks, a couple of golf courses; then more woods. Look for kingfishers, sandpipers, orioles, woodchucks, and muskrats; you might even spot a deer, fox, or raccoon. On your right you'll see Talcott Mountain, Heublein Tower marking its summit. At the bend in the river toward the right, just as you come abreast of the tower, look for the cave at the northern end of the ridge. Legend has it that King Philip directed the burning of Simsbury from this spot in 1676.

Farther west, the upper Farmington River between Riverton and New Hartford is also popular (sometimes too popular—it gets crowded on nice days). You can take a 4½-mile trip, with some small rapids, from the Riverton picnic area west of the Route 20 bridge (across the highway from the Hitchcock Chair Factory), to the bridge on Route 318. Or go on another 5 miles, to the take-out above the Route 44 bridge.

Along the way: some rapids interspersed with flat stretches, islands, woods, and fast water, and several picnic areas and a campground. The general rule seems to be stick to the right side, which is clearer; on the left you'll find rocks. A stand of tall pines on the left bank signals one set of rapids; then, just after the river curves to the left, you'll see a stretch of boulders. The first bridge you come to is Route 318, the site for the first take-out. The second bridge is Route 219; where you'll have to dodge some rocks.

Don't go beyond the bridge at Route 44 unless you're a white-water expert; the heavy rapids in the gorge at Satan's Kingdom demand a rubber raft or inner tube. The Six D's Restaurant and River Run apartments, on the right, signal the take-out. Once you've landed, walk along the shore below the bridge to see what you've missed—the river cascading into the gorge between cliffs on both sides.

From Farmington follow Route 6 into West Hartford. The **Noah Webster House** is now a national historic landmark. When it was built in 1676, the farmhouse had just two rooms; a later addition turned the house into a saltbox. In the museum wing you can buy pewter and apothecary jars at the museum shop.

Don't miss the **Children's Museum**, where kids enjoy the hands-on aquarium, the life-size model of a 60-foot sperm whale, and the **Gengras Planetarium**.

Fort Good Hope was founded by Dutch fur traders from Nieuw Amsterdam in 1623. In 1635 settlers from Cambridge, Massachusetts, arrived with John Steel as their leader. They changed the Indian name for the area—Suckiag—to Newtowne. (It was named Hartford two years later in honor of Reverend Samuel Stone, who hailed from Hertford, England.) A year later Thomas Hooker led more settlers here from Cambridge, on a two-week journey. He bought the land from Sequassen, sachem of the Suckiaug Indians. This was the second time the land was bought: In 1633 the Pequot Indians had sold it for "one piece of duffell (a heavy woolen fabric) 27 ells long (an ell is an old Dutch unit of measurement), six axes, six kettles, eighteen knives, one sword blade, one pair of shears, some toys and a musket."

Settlers from Windsor, Wethersfield, and Hartford drew up a constitution in 1639. The eleven

West Hartford

Children's Museum
960 Trout Brook
 Drive
West Hartford
236-2961

Noah Webster House
227 South Main
 Street
West Hartford
521-5362

Hartford

articles in the Fundamental Orders of Connecticut later served as a model for the Constitution of the United States.

Early settlers made good use of the Connecticut River, their outlet to the sea. Their source of trade: furs, timber, fish, game, and tobacco. This busy trade created a new industry. The people who financed the ships, worried about possible wrecks, storms, and fire damage, began to set aside a portion of their profits to insure against possible losses. When shipping ended during the War of 1812, the insurance companies shifted their focus from marine insurance to fire insurance for homes and buildings. A disastrous fire in New York City in 1835 was a bonanza for the Hartford Fire Insurance Company. Claims in excess of $17 million forced its New York competitors into bankruptcy; the Hartford firm paid every one of its claims. Suddenly new clients wanted policies, and the boom was on. And it's still on. Hartford even today is dominated by insurance and banking companies that retain their reputation for reliability and profitability.

Mark Twain House
351 Farmington Avenue
Hartford
247-0998

As you enter Hartford from West Hartford, your first stop, and our favorite place in the city, is the **Mark Twain House**. The house—"part medieval fortress, part Mississippi riverboat, part cuckoo clock"—was described by Twain this way:

This is the house that Mark built,
   These are the bricks of various hue,
And shape and position, straight and askew,
   With the nooks and angles and gables too,
Which make up the house presented to view,
   The curious house that Mark built.

This is the sunny and snug retreat,
   At once both city and country seat,
Where he grinds out many a comical grist,
   The author, architect, humorist,
The auctioneer and dramatist,
   Who lives in the house that Mark built....

Samuel L. Clemens his maiden name;
    As a humorist not unknown to fame,
As author or architect all the same,
    At auction or drama always game,
An extravagant wag whom none can tame:
    He lives in the house that Mark built.

Here is the Innocent Abroad,
    The patron too of the lightning rod;
And here disports the Jumping Frog,
    Roughing it on his native log;
Tom Sawyer, with his graceless tricks,
    Amuses the horse-car lunatics;
And here is the grim historic sage,
    Who hurled in the facts of the Gilded Age,
In this curious house that Mark built.

And below is the alias autograph
    Over which he has given you many a laugh,
This author, architect, humorist,
    This auctioneer and dramatist,
Who still keeps grinding his comical grist
    In his cozy, sunny and snug retreat,
At once both city and country seat,
    Made up of bricks of various hue,
And shape and position, straight and askew,
    With its nooks and angles and gables too,
The curious house that Mark built.

The Victorian-Gothic house is definitely unusual. It sits on a knoll above Farmington Avenue, a large red and black brick structure with gables, porches, and chimneys. Samuel Langhorne Clemens built the house in 1874. Nostalgia for his days on the Mississippi riverboats later prompted him to add a section in the rear shaped like a wheelhouse, complete with nautical doors and an intercom. The servants' quarters were built on the front of the house, so that they could keep track of anyone passing by without running through the house—a plan Twain claimed saved wear on his rugs. The author's study, which was also known as the billiard room, was on the top floor of the house. He worked here all day at his desk, which faced the wall, not the street, using a pigeonhole system for storage—a system so confusing he actually lost the manuscript for *Huckleberry Finn*. There's a large billiard table in the middle of the room, and stenciled billiard balls, cues, and pipes on the ceiling. In the library there's a 12-foot carved mantelpiece that Twain bought in Scotland. It's decorated with carved flowers, fruits, baronial arms, and a bronze plate inscribed "The ornament of a house is the friends who frequent it." The house was decorated by Louis Tiffany and Company, and is filled with Oriental, Turkish, Indian, and American objects. Every one of the twenty rooms has something unusual or interesting about it. And the guides add flavor to your visit with their repertoire of stories about Twain.

Harriet Beecher Stowe House
Forest Street
Hartford
525-9317

The **Harriet Beecher Stowe House**, nearby, is decorated with her paintings, and some original furnishings, and is filled with the kinds of plants the author loved.

Nook Farm
77 Forest Street
Hartford
525-9317

Both Twain and Stowe houses are part of **Nook Farm**, a nineteenth-century writers' colony. Also here: the **Nook Farm Research Library** (twelve thousand volumes, including valuable manuscripts) and the **Nook Farm Museum Shop** (books and gifts).

Before you go to Hartford, write the Greater Hartford Convention and Tourist Bureau (One Civic Plaza, Hartford) for **The Walk**—a pamphlet that describes a walking tour of the city. Banners on lampposts mark tour highlights in the downtown area.

Hartford Civic Center
One Civic Center Plaza
Hartford
566-6588

Follow Farmington Avenue into downtown Hartford, where you'll find parking, shopping, movies, and restaurants at the **Hartford Civic Center**. This is the downtown sports center—the home of the **Aetna World Cup** tennis tournament (566-6000), the **New England Whalers** (728-3366), and, at times, the **Boston Celtics** (566-6000).

HARTFORD

The Library of the Mark Twain Memorial. Twain wrote many of his greatest works in Hartford.

HARTFORD

The Wadsworth Atheneum, founded in 1842 by Daniel Wadsworth, is the oldest civic art museum in the country with a collection of nearly 40,000 objects.

COVENTRY

The Nathan Hale Homestead (c. 1776).

THE WESTERN CIRCUIT

Old State House
800 Main Street
Hartford
522-6766

Leave your car and walk down Asylum Street to the **Old State House**, on Main Street. Charles Bulfinch designed the building. There's an information center on the first floor; legislative chambers, with original furnishings, on the second.

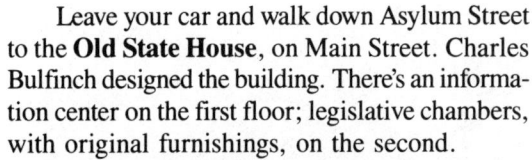

Around the corner, down State Street, you'll see **Constitution Plaza**, one of the first urban-renewal projects in New England, on your left; the **Phoenix Life Insurance Building**, the green curved-glass "hyperbloid" that's stirred up quite a controversy, on your right.

Travelers' Tower
One Tower Square
Hartford
277-0111

Turn down Prospect Street, and head for the **Travelers' Tower** and a bird's eye view of the city. The green light atop the 527-foot tower, the tallest in New England until Boston's Prudential Tower was completed in 1965, is a landmark for visitors and townspeople.

The tower sits on the site of the old Zachary Sanford Tavern. On October 31, 1687, Sir Edmund Andros, the Crown-appointed governor, came to a meeting here and demanded the return of a liberal charter that had been granted the Hartford Colony in 1662 by King Charles II. Before Andros had the charter in his hands, all of the candles "miraculously" blew out, and the charter was gone! One of the colonists, Joseph Wadsworth, took it and hid it in the trunk of an old tree. That tree was called the Charter Oak Tree until it blew down in 1856. Mark Twain once listed some of the objects that were said to have been made from its wood: "A walking stick, dog collar, needle case, three-legged stool, bootjack, dinner table, tenpin alley, toothpick, and enough Charter Oak to build a plank road from Hartford to Salt Lake City."

The arts are alive and well in Hartford. The Connecticut Opera Association, the Hartford Symphony, and the Hartford Ballet all perform at the Horace Bushnell Memorial Auditorium on Capitol Avenue. Also here: films, lectures, Broadway shows, and a rotating art exhibit in the Promenade Gallery.

And there's neighborhood theater and music in town too. Our favorite: the Hartford Stage Company in its new theater on Church Street.

More information? Call the **Hartford Artline** (247-4433).

At the **Wadsworth Atheneum**, right next to the tower, you'll find the Nutting collection of early American furniture, the J. P. Morgan collection of antique bronzes, European porcelains and paintings, ship models, a library of art reference books, a museum shop, and a restaurant. Come for a lecture, a tour, or a special program.

Farther down Main Street is one of the few surviving eighteenth-century houses in Hartford. The **Butler-McCook Homestead**, built in 1782, houses paintings, silver, dolls, toys, and a collection of Japanese armor. Part of the house was once a blacksmith's shop; that room later became Dr. Daniel Butler's kitchen.

Shopping in Hartford? Begin at the civic center, where you'll find **Eastern Mountain Sports** (278-7105), one of our favorites. Then try **Huntington's Book Store** (527-1835) on Asylum Street. **G. Fox** (249-9711) on Main Street, a fixture in town, is a department store carrying just about anything you'd want. And farther out, on Farmington Avenue, there's **Clapp and Treat** (236-0878) for all kinds of sporting goods.

You may wish to take an hour's side trip to see an elaborate recreation of our colonial past in Sturbridge. Leave Hartford headed on I-86 toward Boston. Get off the turnpike at the Sturbridge exit, and follow Route 20 to **Old Sturbridge Village**. Spread out in this recreated nineteenth-century New England town you'll find forty buildings and a farm. (There's a horse-drawn cart for the footweary.) Guides in period costumes demonstrate their skills at weaving, horseshoeing, shearing, printing, candlemaking, and more. Special programs? There are loads. Come for lectures,

Wadsworth Atheneum
600 Main Street
Hartford
278-2670

Butler-McCook
 Homestead
394 Main Street
Hartford
522-1806

Sturbridge

Old Sturbridge
 Village
Route 20
Sturbridge
347-3362

sunrise strolls, sleigh rides, family workshops, Militia Training Day, Fourth of July fireworks, even Thanksgiving dinner.

Before you leave the area, head into town for some shopping. The stores are lovely; their products, distinctive. Then stop at the **Publick House** (347-3313) for a traditional New England meal. We've been back many times, and love it! A special treat: the international dinners on Friday nights during the spring.

Coventry

Nathan Hale
  Homestead
South Street
Coventry
742-6917

Follow Route 84 to Route 44, to Route 31 into Coventry, about 26 miles east of Hartford. This seventeenth-century town is much like its counterpart in England, with woods, hills, lakes, and ponds.

Come mid-May to mid-October, when you can visit the **Nathan Hale Homestead**. Deacon Richard Hale, the patriot's father, built the home in 1776; and the family lived here until 1832. The ten rooms are furnished with family heirlooms and other antiques. The long table in the dining room was originally in a local tavern. It's said that when George Washington came through town, he had breakfast at this table.

During the Revolutionary War, Nathan Hale joined Knowlton's Rangers. When Washington needed information behind the British lines, Hale volunteered. He was caught and executed. His last words on the scaffold: "I regret that I have but one life to lose for my country."

Stop for lunch and more at **Capriland's Herb Farm** (742-7244) on Silver Street, off Route 44A. Your visit (reservations are a must) begins at 12:30 with a lecture and a tour of the twenty-eight herb gardens; the delicious lunch is served at 1:30. During the meal, the owner, Adelma Simmons, appears in a cape and decorated skullcap to talk about each course. After lunch, head for the gift shop for kitchen wreaths, cornhusk scare-

CONNECTICUT

OLD STURBRIDGE VILLAGE

Plowing can be observed in the village fields on most good weather days in April.

OLD STURBRIDGE VILLAGE

Open all four seasons, closed winter Mondays, Christmas, and New Year's Day.

OLD STURBRIDGE VILLAGE

Cheese is made in the summer when pastured cows give an abundance of milk.

Wethersfield

Webb-Deane-Stevens Museum
211 Main Street
Wethersfield
529-0612

Buttolph-Williams House
Broad and Marsh Streets
Wethersfield
529-0460

Rocky Hill

Dinosaur State Park
West Street
Rocky Hill
566-2304

crows, sandalwood powder, handmade soaps, and pomanders.

From Hartford head south on I-91 to Wethersfield. Here you'll find the **Webb-Deane-Stevens Museum**, actually three houses. The **Webb House** was once called Hospitality Hall, because officers of the Continental Army were entertained here during the Revolution. This national historic landmark, built in 1752 by Joseph Webb, was where George Washington and Count de Rochambeau met to plan the Yorktown campaign. It contains period furnishings, silver, and porcelain. Mrs. Webb redecorated in a flurry with a French red-flocked wallpaper just before Washington arrived; you can still see the paper on the walls of the room where he slept. The **Silas Deane House** was built in 1766 by a commissioner to France who was also a member of the First Continental Congress. It's furnished with elegant period pieces. The **Isaac Stevens House**, built in 1788, features toys, ladies' bonnets, handwrought fixtures, and an herb garden.

The **Buttolph-Williams House**, built in 1692, is the oldest restored house in Wethersfield. It was considered a mansion in its day. Look for Pilgrim Century chairs and tables, pewter and Delft, a curved settee, and authentic implements in Ye Greate Kitchin.

From Wethersfield continue south on I-91 to exit 23 in Rocky Hill. At **Dinosaur State Park** you'll see hundreds of tracks from the Triassic period, 200 million years ago. These tracks, left in the soft mud of shallow ponds, later hardened into rock. They were uncovered in 1966, and now are protected by a geodesic dome.

More dinosaur lore? Drive up to Granby, Massachusetts, where you'll find **Granby Dinosaur Museum**. (Take I-91 north to Route 202 east.) There are fine collections nearby at **Amherst College** and **Mount Holyoke**. Or head south to

New Haven, where a gigantic dinosaur skeleton can be found at the **Peabody Museum** (page 6).

At Rocky Hill rejoin I-91 for a fast trip to New Haven, where our first itinerary began. You've now completed a circuit through some of the most interesting areas of New England. That circuit has included astounding variety in small compass — sandy beaches and rocky coastline, historic walks and mountain hikes, idyllic villages and bustling cities. And it's all within a day's drive of Boston, Springfield, Hartford, or New Haven. This is why New Englanders value their small corner of the country! It gives them everything they could possibly want. And it heaps the same rewards on visitors.

APPENDIX I

FRANCONIA NOTCH STATE PARK

New England Under Canvas

Recommended Campgrounds in
   Connecticut 225
Recommended Campgrounds in
   Maine 226
Recommended Campgrounds in
   Massachusetts 227
Recommended Campgrounds in
   New Hampshire 232
Recommended Campgrounds in
   Rhode Island 232
Recommended Campgrounds in
   Vermont 233

Advantages of Camping

Over the past 28 years of traveling together, with children of varying ages, we have found that camping multiplies vacations, extending the time we can afford and increasing our range. Although campsite fees have risen since earlier days when we traveled across country with babies, they are still a bargain. A family can travel comfortably for a fraction of the cost of a motel trip with meals out, thereby freeing unspent money for sports and entertainment. The hidden benefits of this mode of travel are many. You can dress casually, eat at your own convenience, avoid the hassle of checking in and out (plus springing your car from exorbitant garage rates in large cities), change your mind, leave earlier or stay longer without worrying about accommodations, explore beaches and mountains in areas that are remote, choose the campsite with a view that suits you, and enjoy cooking and relaxing with your family. Travel more while paying less and enjoy the ultimate vacation luxury of complete freedom.

Of course, there are times when it is not fun to camp. We had one horrendous night pitching tents in a howling gale after midnight, but the sun did come out the next morning and we quickly dried out our belongings and went off for a day that was truly appreciated after the night before. The "good camper award" went to the best sport that night! On another occasion, while camping at North Truro on the Cape, our long weekend coincided with a particularly nasty three-day northeaster. We simply shifted from spending days on the beach to discovering museums and shops. One time, early in our camping days, we made the mistake of pitching the tent on a slight incline with the entrance on the high side. After spending the day in museums while the storm raged, we returned to find several inches of water lapping along the low side of the tent—inside. Another learning experience!

Campgrounds

Campground facilities vary from minimal pit toilets to imitations of city life, including tables, hot showers, playgrounds, fireplaces, rec rooms, stores, laundries and swimming pools. Many privately owned campgrounds offer hookups for electricity, water and sewer.

Campers may want to consider making advance reservations for a base camp if traveling in peak season. We suggest using a base camp for each regional area to avoid making and breaking camp often. Some campgrounds will accept reservations and some will not. If you do not have a reservation, try to stop early enough to be sure of finding a campsite. Many campgrounds have a "holding" area where you can stay overnight until a vacancy occurs.

Following is a state by state listing of campgrounds that we have found to be desirable. We have listed available facilities and special features for each campground. These lists are selective rather than complete. You may want to check the current *Rand McNally Campground Guide* for a full listing of sites and facilities. State tourist offices often have listings of private campgrounds. You can also make reservations by calling "Camper 800," a computerized system. For a fee of $1 charged to a credit card number, you can obtain a confirmation immediately. Even if you do not know names of specific campgrounds in the area you wish to visit, the service will make arrangements for you. Call 800-828-9280 (in New York 800-462-9220).

Recommended Campgrounds in Connecticut

Cornwall Bridge

Housatonic Meadows State Park, Box 105, Cornwall Bridge, CT 06754 Phone: 203/672-6772. 1 mile north on Route 7. Offers 92 sites on 451 acres, flush toilets, showers (charge), hiking, and fishing. A good base for canoe trips on the Housatonic. Reservations accepted.

East Haddam

Devil's Hopyard State Park, East Haddam, CT 06423 Phone: 203/873-8566. 3 miles north of the junction of Routes 82 and 156. Offers 20 sites on 860 acres, pit toilets, and stream fishing. A wooded setting near scenic Chapman Falls. Reservations accepted.

Litchfield

White Memorial Foundation Family Campground, Box 368, Litchfield, CT 06759 Phone: 203/567-0089. Between Litchfield and Bantam off Route 202. Offers sites in Windmill Hill area (wooded) and Point Folly area (waterfront), pit toilets, store, and boating. Reservations with a deposit accepted.

Madison

Hammonasset Beach State Park, Box 271, Madison, CT 06443 Phone: 203/245-2785. Exit 62 from I-95, 1 mile south on Route 1. Offers 538 sites on 918 acres, flush toilets, showers (charge), snack bar, store, swimming, and fishing. The park sits on Long Island Sound. Reservations accepted.

Mystic	Seaport Campground, Mystic, CT 06372 Phone: 203/536-4044. From I-95, 1½ miles north on Route 27; then a half mile east on Route 184. Offers 130 sites on 30 acres, flush toilets, electricity hookups (charge), water hookups, laundry, store, recreation hall, swimming pool, and fishing. Reservations accepted.
New Preston	Lake Waramaug State Park, New Preston, CT 06777 Phone: 203/868-0220. From Route 45, 2 miles west on town roads. Offers 88 wooded sites on 95 acres, flush toilets, showers (charge), snack bar, swimming, scuba diving, and fishing. Reservations accepted.
Niantic	Rocky Neck State Park, Box 676, Niantic, CT 06357 Phone: 203/739-5471. Exit 72 from I-95, 1 mile south on Route 156. Offers 169 sites on 562 acres, flush toilets, showers (charge), snack bar, swimming, and fishing. Sandy beach a short walk away. Reservations accepted.
Pleasant Valley	American Legion State Forest, Box 161, Pleasant Valley, CT 06790 Phone: 203/485-0226. From Route 318, 2 miles north on West River Road. Offers 30 sites on 738 acres, flush toilets, showers, and hiking trails. Fishing and canoeing on the Farmington River. Reservations accepted with application.
Torrington	Taylor Brook-Burr Pond State Park, Torrington, CT 06790 Phone: 203/482-1817. Exit 46 from Route 8, 1 mile west on town road. Offers 40 sites on 436 acres, flush toilets, showers, hiking, swimming and fishing. Reservations accepted.
Recommended Campgrounds in Maine	
Pownal	Bradbury Mountain State Park, Pownal, ME 04069 Phone: 207/688-4712. Freeport exit from I-95, 2 miles west. Offers 54 sites on 272 acres, pit toilets, nature trails and a playground. Features a view of Casco Bay and the White Mountains from the mountaintop (an easy hike). No reservations.
Damariscotta	Lake Pemaquid Camping, Box 599, Damariscotta, ME 04543 Phone: 207/563-5202. From Damaris-

cotta, 1 mile north to Biscay Road (Route 32), 2 miles south to Egypt Road. Offers 200 sites on 150 acres, flush toilets, showers (charge), electricity and water hookups, laundry, swimming, fishing, boating, tennis, and a playground. The spring-fed lake is 7 miles long with a sandy beach. Reservations accepted.

Camden Hills State Park, Camden, ME 04843 Phone: 207/236-3109. From Camden, 2 miles north on Route 1. Offers 112 sites on 5,004 acres, flush toilets, showers, and nature trails. The area features scenic views of Maiden Cliff, the Megunticook range, and 1,700 feet of typical rocky Maine coastline. No reservations.

Camden

Black Woods Campground, RFD 1, Box 1, Bar Harbor, ME 04609 Phone: 207/288-3274. From Bar Harbor, 5 miles south on Route 3. Offers 297 sites, flush toilets, swimming, fishing, boating, riding, and recreational programs. Reservations required.

Bar Harbor

Baxter State Park. There are several campgrounds in the park. For information write: Reservation Clerk, Baxter Park Authority, 64 Balsam Drive, Millinocket, ME 04462. Mount Katahdin, the Appalachian Trail, and the many lakes make this a beautiful place to camp and hike.

Millinocket

Boston Harbor Island State Park, c/o Wompatuck State Park, Union Street, Hingham, MA 02043 Phone: 617/749-7160. Accessible by boat. Sites on Lovells, Bumpkin, and Grape islands. Permits required.

Recommended Campgrounds in Massachusetts

Boston

Sweetwater Forest, Drawer FF, Brewster, MA 02631 Phone: 617/896-3773. Exit 10 from Route 6, 3 miles north on Route 124. Offers 250 sites (a few on the lake), on 60 acres. Flush toilets, showers, electricity and water hookups (charge), swimming pool and children's beach, fishing, boating and a playground. Reservations with a deposit accepted.

Brewster

Charlemont Mohawk Trail State Forest, Box 7, Charlemont, MA 01339 Phone: 413/339-5504. From Charlemont, 5 miles west on Route 2. Offers 56 sites on 6,457 acres, flush toilets, store, hiking trails, swimming, and fishing. Spectacular mountain scenery. No reservations.

East Brewster Nickerson State Park, Box 787, East Brewster, MA 02631 Phone: 617/896-7695. From Brewster, 2 miles east on Route 6A. Offers 400 wooded sites on 1,788 acres, flush toilets, showers, store, nature trails, swimming, fishing, boat-launching facility, and bike rentals. Features separate camping areas surrounding ponds with swimming, boating, and fishing. No reservations.

Falmouth Sippewissett Cabins/Family Campground, 836 Palmer Avenue, Falmouth, MA 02540 Phone: 617/548-2542. From Bourne Bridge, 12 miles south on Route 28; exit at Sippewissett cutoff, left at blinker, driveway on right. Offers 95 wooded sites and several cabins on 13 acres, flush toilets, showers, electricity and water hookups, laundry, and a playground. The area is wooded with access to the ocean. Reservations with a deposit accepted.

Florida Savoy Mountain State Forest, Florida, MA 01247 Phone: 413/663-8469. From North Adams, 5 miles on Route 2, 3 miles south on Route 116. Offers 45 sites on 11,721 acres, flush toilets, showers, hiking trails, swimming, fishing and bridle paths. No reservations.

Hingham Wompatuck State Park, Union Street, Hingham, MA 02043 Phone: 617/749-7160. Exit 30 from Route 3, 7 miles north on Route 228. Offers 400 sites on 2,900 acres, flush toilets, showers, electricity hookup (charge), visitor center, nature trails, riding and bike paths. No reservations.

Lanesboro Greylock Mountain State Reservation, Box 138, Lanesboro, MA 10237 Phone: 413/499-4262. From North Adams, 1½ miles west on Route 2, 5 miles south on Route 8. Offers 35 sites on 11,119 acres, pit toilets, hiking trails, fishing, riding, and bike paths. No reservations.

Lee

October Mountain State Forest, Woodland Road, Lee, MA 01238 Phone: 413/243-1778. 3 miles north on Route 20. Offers 50 sites on 15,711 acres, flush toilets, showers, hiking, fishing, boating and riding. Views of streams and mountains. No reservations.

Littleton

Minuteman KOA Kampground, Box 122, Littleton, MA 01460 Phone: 617/772-0042. From I-495, 3 miles west on Route 110. Offers 5 sites on 20 acres, flush toilets, showers, electricity hookup (charge), water hookup, laundry, store, recreation hall, swimming pool, and a playground. Reservations with deposit accepted.

North Reading

Harold Parker State Forest, North Reading, MA 01810 Phone: 617/686-3391. 3 miles north of Middleton on Route 114. Offers 134 sites on 2,800 acres, flush toilets, snackbar, store, swimming, fishing in five stocked ponds, boating, and riding.

North Truro

Horton's Park, Box 308, North Truro, MA 02652 Phone: 617/487-1220. From Route 6, 1 mile east on South Highland Road. Offers 200 wooded sites (some with a view of the bay) on 40 acres, flush toilets, showers (charge), electricity and water hookups (charge), laundry, snack bar, store, and a playground. Within the National Seashore, next to a nine-hole golf course and a mile from an ocean beach. Reservations with a deposit accepted.

North Truro Camping Area, Highland Road, North Truro, MA 02652 Phone: 617/487-1847. From Truro, Route 6 to Highland Road. Offers 250 wooded sites on 20 acres, flush toilets, showers (charge), electricity and water hookups (charge), laundry, and a store. Access to the ocean. Reservations accepted.

Plymouth	Indianhead Resort, RFD 8, Plymouth, MA 02360 Phone: 617/888-3688. Exit 2 from Route 3, 2 miles north on Route 3A. Offers 200 sites on 100 acres, flush toilets, showers (charge), electricity and water hookups, laundry, snack bar, store, fishing, boating, and a playground. Ocean swimming nearby. Reservations with a deposit accepted.

Provincetown	Dune's Edge, Box 875, Provincetown, MA 02657. Phone: 617/487-9815. From Provincetown, a half mile west on Route 6. Offers 100 sites on 13 acres, flush toilets, showers (charge), electricity hookup (charge), store, and a playground. Access to the ocean. Reservations with a deposit accepted.

Rochester	Cape Cod KOA Kampground, High Street, Box 265, Rochester, MA 02770 Phone: 617/763-5911. Exit 20 from I-95, north on Route 105, 4 miles east on county road. Offers 200 sites on 80 acres, flush toilets, showers (charge), electricity hookup (charge), water hookup, laundry, store, swimming pool, fishing, boating, tennis and a playground. Reservations with deposit accepted.

Sagamore	Scusset Beach State Reservation, Box 65, Sagamore, MA 02561 Phone: 617/888-0859. From Route 3, 2 miles east on Scusset Beach Road. Offers 100 sites on 380 acres, flush toilets, showers, electricity and water hookups, snack bar, swimming, fishing, and a playground. Friends recommend the jetty for pollock fishing; also great boat watching on the canal! No reservations. Two-week stay limit.

Salisbury	Salisbury Beach State Reservation, Salisbury, MA 01950 Phone: 617/462-4481. 2 miles east of Salisbury on Route 1A. Offers 500 sites on 520 acres, flush toilets, showers, snack bar, visitors' center, swimming, fishing, boat-launching facilities, and a playground. No reservations.

Sandwich	Peters Pond Park, Box 999, Sandwich, MA 02563 Phone: 617/477-1775. Exit 2 off Route 6, right for

2 miles on Route 130, left on Cotuit Road. Offers 498 sites (some shaded and some along the lake) on 87 acres, flush toilets, showers, electricity and water hookups (charge), store, swimming, fishing, boating and a playground. Site located on a lovely spring-fed lake. Reservations with deposit accepted.

Myles Standish State Forest, Box 66, South Carver, MA 02366 Phone: 617/866-2526. 3 miles southeast of South. Carver (follow signs). Offers 475 sites on 16,000 acres, flush toilets, showers, snack bar, hiking and nature trails, swimming, fishing, boat-launching facilities, and bike paths. No reservations.

South Carver

Martha's Vineyard Family Campground, Box 1557, Vineyard Haven, MA 02568 Phone: 617/693-3772. From Vineyard Haven ferry dock, 1½ miles on the road to the airport. Offers 175 sites on 20 acres, flush toilets, showers, electricity and water hookups, laundry, store, and a playground. The area is wooded with access to the ocean. Reservations accepted.

Vineyard Haven

Webb's Camping Area, RFD, Vineyard Haven, MA 02568 Phone: 617/693-0233. From Vineyard Haven, 3 miles east on Edgartown Road, a quarter mile north on Barnes Road. Offers 108 sites (a few overlooking the pond) on 90 acres, flush toilets, showers, electricity and water hookups, laundry, store, and a playground. Reservations with a deposit accepted.

Horseneck Beach State Reservation, Westport Point, MA 02791 Phone: 617/636-8816. From I-95 south on Route 88. Offers 100 sites on 560 acres, flush toilets, showers, swimming, and fishing. No reservations.

Westport Point

Recommended Campgrounds in New Hampshire

Berlin

Moose Brook State Park, RFD 1, Berlin, NH 03570 Phone: 603/466-3860. From Gorham, 2 miles west on Route 2. Offers 42 sites on 755 acres, flush toilets, showers (charge), hiking trails and swimming. Nearby Pine Mountain offers a particularly lovely climb with spectacular views. No reservations.

Conway

Eastern Slope Camping Area, Conway, NH 03818 Phone: 603/447-5092. From Conway, 1 mile north on Route 16. Offers 260 sites on 32 acres, flush toilets, showers (charge), store, tennis, and a playground. Good for small children. Spectacular scenery. Reservations accepted.

Franconia

Lafayette Campground, Franconia Notch State Park, Franconia, NH 03580 Phone: 603/823-5563. From North Woodstock 8 miles north on Route 3. Offers 98 campsites on 6,440 acres, flush toilets, showers, hiking trails, fishing, playground, and a naturalist program. No reservations.

North Conway

Saco River Camping Ground, Box 546, North Conway, NH 03860 Phone: 603/356-3360. From North Conway, 1 mile south on Route 16. Offers 139 sites on 50 acres, flush toilets, showers (charge), electricity and water hookups (charge), laundry, store, recreation hall, swimming, fishing, square dancing, and community sings. Reservations accepted.

Recommended Campgrounds in Rhode Island

Charlestown

Burlingame State Park, Cookestown Road, Charlestown, RI 02813 Phone: 401/322-7337. Off Route 1. Offers 755 sites on 2,100 acres, flush toilets, showers, laundry, swimming, fishing, and boating. The area is wooded, only a few minutes drive from ocean beaches and the Ninigret Wildlife Refuge. For privacy, you may prefer the north camp, which is on the far side of Watchaug Pond. No reservations.

Narragansett

Fisherman's Memorial State Park, Point Judith Road, Narragansett, RI 02882 Phone: 401/789-

8374. From Route 1 south on Route 108 to Galilee Road; then west to the campground. Offers 182 sites on 91 acres, flush toilets, showers, electricity and water hookups, swimming, tennis, basketball, volleyball, and a playground. Reservations accepted for a minimum of two days.

Long Cove Marina, RR 9, Box 76, Narragansett, RI 02882 Phone: 401/783-4902. From Route 1, south on Route 108 beyond Fisherman's Memorial State Park. Offers 150 sites on 100 acres, flush toilets, showers, electricity and water hookups (charge), fishing, and boat-launching facilities. Ocean swimming nearby. On the grounds is a native stone house and an old factory that once made bayberry wax. Reservations with deposit accepted.

Recommended Campgrounds in Vermont

Arlington

Camping on the Batten Kill, Arlington, VT 05250 Phone: 802/375-6663. From Arlington, 1 mile north on Route 7. Offers 100 sites on 35 acres, flush toilets, showers, electricity hookups (charge), water hookups, swimming, fishing and a playground. Both shaded and open sites available. Reservations accepted.

Bennington

Woodford State Park, Bennington, VT 05201 Phone: 802/773-6691. From Bennington, 11 miles east on Route 9. Offers 104 sites on 400 acres, flush toilets, showers (charge), hiking and nature trails, swimming, fishing and boating. Reservations accepted.

Brattleboro

Fort Dummer State Park, RD 3, Brattleboro, VT 05301 Phone: 802/254-2610. From Brattleboro, drive north on Route 5 to the first traffic light, a half mile east on Fairground Road, 1 mile south on South Main Street and Old Guilford Road. Offers 61 sites and 9 lean-tos on 217 acres, flush toilets, showers (charge), and hiking trails. The sites are large, well screened, and wooded, and more private than many campgrounds. Reservations accepted.

Burlington Burlington Beach, Superintendent of Parks, City Hall, Burlington, VT 05401 Phone: 802/862-0942. From Burlington follow "City Beach Campsite" signs north on Route 2, left on North Street, right on North Avenue, left on Institute Road. Offers 112 sites on 65 acres, flush toilets, showers, electricity and water hookups (charge), snack bar boathouse and a playground. Right on Lake Champlain.

East Dorset Emerald Lake State Park, East Dorset, VT 05253 Phone: 802/362-1655. From Danby, 6 miles south on Route 7. Offers 105 sites and 36 lean-tos on 430 acres, flush toilets, showers (charge), museum, snack bar, hiking and nature trails, and boating. There is a sandy beach with roped-in shallow area perfect for toddlers. Reservations for a minimum of six nights.

Grand Isle Grand Isle State Park, Grand Isle, VT 05458 Phone: 802/372-4300. From South Hero, 3 miles north on Route 2, 1 mile east on unpaved access road. Offers 154 sites and 30 lean-tos on 226 acres, flush toilets, showers (charge), snack bar, stove, recreation hall, swimming and boating. Right on the water, with scenic views, a center green for playing and secluded sites. Reservations are accepted.

Silent Cedars Campground, Route 314, Grand Isle, VT 05458 Phone: 802/372-8298. From Route 2, 3 miles west on Route 314. Offers 70 sites and 4 cottages on 20 acres, flush toilets, showers (charge), electricity and water hookups (charge), laundry, swimming, fishing, boat launching facilities and a playground. Some sites on the lake, others in the orchard.

Killington Gifford Woods, Killington, VT 05751 Phone: 802/775-5354. From Rutland, 10 miles east on Route 4, half a mile north on Route 100. Offers 47 sites on 114 acres, flush toilets, showers (charge), and boat-launching facilities. Reservations accepted.

Mount Philo State Park, North Ferrisburg, VT 05473 Phone: 802/425-2390. From Vergennes, 1 mile north on Route 22A, 6 miles north on Route 7, 1 mile east on town road. The entrance road is steep and not recommended for large trailers and RVs. Offers 16 sites on 163 acres, flush toilets, picnic area, and a recreation building. Scenic views.

North Ferrisburg

North Hero State Park, North Hero, VT 05474 Phone: 802/372-8727. From North Hero, 8 miles north on Route 2 and a town road. Offers 117 sites and 9 lean-tos on 399 acres, flush toilets, showers (charge), nature trail, swimming, fishing and boat launching facilities.

North Hero

Burton Island State Park, Box 123, St. Albans Bay, VT 05481 Phone: 802/524-6353. On an island in the upper part of Lake Champlain, accessible by boat or ferry from the Kill Kare Area. Offers 42 sites and 19 lean-tos on 253 acres, flush toilets, showers (charge), museum, hiking trails, swimming, fishing and a marina. Reservations accepted.

St. Albans Bay

Apple Tree Bay Campground and Marina, South Hero, VT 05486 Phone: 802/372-5398. Exit 17 from I-89, 6 miles west on Route 2. Offers 250 sites on 200 acres, flush toilets, showers, electricity and water hookups (charge), laundry, store, recreation hall, swimming pool, fishing, marina, and a playground. The lake is across the road. Reservations accepted.

South Hero

Little River Camping Area, Box 86, RD 1, Waterbury, VT 05676 Phone: 802/244-7103. Exit 10 from I-89, 1½ miles west on Route 2, 3½ miles southwest on town road. Offers 101 sites and 6 lean-tos in Mount Mansfield State Forest, flush toilets, showers (charge), museum, hiking and nature trails, swimming, fishing, boating and a playground. Reservations accepted.

Waterbury

White River Junction	Quechee Gorge RA, RFD, White River Junction, VT 05001 Phone: 802/295-2990. From White River Junction, 7 miles west on Route 4. Offers 30 sites on 76 acres, flush toilets, and showers (charge). Reservations accepted.
Wilmington	Molly Stark State Park, Wilmington, VT 05363 Phone: 802/464-5460. From Brattleboro, west on Route 9. Offers 34 sites on 158 acres, flush toilets, showers (charge), hiking trails, swimming, and boating. Reservations accepted.

National Parks

For information on National Parks you may want to write to:

National Park Service, North Atlantic Region, 15 State Street, Boston, Massachusetts 02109.

National Park Service, U.S. Department of the Interior, Washington, D.C. 20240.

National Forest Service, U.S. Department of Agriculture, Washington, D.C. 20250.

The National Park Service charges entrance fees at designated national parks, monuments, recreation areas, seashores, historic sites and memorial parks. You can purchase a "Golden Eagle Passport" for $10 which is valid for one year and covers entrance fees in any of the designated areas. The fees range from $.50 to $3 at each site. Persons who are over 62 years of age may receive a free lifetime entrance permit to the designated areas. The permit holder, his spouse and children are all included when traveling together. If you are over 62 years of age bring proof of age. "Passports" and permits are available at most federally operated recreation areas. They cover entrance to parks but not campground fees.

State Parks

Some of the best campsites in New England are located in state parks. Reservation procedures vary by state. For full information on locations, facilities, and reservation policies, write to:

Connecticut: Department of Environmental Protection, Office of Parks & Recreation, 165 Capitol Avenue, Hartford, Connecticut 06115.

Maine: Bureau of Parks & Recreation, State Office Building, August, Maine 04333.

Massachusetts: Department of Environmental Management, Division of Forests and Parks, 100 Cambridge Street, Boston, Massachusetts 02202.

New Hampshire: Division of Parks & Recreation, Box 856, Concord, New Hampshire 03301.

Rhode Island: Division of Parks & Recreation, 83 Park Street, Providence, Rhode Island 02903.

Vermont: Department of Forests, Parks & Recreation, Montpelier, Vermont 05602

Appalachian Mountain Club

The Appalachian Mountain Club offers bunks in huts located in the White Mountains National Forest of New Hampshire, one of the most magnificent mountain hiking regions in the East. You can make reservations by writing: Reservations Secretary, AMC Pinkham Notch Camp, Gorham, New Hampshire 03581. The Pinkham Notch Camp serves as AMC headquarters for that area. Check for special discounts that are often available.

Camping Equipment

To get organized, you will probably want to list the equipment you will need for camping. The following relatively complete list of camping equipment was compiled for our book *Europe Under Canvas* (Prentice-Hall, Inc., Englewood Cliffs, New Jersey, 1980). You will probably find about half of the items necessary or useful. We select from this list according to the focus of our trip, keeping unused items at home in a box or duffle bag ready for the next trip.

air mattresses
asbestos mitts (*for charcoal grilling*)
breadboard (*for slicing bread, cheese, salami as well as using as a server for cheese and crackers before dinner*)
broom (*small, for sweeping out your tent*)
can opener
clothesline and pins
cook kit
corkscrew
corn tongs (*for turning bacon*)
dishcloth or sponge
dishpans
dishtowels
dishwashing liquid
funnel (*for stove if you need to pour fuel*)
ground sheet
juice container
kettle
knives
lanterns and flashlights
mallet (*for pounding tent stakes*)
matches
paper towels
plastic bags
plates, cups, bowls
pump for air mattresses
rope
salt and pepper
scissors
scouring pads
silverware
sleeping bags
string
stove
tablecloth, plastic or terrycloth
tent
tent stakes
tools for cooking (*long-handled spoon, slotted spoon, pancake turner, soup ladle*)
tools for repairs (*hammer, pliers, wrenches, screwdrivers, knife, grommet kit, sewing kit*)
water jug
waxed paper
windshield for stove

Organizing Equipment

During the trip we like to keep our equipment in order so that any member of the family will know where an item is. We use three large square plastic boxes to contain our dishes, utensils and miscellaneous cooking items. These stack neatly in a single packsack. A second packsack holds two plastic dishpans, the cook kit, and the kettle on top, with everything else fitting around the circular items. When setting up the kitchen on the ground sheet at one end of our tent extension, we line the boxes and everything else up in a regular pattern so anyone can cook or clean up with ease. Those less orderly by nature may think we overdo organization in our camping life, but it beats searching for some little item with a flashlight on a moonless night!

Eating

Campsite cooking can be fun as well as save a great deal of money. Bring staples from home, then shop at local markets where you can look for special food native to the area. Check the local fish market, fruit and vegetable stands. Depending upon the activity planned for the day, you can pack a trail lunch for hiking, buy a lobster roll for the beach, or lunch in a village restaurant with local residents. We occasionally go to a restaurant for lunch rather than dinner. The prices are cheaper at noon, and it is pleasant to sit in the sun overlooking a lovely view.

After a day of activity we enjoy cooking at our campsite, sometimes with a special local treat. We often sit around sipping sherry while soup warms on the stove, then charcoal grill meat, chicken or fish with vegetables, toss a salad, and open a bottle of wine. There isn't a better way.

Camping Stoves

If you are camping by car you can take any size of stove you wish. We used a two-burner Coleman stove for years, but have now switched to two small butane Gaz picnic stoves which produce just as much heat and are more compact. They are also small and light enough to be used for backpacking trips. Over the years we have tried various stoves that used gas, white gas and alcohol. Butane produces high heat quickly and is easy to handle and store, although the replacement cannisters cost slightly more than other fuels. If you plan on boiling lobster remember to bring a large pot and a stove sturdy enough to accommodate it. We also take a very small charcoal grill along for variety.

Tents

Unless you have an RV or camping trailer, you will probably use one or more tents. We have gathered an assortment of tents and choose among them according to the type of trip we are taking. Twenty years ago I made a 9 x 9 canvas tent for wilderness canoe camping that requires only one tree limb to erect. We even have a special stone with a hole in the middle (found in the woods years ago) to tie on the end of the heaving line, throw over the limb, and secure the tent. This tent has a diamond shape with one high corner reaching up toward the limb (even a tall person has head room to stand up while dressing) and three low corners (3 feet off the ground) supporting back walls. The high corner has nylon netting and canvas doors with long zippers so that you can lie in your sleeping bag and gaze at the moon and stars on beautiful nights or completely zip it up in bad weather. This tent originally weighed only 12 pounds for easy packing but we had to replace the floor with heavier, sturdier fabric when we were faced with constant wet weather in England.

The next tent we bought was a light mountain tent suitable for backpacking. We eventually bought one for each child to provide some relief from constant togetherness. Then, after a great deal of research, we found a light, easily erected (no trees required) French tent that would serve us for sleeping and dressing and provide a family center. It also has a fly sheet, now standard on most tents, which we found a welcome relief after years of dodging drips created when occupants touched the canvas. This main tent and extension system, surrounded by satellite sleeping tents, is flexible and can be put together quickly with no complicated tubing to assemble. Other tents are fancier—especially big ones with walk-in "bedrooms," but we prefer lighter, simpler tents that can be assembled quickly and will also double for backpacking, hiking, and canoeing expeditions.

APPENDIX II

Bed and Breakfast in New England

Reservation Services
   and Directories 242
Bed and Breakfast in
   Connecticut 244
Bed and Breakfast in
   Maine.......................245
Bed and Breakfast in
   Massachusetts 247
Bed and Breakfast in
   New Hampshire 250
Bed and Breakfast in
   Rhode Island 251
Bed and Breakfast in
   Vermont.....................252
Bed and Breakfast
   Bibliography 254

Bed and Breakfast Accommodations

The following listing of bed-and-breakfast accommodations includes a selection of the many houses scattered throughout New England that are available to travellers seeking inexpensive and interesting places to stay overnight. It is not intended to be comprehensive; there are many more you may discover. Most B-&-B proprietors are extremely helpful and will refer you to other houses in the area if they are full.

Defining "bed-and-breakfast" is somewhat difficult because accommodations range from small family homes to country inns. We have tried to include those with known interesting features – restored architecture or an unusual setting – but have avoided larger country inns that tend to be expensive. Prices still will vary considerably from budget homes to moderately priced lodgings, particularly in resort areas. Prices also vary according to season.

The personal attention you will receive may surprise you. Your host or hostess may offer you wine on the porch when you arrive, fresh fruit in your room, flowers by your bed, bath oil in the bathroom, or a foil-wrapped chocolate on your pillow. On the other hand, don't be disappointed with the lack of one of these gestures. You may find that your hosts will offer you an hour of conversation during an evening; you may become friends and return year after year.

A list of reservation services and directories follows. Each of them has a range of accommodations to offer you. Some will help you plan your trip by reserving rooms along your route. Others will offer suggestions for specific areas you wish to visit; or a directory to help you choose your own accommodations.

Reservation Services and Directories

Nutmeg Bed & Breakfast, 56 Fox Chase Lane, West Hartford, CT 06107. Phone: 203/236-6698. Offers the best in Connecticut including modest homes to oceanfront retreats, farmhouses, and suburban homes. List of 120 homes. Send $2 and self-addressed, stamped, business size envelope with inquiry.

Pineapple Hospitality: Bed & Breakfast in all New England, 384 Rodney French Blvd., New Bedford,

MA 02744. Phone: 617/997-9952 or 990-1696. Offers a New England experience which can include placing guests in a 200-year-old farmhouse, a sea captain's house, a beach house, and more. They will reserve accommodations for you in eight or nine homes around New England, if you wish. People find this personalized service helpful in planning a trip. Send a stamped, self-addressed, business envelope.

New England Bed & Breakfast, 1045 Centre Street, Newton, MA 02159. Phone 617/244-2112. John Gardiner started this reservation service years ago—the first in New England. Homes are available in Newton, Boston, and Cambridge; there is a growing list of homes in other New England resort areas. Send a stamped, self-addressed, business envelope.

Bed & Breakfast Cape Cod, Box 341, West Hyannisport, MA 02672. Phone: 617/775-2772. This reservation service has homes all over the Cape. There is a contemporary oceanfront 20-room estate, lots of charming cottages, and some small inns. Some are year-round in case you will be traveling during the colder months.

House Guests—Cape Cod, 65 Hokum Road, Dennis, MA 02638. Phone: 617/385-8332. Offers the oldest home in Harwich, and other homes built in the 1700's, many furnished with antiques. Includes Martha's Vineyard and Nantucket. Send a stamped, self-addressed envelope.

Berkshire Bed & Breakfast Connection, 141 Newton Road, Springfield, MA 01118. Phone: 413/783-5111. Offers 32 homes including renovated colonials, mansions, and a contemporary with a geodesic dome. They have added two other reservation services with the same address and phone. Pioneer Valley B & B: 12 homes; Sturbridge B & B: colonials, an alpine house on a lake.

American Bed & Breakfast, Inc., Box 983, Saint Albans, VT 05478. Phone: 802/524-4731. Listings include dairy farms, and homes in quaint villages, some high in the mountains. They do not reserve for you but will send a directory. Send $3 plus a stamped, self-addressed envelope.

Bed & Breakfast Associates Bay Colony, Ltd., Box 166, Babson Park Branch, Boston, MA 02157. Phone: 617/872-6990. Range of homes from old New England filled with antiques to typical suburban homes.

New Hampshire Bed & Breakfast, RFD 3, Box 53, Laconia, NH 03246. Phone: 603/536-4347. Listings in all of New Hampshire include country classics and in-town houses, old colonials and lakefront contemporaries, some with pool and tennis courts, other with magnificent views of the ocean.

The National Bed & Breakfast Association, 148 East Rocks Road, Box 332, Norwalk, CT 06852. Phone: 203/847-5038. Call for free information on any of their listings. You can purchase *The Bed and Breakfast Guide* by Phyllis Featherston by sending $9.95 plus $1.25 postage.

Bed and Breakfast in Connecticut

East Haddam

Bishop's Gate Inn, Goodspeed Landing, East Haddam, CT 06423. 203/873-1677. An 1818 shipbuilder's home with lots of fireplaces. It is furnished with antique period pieces. Breakfast features home-baked specialties.

Glastonbury

Butternut Farm, 1654 Main Street, Glastonbury, CT 06033. 203/633-7197. An eighteenth-century jewel of a colonial home. It is furnished with period antiques. Continental breakfast includes delicious homemade jam.

Groton Long Point

Shore Inne, 54 East Shore Road, Groton Long Point, CT 06340. 203/536-1180. Beautiful views of the water from this lovely residential setting. The rooms are furnished with handmade bedspreads; one has hand-stencilled walls. Breakfast features home-baked muffins.

Kent

The Candlelight Main Street, Kent, CT 06757. 203/927-3407. This colonial home was built in 1948. It is popular with visitors to the Kent School.

Mystic

1833 House, 33 Greenmanville Avenue, Mystic, CT 06355. 203/572-0633. This home is located at the entrance to Mystic Seaport. It is simple and homelike. People especially enjoy getting together in the kitchen for a continental breakfast of hot muffins before touring the Seaport.

Bed and Breakfast in Maine

Bar Harbor

Thornhedge, 47 Mount Desert Street, Bar Harbor, ME 04609. 207/288-5398. This home recaptures the "spirit of Bar Harbor" from the turn of the century. It is furnished with Victorian furniture. Wine and cheese are served in the afternoon. Breakfast features home-baked muffins and breads, fruit, and delicious coffee.

Hearthside Inn, 7 High Street, Bar Harbor, ME 04609. 207/288-4533. Built by a doctor, this house has a lovely fireplace and beautiful antiques. There is an old Chickering piano in the living room, where evening wine is served. Breakfast includes home-baked muffins.

Boothbay Harbor

Hilltop House, McKown Hill, Boothbay Harbor, ME 04538. 207/633-2941. Located on the top of a hill overlooking the town and the harbor, this home is within walking distance of shops, restaurants, and theater. It was built 150 years ago by

Captain Mitchell Reed. Because he was sailing for much of the year his wife decided to rent rooms; the roof was removed and a third floor was added to the house. During World War II troops lived here; the present owners bought it after the war and completely renovated it.

Kennebunkport The Chetwynd House, Chestnut Street, Kennebunkport, ME 04046. 207/967-2235. This home was built in 1840 by Captain Seavey. It is in the village and the ocean is nearby. The house features ceiling to floor windows and wideboard pine floors. Breakfast includes such specialties as quiche and cheese souffle.

Ogunquit Blue Shutters, 6 Beachmere Place, Ogunquit, ME 03907. 207/646-2163. This colonial home overlooks the ocean; in fact, all bedrooms have an ocean view. A path leads you to Marginal Way and a private beach. Breakfast is served on English china and arrives at your door when you wish. One room has a private deck and two have fireplaces.

Pemaquid Falls Little River Inn, Route 130, Pemaquid Falls, ME 04558. 207/677-3678. Located on top of Pemaquid Falls, this house has a view of the river as well as a saltwater view. It is in a coastal area that has not been highly developed. This is a great place to relax. Guests receive a complimentary glass of wine. Breakfast includes frittata, baked Swiss eggs, quiche, or other special treats.

South Harpswell The Maine Stay, RD 2, Box 355, South Harpswell, ME 04079. 207/729-1373. This 1847 classic Cape has been completely modernized. It is located one-quarter mile from the water and there is a forest behind it. A full breakfast is served.

Wiscasset Roberts House Bed and Breakfast, Main Street, Box 413, Wiscasset, ME 04578. 207/882-5055. This 1799 foursquare federal house was built by Ebenezer Whittier. There are old brick footpaths to restaurants and shops. The bedrooms are furnished with antiques and handmade quilts.

York Beach

Jo-Mar Guest House, 41 Freeman Street, Box 838, York Beach, ME 207/363-4826. Located on the ocean, this house offers appealing views up to Nubble Light. It is located on a bluff overlooking Short Sands Beach. Continental breakfast includes blueberry muffins or coffee cake.

Nirvana By-the-Sea, Nubble Road, York Beach, ME 03910. 207/363-3628. Built by the Governor of Maine, this house was especially designed for the view. All bedrooms have a view of the ocean; some have private terraces. Kitchen privileges for light meals are offered. You can organize your own lobster cookout on the patio if you wish.

Bed and Breakfast in Massachusetts

Brewster

Old Sea Pines Inn, 2553 Main Street, Brewster, MA 02631. 617/896-6114. This turn-of-the-century home on 3½ acres of wooded land was originally a girls' school. Its furnishings reflect the Twenties and Thirties. The emphasis is on tranquil old Cape Cod.

Concord

Hawthorne Inn, 462 Lexington Road, Concord, MA 02554. 617/369-5610. Originally this land belonged to Emerson, who deeded it to Bronson Alcott and later to Nathaniel Hawthorne. Hawthorne planted trees on the land; his larch trees are still standing. He died in 1864 and the house was built in 1870. The house is furnished with antiques, oriental and rag rugs, paintings, and some Japanese block prints from the 1800s. Home-baked breads are served with the continental breakfast.

Falmouth

Sea Gull Lodge, 41 Belvidere Road, Box 564, Falmouth, MA 02540. 617/548-0679. This centrally located home has a patio and a large yard. Swedish antiques are everywhere in the house.

Silver Shores on the Ocean, Old Silver Beach Road, North Falmouth, MA 02556. 617/548-0846. This home is right on a lovely white beach. It faces west, and from comfortable chairs you can enjoy watching the sun dip down into the ocean.

Gloucester

Williams Guest House, 136 Bass Avenue, Gloucester, MA 01930. 617/283-4931. This colonial revival home is located right on Good Harbor beach. Some of the rooms have balconies. Breakfast includes home-baked treats.

Hyannis

Sea Witch Inn, 363 Sea Street, Hyannis, MA 02601. 617/771-4261. Built in 1900, this home features a wraparound porch. The rooms are furnished with antiques, including brass beds.

Marblehead

Nasutilus Guest House, 68 Front Street, Marblehead, MA 01945. 617/631-1703. This 175-year-old house has a view of the harbor. It is located across from the public landing.

Nantucket

Cliff Lodge, 9 Cliff Road, Nantucket, MA 02554. 617/228-0893. This sea captain's home built over 200 years ago has sitting rooms, a library, a living room filled with antiques, and a large yard with comfortable chaises.

Periwinkle Guest House, 9 North Water Street, Nantucket, MA 02554. 617/228-9267. Just two minutes from the center of town, this guest house has a nice view of the harbor. It is an old colonial, filled with antiques. Continental breakfast is included.

Nantucket Landfall, 9 Cliff Road, Nantucket, MA 02554. 617/228-0500. This home is located on a side street across from Children's Beach (so-called because of the gradual slope into the water). Children may take lifesaving classes there. The rooms are casual and summery.

Newburyport

Benjamin Choat House, 25 Tyng Street, Newburyport, MA 01950. 617/462-4786. This house was built in 1794 by a shipbuilder and contains the largest fireplace in the area. Original artwork, oriental rugs, and antiques fill the house. Guests are offered wine when they register. A full breakfast is included.

Morrill Place, 209 High Street, Newburyport, MA 01950. 617/462-2808. This home features a staircase with six-inch risers built when women wore hoop skirts. There is a music room, library, and porches for you to enjoy. Afternoon tea, as well as a continental breakfast, is offered.

Provincetown

Joshua Paine, 15 Tremont Street, Provincetown, MA 02657. 617/487-1551. The descendants of Joshua Paine sold this house to its present owners. It is furnished with lovely antiques, and is just one block from the water.

Twelve Center Guest House, 12 Center Street, Provincetown, MA 02657. 617/487-0381. Captain Josiah Snow built this Victorian house in 1872. The rooms are very large, and each is done in a different color scheme. Breakfast includes home-baked muffins. The water is one block away.

Rockport

Linden Tree, 26 King Street, Rockport, MA 01966. 617/546-2494. This white Victorian house is 145 years old. It is on a side street and has a pleasant porch from which to enjoy the view. The beach is 2½ blocks away. Continental breakfast may include homemade apricot bread, blueberry cake, or lemon nut bread.

Seafarer, 86 Marmion Way, Rockport, MA 01966. 617/546-6248. Located on the easternmost point of Cape Ann, this house has a 180° view of the water. Cool breezes waft even when the temperature soars in town. Each room has at least three paintings by local artists.

Stockbridge

The Norris Putnam House, Route 7, Stockbridge, MA 01262. 413/298-3337. This Georgian colonial,

Swampscott

secluded on 12 acres, provides "easy elegance in country living." A full gourmet breakfast, served on china and crystal, is included for your pleasure. Cross-country ski trails are available on the grounds.

Cap'n Jack's, 253 Humphrey Street, Swampscott, MA 01907. 617/595-9734. The house overlooks the harbor, filled in the summer with many sailboats. There is a pool and a sauna. Boats are available for your use.

Williamstown

Victorian Tourist Home, 1120 Main Street, Williamstown, MA 01267. 413/458-3121. This 1804 home is located in the center of the town, off Field Park. It is furnished with antiques and oriental rugs.

Woods Hole

The Marlborough, 320 Woods Hole Road, Woods Hole, MA 02543. 617/548-6218. In this seven-room Cape you will find each room individually decorated with collectibles and antiques. There is a private beach nearby. Full breakfast is offered.

Bed and Breakfast in New Hampshire

Franconia

Cannon Mountain House, Easton Road, Route 116, Franconia, NH 03580. 603/823-9574. This renovated farmhouse has a big porch for your relaxation while you take in the view. This is a great area for hiking.

Pinestead Farm Lodge, Route 116, Franconia, NH 03580. 603/823-8121. From this working farm the views include a meadow with cows, Cannon Mountain, and Kinsman Ridge. Rooms are in the farmhouse, where you may share the kitchen.

Hampton Beach

The Grayhurst, 11F Street, Hampton Beach, NH 03842. 603/926-2584. This 1890 gambrel-roofed beach house has flower boxes totalling thirty feet in length. Champagne breakfasts are available at quiet times during their three-month open season.

Blake House, Route 16, Jackson, NH 03846. 603/383-9057. An intimate guest house in European tradition. Cozy bedrooms, paneled living room, fieldstone fireplace, cathedral ceilings. A full breakfast is served buffet-style. Downhill and cross-country skiing nearby.

Jackson

Wildflowers Guest House, Route 16, North Main Street, North Conway, NH 03860. 603/356-2224. This century-old country home has a lovely view of Mount Washington. The "wildflower" theme is carried out into the bedrooms, each with different wildflower wallpaper. Guests are invited to enjoy the living room during the evenings. Complimentary breakfast includes home-baked coffee cakes and special breads.

North Conway

Bed and Breakfast in Rhode Island

Gables Inn, Old Harbor, Block Island, RI 02807. 401/466-2213. This house is over 125 years old and is furnished with antiques and floral wallpaper. Beaches are just a few minutes walk from the inn. There are picnic tables and barbecues for your use.

Block Island

The Guest House, Center Road, Block Island, RI 02807. 401/466-2676. Located off the road, this house offers peace and quiet and a beautiful panoramic view of the ocean. It is within walking distance of beaches, docks, and restaurants.

Sea Gull Guest House, 50 Narragansett Avenue, Narragansett, RI 02882. 401/783-4636. This Victorian house was built in 1904. It is located just one block away from the beach.

Narragansett

Cliffside Guest Villa, 2 Seaview Avenue, Newport, RI 02840. 401/847-1811. Located just off Cliff Walk, this house overlooks the ocean and Cliff Walk. You can walk to East and First beaches in five minutes. The house was built by Governor Swann of Maryland in 1880 as a summer residence.

Newport

Watch Hill

Wayside, Bellevue Avenue, Newport, RI 02840. 401/847-0302. Wayside was one of the summer "cottages" on Bellevue Avenue. It was built for Elisha Dyer who was a cotillion dance master. The bedrooms are large. Continental breakfast is served.

Hartley's Guest House, Larkin Road, Watch Hill, RI 02891. 401/348-8253. Hartley's is located high on a hill overlooking the water. There is a large wraparound porch—a perfect spot to relax and enjoy the view.

Bed and Breakfast in Vermont

Bennington

Colonial Guest House, North and Orchard Road, Bennington, VT 05201. 802/442-2263. This house sits on a hill with a view of the Bennington Monument on an adjacent hill. It is 100 years old, beautifully restored and furnished with antiques. Breakfast includes home-baked treats.

Burlington

Hedgemeer, 565 Main Street, Burlington, VT 05401. 802/862-5320. This colonial home is painted white, with a hedge around it and wonderful hospitality inside. It is across from the University of Vermont and is near shops and restaurants.

Londonderry

The Highland House, Route 100, Londonderry, VT 05148. 802/824-3019. This house is located on a hill with a view of Magic Mountain. There are 26 acres to roam in. A full country breakfast is served.

Ludlow

The Red Door, 7 Pleasant Street, Ludlow, VT 05149. 802/228-2376. This quaint house is 150 years old. It is located one mile from the Okemo ski area; lakes are nearby.

Manchester

Brook-n-Hearth, Box 508, Manchester, VT 05255. 802/362-3604. This homey, family-style house is perfect for winter or summer visitors. You can cross-country ski or hike all over the property. There is also a trout stream. Enjoy the views of the countryside, including Mount Equinox.

1811 House, Main Street, Manchester, VT 05224. 802/362-1811. This house once belonged to Abraham Lincoln's granddaughter. Full breakfast is served in winter, continental in summer.

The Waybury Inn, Route 125, East Middlebury, VT 05740. 802/388-4015. If this one looks familiar it's because it is used on the Bob Newhart show! The house was built in 1810 as a stagecoach stop. A home-cooked breakfast is available. *Middlebury*

The Hillcrest Tourist House, McKinley Avenue, Rutland, VT 05701. 802/775-1670. This 100-year-old farmhouse is furnished with country antiques. Continental breakfast is included. *Rutland*

Green Mountain Tea Room and Guest House, Route 7, South Wallingford, VT 05771. 802/446-2611. This house was built in 1792 as a stagecoach stop. Home-cooked meals are available. You can swim and fish in Otter Creek on the edge of the property. The Appalachian Trail is nearby. *South Wallingford*

Timberholm, Cottage Club Road, Stowe, VT 05672. 802/253-7603. The views from this home include the valley and the Worcester Mountain range. The living room has a large fieldstone fireplace and plenty of comfortable chairs. Homemade soup is served for skiers who return with hearty appetites in the afternoon. *Stowe*

The Darling Family Inn, Route 100, Weston, VT 05161. 802/824-3223. This restored 1830 farmhouse exhibits both European and American antiques. Breakfast includes home-baked breads and muffins. Hiking and fishing are available near *Weston*

Wilmington — the house. There is a view of the mountains as well.

Nutmeg Inn, Route 9 (Molly Stark Trail), Wilmington, VT 05363. 802/464-3351. This 1700's farmhouse has been restored and furnished with antiques. Country-style breakfast is available.

Bed and Breakfast Bibliography

America's Wonderful Little Hotels and Inns, 2nd ed., edited by Barbara Crossette. Published by Congdon & Lattes, NY, NY. 1981. $8.95.

Bed and Breakfast American Style, by Norman T. Simpson. Published by The Berkshire Traveller Press, Stockbridge, MA. 1981. $6.95.

Bed and Breakfast in the Northeast, by Bernice Chesler. Published by The Globe Pequot Press, Chester, CT. 1985. $10.95.

Bed and Breakfast USA, by Betty Rundback & Nancy Ackerman. Published by E. P. Dutton, Inc., NY, NY. 1983. $5.95.

Christopher's Bed and Breakfast Guide to the U.S. and Canada, by Bob & Ellen Christopher. Published by Travel Discoveries, Milford, CT. $3.95.

Compleat Traveler's Guide to Inns & Guesthouses of Country New England, by Anthony Hitchcock & Jean Lindgren. Published by B. Franklin. $4.95.

Guest Houses/Bed & Breakfasts/Inns & Hotels in Newport, RI., by Marguerite Vauclair. Published by Port Quarters Publishing, Newport, RI. 1982. $3.75.

Great American Guest House Book, by John Thaxton. Published by Burt Franklin & Co., NY. 1982. $7.95.

Morrow Book of Havens & Hideaways. A Guide to America's Unique Lodgings, by Thomas Tracy & James O. Ward. Published by William Morrow & Co., Inc., NY. 1980. $6.95.

National Guide to Guest Homes, by Maxine Coplin. Published by Home on Arrange. 1981. $4.95.

Index to Attractions

Abbe Museum, 154
Abbot Hall, 108
Abel's, 154
Acadia Mountain Trail, 157
Acadia National Park, 153
Adams National Historic Site, 83-84
Adventure-Wilderness Trail Camp, 170
Aetna World Cup, 212
Alden House, 80
Allen House, 195
Allenholm Farm, 177
Alpine Slide, 173
American Youth Hostels, xvii
America's Cup races, 28, 31
Amherst College, 218
Andrew-Safford House, 112
Annisquam Lighthouse, 123
Annual Cobble Day, 200
Antique Exposition (Orleans, MA), 63
Appalachian Mountain Club, xvii, 163, 237
Appledore, 133
Apprenticeshop (Bath, ME), 146
Archives Museum (Boston, MA), 88
Armchair Sailor Bookstore, 30
Arrowhead, 195
Arthur D. Story Shipyard, 124
Artists and Craftsmen's Guild Art and Craft Shows (Orleans, MA), 63
Arts and Crafts Fair (Sandwich, MA), 70
Arundel Wharf, 140
Ashumet Holly Reservation, 46
Assembly House, 112
Atlantic White Cedar Swamp Trail, 66
Author's Ridge, 102
Avalanche Falls, 165
Avon Old Farms Inn, 207

Back Beach (Rockport, MA), 115
Back Home Cafe, 180
Bagel Factory, 176

Bald Rock Mountain Trail, 151
Bannister's Wharf, 30
Bar Harbor, 154
Barker Tavern, 82
Barn, The, 181
Bartholomew's Cobble, 200
Bash Bish Falls, 199
Basin (Franconia Notch, NH), 165
Bass Shoe Outlet, 164, 181
Battery Park, 174
Battle Green, 100
Battle Road Visitor Center, 101
Baxter State Park, 157
Bay State-Spray & Provincetown Steamship Company, 96
Bayside Restaurant, 40
Bearskin Neck, 122
Beauport, 122
Beaver Tail Lighthouse, 27
Bed and Bath, 94
Beech Forest Nature Trail, 67
Beinecke Rare Book and Manuscript Library, 6
Belcourt Castle, 31
Ben & Jerry's Ice Cream, 176
Benjamin Franklin Statue, 87
Bennington Battle Monument, 187
Bennington Museum, 187
Bennington Pottery, 187
Berkshire Athenaeum, 195
Berkshire Center for the Performing Arts, 196
Berkshire Museum, 195
Berkshire Theatre Festival, 196
Berkshire Vacation Bureau, 195
Bermuda Race, 28
Bill's Country Store, 170
Bittersweet Farm, 8
Bittersweet Farm Arts and Crafts Festival, 8
Black Pearl, 30

INDEX TO ATTRACTIONS

Blacksmith House, 98
Blessing of the Fleet (New Bedford, MA), 43
Blessing of the Fleet (Provincetown, MA), 68
Block Island State Beach, 25
Block Island Week, 24
Bonded Warehouse, 114
Boon Island Lighthouse, 138
Boothbay Harbor Chamber of Commerce, 148
Boothbay Railway Museum, 148
Boothbay Region Historical Society, 148
Boston Celtics, 212
Boston Common, 88
Boston Common Information Booth, 85
Boston Convention & Tourist Bureau, 84–85
Boston Harbor Cruises, 96
Boston Massacre site, 86
Boston Public Garden, 88
Boston Tea Party Ship and Museum, 93
Botanical Museum, 97
Bowdoin College, 141
Bowen's Wharf, 30
Branford Trolley Museum, 8
Breakers, The, 30
Breakwater, 140
Brick Dwelling, 196
Brick Market, 30
Brick Store Museum, 139
Bridgewater Mill Mall, 169
Brigham's, 83
Bristol County Development Council, 45
Bucklin Trail, 172
Buckman Tavern, 101
Bunch of Grapes, 51
Bunker Hill Monument, 93
Burlingame State Park, 22
Burying Ground, 87
Busch-Reisinger Museum, 97
Butler-McCook Homestead, 215
Buttery, 182
Buttolph-Williams House, 218
Buttonbush Trail, 66
Cadillac Mountain, 154
Cafe L'Espresso, 114
Calverts, 94
Calvin Coolidge State Forest, 169
Cambridge Historical Commission, 98
Camden Hills, 150
Camden Hills State Park, 150
Camden Information Booth, 150
Cannon Mountain Aerial Tramway, 165

Cape Ann Chamber of Commerce, 121
Cape Cod Chamber of Commerce, 45
Cape Cod Museum of Natural History, 68
Cape Cod National Seashore, 45, 66
Cape Hedge Beach, 115
Capriland's Herb Farm, 216
Captain Linnell House, 64
Captain's Courageous, 121
Carbur's Restaurant, 176
Carols, 40
Carroll Read, 163
Castle Hill, 124
Castle Tucker, 147
Cathedral Ledge, 164
Cathedral Pines, 204
Champlain Shakespeare Festival, 175
Chandler Hovey Park, 109
Chantey Festival, 18
Chapin Library, 193
Chapman Falls, 11
Chapman-Hall House, 148
Charles Hayden Memorial Library, 98
Charlestown Community Beach, 23
Chart Room, 47
Chase Park, 58
Château-sur-Mer, 30
Chatham Chamber of Commerce, 58
Chatham Cooperative Seafood Fish Market, 58
Chatham Lighthouse, 58–59
Chatham Railroad Museum, 58
Cheese Outlet, 176
Chello Oyster House, 10
Chesterwood, 199
Children's Museum (Boston, MA), 93
Children's Museum (West Hartford, CT), 209
Children's Services Horse Show and Country Fair, 207
China Fair, 94
Chowder Race, 149
Chowderworks, 58
Christmas Farm Inn, 163
Christmas Lantern Light Tours, 18
Chuck Roast Outlet, 164
Clapp and Treat, 215
Clarke Outdoors, 204
Cliff Walk (Newport, RI), 31
Cliff Walk (York Harbor, ME), 138
Clipper Inn, 154
Clock Tower, 202
Clothesline Art Show, 202
Cohasset Historical Society, 82
Colonel John Asley House, 200

INDEX TO ATTRACTIONS

Colonial Candleshop of Cape Cod, 57
Colonial Pemaquid Restoration State Park, 148
Common Burying Ground, 31
Commons Lunch, 33
Commonwealth Winery, 79
Concord Chamber of Commerce, 103
Congregational Church (Litchfield, CT), 205
Congregational Church (Sharon, CT), 202
Congregational Church (Townshend, VT), 184
Connolly and Wellington, 114
Constitution Plaza, 214
Conway Scenic Railroad, 163
Cookies, 68
Coolidge Birthplace, 169
Coolidge Homestead, 169
Coonamesset Inn, 47
Copp's Hill Burying Ground, 89
Country Kitchen Restaurant, 185
Cranberry World, 78
Crane's Beach, 124
Crocker Park, 108
Crowninshield-Bentley House, 112
Cushing Museum, 125
Custom House (Newburyport, MA), 125
Custom House (Salem, MA), 114

Daken Mills Outlet, 181
Dana Place Inn, 163
Dansk Factory Outlet, 163
Dartmouth College, 166
Dartmouth Row, 166
Davidson's Dress Shop, 205
Deerfield (Historic), 195
Department of Environmental Affairs, 96
Department of Forests and Parks (Montpelier, VT), 176
Derby House, 114
Deshon-Allyn House, 14
Devil's Hopyard State Park, 11
Devil's Oven, 11
Dewey's, 168
Dexter Footwear, 180
Dexter's Grist Mill, 70
Dinosaur State Park, 218
Dock Square, 139
Dog Bar Breakwater, 122
Dogtown Commons, 120
Donald G. Trayser Museum, 69
Dorothy Quincy Homestead, 84
Dorset Inn, 184
Dorset Playhouse, 182

Drake's Island, 136
Drummer Boy Museum, 68
Dudleytown, 202
Dunhams Footwear, 180
Durgin Park, 96
Duxbury Beach, 80

Eagle Lake, 156
East Beach (Charlestown, RI), 23
East Matunuck State Beach, 23
Eastern Historical Society, 64
Eastern Mountain Sports, 163, 186, 215
Eastern Point Light, 122
Eastern Promenade, 140
Eastham Historical Society, 64
Eastham Lobster Pool, 66
Echo Lake State Park, 164
Edgartown Regatta, 51
Eight Mile River, 11
1800 House, 55
Elbow Trail, 199
Elizabeth Perkins House, 138
Ellie's Place, 40
Elms, The, 30
Emerald Lake State Park, 182
Emerson-Wilcox House, 137
Essex Institute, 112
Essex Shipbuilding Museum, 124
Essex Street Mall, 114
Ethan Allen Park, 174
Eugene O'Neill Memorial Theater Center, 15

F. Parker Reidy's, 140
Fall River Knitting Mills, 43, 57
Falmouth Foreside, 141
Falmouth Historical Society, 46
Faneuil Hall, 86
Farmer's Market, 176
Farmington Museum, 207
Farmington Valley Arts Center, 207
Farnhams, 123
Farrar-Mansur House, 181
Faulkner Nature Trail, 169
Finally Hand Weavers, 11
First Congregational Church (Falmouth, MA), 46
First Meetinghouse (Brunswick, ME), 141
First Parish Church (Cohasset, MA), 82
First Parish Congregational Church (York, ME), 137
Fisherman's Museum, 148
Fisherman's Statue, 116
Flume, 165
Flying Horse Carousel, 22

INDEX TO ATTRACTIONS

Fogg Art Museum, 97
Folkway Restaurant, 186
Fort Foster, 136
Fort George, 152
Fort Hill Trail, 66
Fort McClary Memorial Park, 136
Fort Popham Memorial, 146
Fort Sewall, 108
Frances Russell Hart Nautical Museum, 98
Franconia Notch State Park, 164
Franklin Park Zoo, 96
Frenchman's Bay Boating Company, 154
Fresh Ground Coffeehouse, 175
Friendship Sloop Days, 148
Friendship Sloop Race, 149
Front Beach (Rockport, MA), 115

G. Fox, 215
Gardner Museum, 94
Gardner-Pingree House, 112
Gay-Hoyt House, 202
Gazebo, 170
Gengras Planetarium, 209
Georges, 23
Giant Pothole, 165
Gillette Castle State Park, 12
Glass Basket, 11
Gloucester Fishermen's Museum, 121
Good Harbor Beach, 115
Goodspeed Opera House, 11
Gorham Mountain Trail, 156
Granary Burying Ground, 88
Grand Banks Schooner Museum, 148
Grand Isle State Park, 176
Granby Dinosaur Museum, 218
Grapevine Cottage, 102
Greater Westerly-Pawcatuck-Charlestown Chamber of Commerce, 23
Green Mountain Club, xvii, 173
Greenbrier, 170
Greylock Mountain State Reservation, 193
Gristmill (Sudbury, MA), 106
Griswold Inn, 11
Guilder Pond, 199
Guilford Handcraft Center, 9
Guilford Handcraft Exposition and Sale, 10
Guilford Recreation Department, 10

Hadwen House-Satler Memorial, 55
Haight Vineyards and Winery, 206
Halibut Point Reservation, 123
Hall Tavern, 195
Hammersmith Farm, 31
Hammond Castle Museum, 116

Hancock Cemetery, 84
Hancock-Clarke House, 101
Hancock Shaker Village, 196
Hanging Rock (Middletown, RI), 32
Hanover Inn, 166
Harbor Sweets, 109
Harbor View Restaurant, 21
Harkness Memorial State Park, 15
Harkness Tower, 6
Harpswell House, 142
Harriet Beecher Stowe House, 212
Harrington's, 178
Hartford Artline, 215
Hartford Civic Center, 212
Harvard Information Center, 97
Harvard University, 97
Harvard University Museum, 97
Harvard Yard, 97
Hathaway Shirts, 180
Hayden Gallery, 98
Hayden Planetarium, 94
Hempstead House, 15
Henry Whitfield Museum, 9
Heritage Plantation, 70
Herman Melville Memorial Room, 195
Herring Run Diner, 71
Heublein Tower, 207
High Island, 9
High Street (Newburyport, MA), 125
Highland Light, 67
Hildene, 181
Hill-Stead Museum, 207
Hingham Chamber of Commerce, 83
Historic House (Cohasset, MA), 82
Hitchcock Chair Factory, 206
Hollow Reed, 140
Homer Noble Farm, 179
Hoosac Community Resources Corporation, 194
Hopkins Center, 166
Hopkins Observatory, 193
Horseneck State Beach, 40
Housatonic Meadows State Park, 203
House of the Seven Gables, 114
Hoxie House, 70
Hugo's Lighthouse, 82
Hunter House, 28
Huntington's Book Store, 215
Hyde Log Cabin, 177
Hyland House, 9
Hy-Line Hyannis Harbor Tours, 48, 50

Ice House, 176
Independence Gown Museum, 82

258

INDEX TO ATTRACTIONS

Indian Cedar Swamp, 23
Interstate Navigation, 26
Ipswich River Wildlife Sanctuary, 124
Isaac Stevens House, 218
Island Commuter Corporation, 48
Island Voyage, 50

Jack Frost Shop, 163
Jackson Village Store, 163
Jacob's Pillow Dance Festival, 196
Jamestown Museum, 27
Jared Coffin House, 55
Jefferds' Tavern, 137
Jelly Mill, 182
Jenney Grist Mill, 79
Jeremiah Lee Mansion, 108
John F. Kennedy Library, 94
John Fitzgerald Kennedy Memorial, 57
John Hancock Observatory, 85
John Hancock Warehouse, 137
John Paul Jones House, 132
John Wanamaker (Camden, ME), 151
John Ward House, 112
John Whipple House, 124
Jolly Butcher's Tavern, 185
Jordan Cliffs Trail, 156
Jordan Pond House, 156
Judges' Cave, 7

Kancamagus Highway, 164
Kate Gould Park, 58
Kelley House, 52
Kendall Whaling Museum, 98
Kennebunkport Historical Society, 139
Killington Peak, 170
Killington Playhouse, 170
Killington Ski Area, 170
Kimball Wildlife Refuge, 22
King's Chapel, 87
Kittery Point, 136
Knight Point State Park, 176

L. L. Bean, 141
Lady Pepperell House, 136
Lake Champlain Regional Chamber of Commerce, 174
Lake Champlain Transportation, 174
Land's End, 145
Laura B, 149
League of New Hampshire Craftsmen, 164
Legal Seafoods, 96
Lexington Chamber of Commerce, 100
Lexington Historical Society, 100
Liberty Belle, 8

Lightship Nantucket, 55
Lighthouse Park Community Beach, 8
Lilly Pulitzer, 63
Lime Rock Raceway, 201
Lincoln County Fire Museum, 147
Litchfield Historical Society, 205
Little Compton, 33
Lobster Claw, 63
Lobster Pound, 151
Long Trail, The, 172
Long Wharf Theater, 8
Longfellow National Historic Site, 98
Longfellow's Wayside Inn, 105
Loon Mountain, 164
Loop Road Trail, 154
Lost River Reservation, 165
Lothrop House, 82
Lowell National Historical Park, 99
Luethi-Peterson International Camp, 164
Lyceum (Salem, MA), 114
Lyman Allyn Museum, 14

MacMillan Wharf, 67
Maiden Cliff, 151
Maiden Cliff Trail, 151
Maine Art Gallery, 147
Maine Maritime Academy, 152
Maine Maritime Museum, 145
Maison Robert, 97
Man o'War Brook, 157
Manchester Sail Makers, 40
marble bridge (North Adams, MA), 194
Marble Exhibit, 179
Marble House, 31
Marblehead, 108
Marblehead Light, 109
Marblehead Neck, 108
Marblehead Neck Sanctuary, 108
Marginal Way, 138
Maria Mitchell Association, 55
Marine Biological Laboratory, 47
Mariner's Home, 42
Maritime Museum, 82
Mark Twain House, 210
Market Barn Gallery, 46
Market Bookshop, 46
Market Square, 125
Martha-Mary Chapel, 106
Martha's Restaurant, 52
Martha's Vineyard Chamber of Commerce, 45
Massachusetts Audubon Society, 45
Massachusetts Bay Line, 96
Massachusetts Institute of Technology, 97

259

INDEX TO ATTRACTIONS

Mattapoisett Inn, 43
Mattatuck Trail, 204
Mayflower II, 78
Mayor's Festival (New Haven, CT), 7
McDowell Colony, 186
Merck Forest, 184
Metacomet Trail, 207
Miacomet Fair, 55
Middlebury College, 178
Miles Standish Monument, 80
Mineralogical Museum, 97
Minots Ledge Lighthouse, 83
Minute Man National Historical Park, 101
Minutemen Statue, 100
Misquamicut State Beach, 22
MIT Chapel, 97
Moby Dick Trail, 42
Moby Dick Wharf, 39
Moffatt-Ladd House, 132
Mohawk State Forest, 204
Mohawk Trail, 193
Mohawk Trail State Forest, 194
Mohegan Bluffs, 24
Molly Stark State Park, 186
Monadnock State Park, 185
Money Island, 9
Monhegan Museum, 149
Monte Cristo Cottage, 15
Moody Beach, 136
Moore's Rocks Reservation, 82
Morgan Horse Farm, 178
Motif Number 1, 122
Mount Battie South Trail, 150
Mount Cranmore Skimobile, 164
Mount Equinox, 184
Mount Everett, 199
Mount Holyoke, 218
Mount Katahdin, 157
Mount Mansfield, 173
Mount Mansfield Gondola, 173
Mount Megunticook Trail, 150
Mount Peg Nature Trail, 169
Mount Riga Furnace, 201
Mount Riga State Park, 201
Mount Tom State Park, 206
Mount Washington Cog Railway, 162
Mount Washington State Forest, 199
Mount Washington Toll Road, 162
Mozart Festival, 175
Munroe Tavern, 101
Museum of Art (Brunswick, ME), 141
Museum of Comparative Zoology, 97
Museum of the Concord Antiquarian Society, 102

Museum of Fine Arts (Boston, MA), 94
Museum of Our National Heritage, 101
Museum of Science (Boston, MA), 94
Musical Wonder House, 147
Mystic Marinelife Aquarium, 16
Mystic Seaport, 16
Mystic Whaler, 20

Nantucket Historical Association, 54
Nantucket Island Chamber of Commerce, 46
Nantucket Kiteman, 55
Nathan Hale Homestead, 216
Nathan Hale Schoolhouse, 15
Nathaniel Hempstead House, 15
National Audubon Society, xvii
National Board of YMCAs, xv
National Board of YWCAs, xv
National Historical Park Visitor Center, 84
National Marine Fisheries Service, 48
National Park Tours (Bar Harbor, ME), 154
National Survey, 172
Natural Bridge (East Dorset, VT), 182
Naulahka, 185
Naumkeag, 198
Nauset Light Beach, 64
Navigator Restaurant, 52
New Bedford, 43
New Bedford Chamber of Commerce, 42
New Bedford Whaling Museum, 42
Newburyport Chamber of Commerce, 125
New England Aquarium, 93
New England Fire and History Museum, 68
New England Maple Museum, 179
New England Whalers, 212
New Harbor (Block Island, RI), 24
New London Chamber of Commerce, 15
Newfane Country Store, 185
Newfane Flea Market, 185
Newfane Inn, 185
Newport Chamber of Commerce, 28
Newport Jazz Festival, 28
Newport Sailboat Show, 28
Nickels-Sortwell House, 147
Noah Webster House, 209
Nobska Lighthouse, 46
Nook Farm, 212
Nook Farm Museum Shop, 212
Nook Farm Research Library, 212
Norman Bird Sanctuary, 32
North Beach (Burlington, VT), 174
North Bridge Visitor Center, 101–102

INDEX TO ATTRACTIONS

North Cemetery (North Truro, MA), 68
North Hero State Park, 176
North Ridge Trail, 156
Norumbega Mountain Trail, 156
Nubble Light, 138

Ogunquit Beach, 136, 138
Okemo Mountain, 181
Old Atwood House, 58
Old Burying Ground (Duxbury, MA), 80
Old Burying Ground (York, ME), 136
Old Cemetery (Chatham, MA), 58
Old Colony House, 28
Old Corner Bookstore, 87
Old Corner House, 198
Old Crocker Tavern, 69
Old Farm Inn, 123
Old First Church (Bennington, VT), 187
Old Friends Burial Ground, 27
Old Gaol Museum, 137
Old Grist Mill (Chatham, MA), 58
Old Grist Mill (Kennebunkport, ME), 140
Old Home Week (Freedom, NH), 164
Old Man of the Mountains, 165
Old Manse, 103
Old Mill, 55
Old North Bridge, 102
Old North Church, 89
Old Ordinary, 83
Old Port Exchange, 140
Old Schoolhouse (York, ME), 137
Old Ship Church, 83
Old South Meeting House, 87
Old State House (Boston, MA), 86
Old State House (Hartford, CT), 214
Old Stone Tower, 28
Old Sturbridge Village, 215
Old Yankee Marketplace, 199
Olde Mistick Village Art and Handcrafts Show, 16
Oldest House (Nantucket, MA), 55
Open House Day (Litchfield, CT), 205
Orchard House, 102
Orleans Historical Society, 63
Orleans Information Center, 63
Orvis Company, 181
Otter Cliffs, 154

Packet, 40
Pairpoint Glass Works, 70
Palatine Graves, 24
Paper House, 123
Paradise Falls, 165
Park Street Church, 88

Parke-McCullough House, 187
Parker River National Wildlife Refuge, 125
Pasta House, 43
Patriot's Trail, 84
Paul Revere House, 89
Paul Revere Mall, 89
Peabody Museum (Cambridge, MA), 97
Peabody Museum (New Haven, CT), 6, 219
Peabody Museum (Salem, MA), 112
Peacock Alley, 63
Peary-MacMillan Artic Museum, 141
Pebbly Beach, 115
Peirce-Nichols House, 112
Pemaquid Point Lighthouse, 148
Pemetic Mountain Trail, 156
Penobscot Mountain Trail, 156
Pepe's Wharf, 68
Percy and Small Shipyard, 146
Perkins Cove, 138
Phoenix Life Insurance Building, 214
Pickering Wharf, 114
Piel Craftsmen, 125
Pier II Restaurant, 132
Pilgrim Hall, 79
Pilgrim Memorial Monument, 68
Pilgrim Spring Trail, 67
Pilgrim Village, 79
Pine Hollow Trail, 124
Pinkham Notch, 162
Pioneer Valley, 194
Pioneer Village, 115
Plimoth Plantation, 79
Plum Island, 125
Plum Island Lighthouse, 125
Plymouth Cheese, 170
Plymouth County Development Council, 78
Plymouth Rock, 78
Plymouth Town Information Booth, 78
Popham Beach State Park, 147
Portland Chamber of Commerce, 140
Portland History Trail, 140
Portsmouth Chamber of Commerce, 132
Powder House Day, 7
Powder Point Bridge, 80
Prescott Park, 132
Preservation Society of Newport County, 30
Presidential Range, 162
Profile Lake, 165
Province Lands Visitor Center, 67
Provincetown Chamber of Commerce, 68
Provincetown Museum, 68
Prudential Tower, 85

INDEX TO ATTRACTIONS

Publick House, 216
Puddle Dock Pub, 132

Quail Hollow Farm, 70
Quarterdeck Restaurant, 154
Quechee Gorge, 168
Quechee Gorge Trail, 168
Quincy Market, 86
Quincy-South Shore Chamber of Commerce, 83
Quisset Harbor, 46

Race Point Beach, 68
Race Week (Marblehead, MA), 109
Rachel Carson National Wildlife Refuge, 139
Rafe's Chasm, 115
Ragged Mountain Trail, 151
Red Lion Inn, 198
Redstone School, 106
Regatta, The, 47
Regicides Trail, 7
Reluctant Panther Inn, 182
Restaurant Swisspot, 173
Revereware Factory Store, 43
Rhode Island Tuna Tournament, 23
Richard Robbins, 174
Riverrunning Expeditions, 204
Roaring Brook Nature Center, 206
Robert Frost Interpretive Trail, 179
Robert Frost Place, 165
Robert Hull Fleming Museum, 175
Rock Harbor, 63
Rockport Art Association, 122
Rocktide Inn, 154
Rocky Neck, 121
Roebuck Caterers, 83
Roger Wheeler Memorial Beach, 23
Rosecliff, 30
Round Stone Barn, 196
Royal Indian Burial Ground, 22
Royall Tyler Theater, 175

Sabino, 20
Sagamore Bridge, 70
Sail Loft, 40
Saint Stephen's Episcopal Church, 82
Salas' Dining Room, 30
Salem Chamber of Commerce, 112
Salem Maritime National Historic Site, 114
Salem Witch Museum, 112
Salt Pond Visitor Center, 66
Sand Beach, 154, 156
Sandwich Glass Museum, 70

Savoy Mountain State Forest, 194
Scarborough State Beach, 26
Scargo Hill Tower, 69
Scenic Trail (Camden, ME), 151
Scott Bridge, 184
Sea Education Association, 48
Sea Point Beach, 136
Seal Harbor Beach, 156
Sealand of Cape Cod, 68
Seamen's Bethel, 42
Seamen's Inne, 20
Seashore Trolley Museum, 140
Second Beach (Middletown, RI), 32
Seth Thomas Clock Shoppe, 206
Sewall House, 146
Shaker Kitchen Festival, 196
Shakespeare & Company at the Mount, 196
Sharon Audubon Center, 202
Sharon Audubon Festival, 202
Sharon Playhouse, 202
Shaw Mansion, 15
Shed, The, 94
Shelburne Country Store, 178
Shelburne Museum, 178
Sheldon's Tavern, 205
Shining Sea Bikeway, 46
Siasconset, 56
Sieur de Monts Spring, 154
Silas Deane House, 218
1690 House, 125
Ski Shack, 170
Sky Walk, 85
Skyline Drive, 184
Sleepy Hollow Cemetery, 102
Small Swamp Trail, 67
Smugglers Notch, 173
Smuttynose Island, 134
Somes Sound, 156
South Bridge Boat House, 102
South Ridge Trail, 156
Stanley-Whitman House, 207
Star Island, 133
State House (Boston, MA), 88
State of Maine Ferry Service, 149
State Pier (New Bedford, MA), 43
State Street Landing (Marblehead, MA), 108
Steamboat Cafe, 20
Steamship Authority (Woods Hole, MA), 48
Sterling and Francine Clark Art Institute, 193
Sterling Memorial Library, 6

262

INDEX TO ATTRACTIONS

Stonebridge Dishes, 33
Stony Brook Mill, 69
Stowe Area Association, 173
Stowehof, 173
Straight Wharf, 55
Strawberry Court, 132
Strawbery Banke, 132
Striped Bass and Bluefish Derby, 52
Sturgis Library, 69
Surfside, 56
Sweater Store, 168
Sylvan Gardens, 58

Tablelands Trail, 151
Talbots, 83
Tanglewood, 196, 198
Tapping Reeve House and Law School, 205
"Target Ship," 63
Third Beach (Middletown, RI), 32
Thomas Cooke House, 51
Thomas Franklin Waters Memorial, 124
Thomas Griswold House Museum, 9
Thompson Memorial Chapel, 193
Thoreau Lyceum, 103
300 Derby Street, 114
Thunder Hole, 154
Topnotch at Stowe, 173
Touro Synagogue, 28
Trails of the Guilford Westwoods, 10
Trapp Family Lodge, 173
Travelers' Tower, 214
Trinity Church (Newport, RI), 28, 31
Tuckerman's Ravine, 162
Tugboat Inn, 154
Tunxis Trail, 206

Union Cemetery (Chatham, MA), 58
Union Oyster House, 96
University of Vermont Outing Club, 173
U.S. Coast Guard Academy, 14
U.S. Geological Survey, 170
U.S. Naval Submarine Base, 14
USS *Cassin Young*, 92
USS *Constitution*, 90–91
USS Constitution Museum, 91
USS *Croaker*, 14

Valcour Island, 176
Valley Railroad, 11
Vermont Country Store, 181
Vermont State Craft Center, 178
Viking Queen, 132
Volsunga III, 9

Wadsworth Atheneum, 215
Wadsworth-Longfellow House, 141
Walden Pond State Reservation, 103–104
Walk, The, 212
Wanton-Lyman-Hazard House, 28
Waterfront (Camden, ME), 151
Waterfront Historic District (New Bedford, MA), 42
Way Station (Rutland, VT), 180
Wayside, The, 102
Webb-Deane-Stevens Museum, 218
Webb House, 218
Wedding Cake House, 139
Wellfleet Bay Wildlife Sanctuary, 66
Wells Auto Museum, 139
Wells Beach, 136
Wentworth-Coolidge Mansion, 131
Wesley House, 51
West Face Trail, 156
West Rock Nature Recreation Center, 7
West Rock Park, 7
Weston Bowl Mill, 181
Weston Playhouse, 181
Weston Village Store, 181
Whaling Museum, 54
White Barn Inn, 140
White Flower Farm, 205
White Horse Ledge, 164
White Memorial Conservation Center, 206
Whites of Their Eyes, The, 92
Widener Library, 97
Widow Bingham's Tavern, 198
Wilderness Shop, 205
William A. Farnsworth Library and Art Museum, 149
William Pratt House, 11
Williams Beach, 20
Williams College, 193
Williams College Museum of Art, 193
Williams Inn, The, 193
Williamstown Theatre Festival, 196
Wilson Castle, 180
Windham County Court House, 185
Windjammer Festival, 148
Windmill Weekend, 64
Winter Street Center, 146
Witch House, 112
wolf stones (Stonington, CT), 20
Woodbury Pewterers, 205
Woodman's, 123
Woods Hole Oceanographic Institute, 47
Woodstock Chamber of Commerce, 169
Woodstock Historical Society, 168
World's End Reservation, 83

INDEX TO ATTRACTIONS

Yale University, 6
Yale Center for British Art, 6
Yale Collection of Musical Instruments, 6
Yale Information Office, 6
Yale University Art Gallery, 6
Yankee Fleet, 122
Yesteryear's Museum, 70
Yield House, 163
Yodler, 173

Other Globe Pequot books of interest to the Northeast traveler are available at your bookstore or direct from the publisher. For a free catalogue, call 1-800-243-0495 (in Connecticut, 1-800-962-0973) or write to: The Globe Pequot Press, Old Chester Road, Box Q, Chester, Connecticut 06412.